Drug Scenes

Withdrawn from
Jbck 16/4/24

Drug Scenes

A Report on Drugs and Drug Dependence by
the Royal College of Psychiatrists

Foreword by
Dr J. L. T. Birley
President of the College

Royal College of
Psychiatrists

Gaskell

Gaskell is an imprint of the Royal College of Psychiatrists, 17 Belgrave Square, London SW1 8PG

Distributed in North America by American Psychiatric Press, Inc.

ISBN 0-88048-306-7

Index compiled by Stanley Thorley
Typeset by Dobbie Typesetting Limited, Plymouth, Devon
Printed in Great Britain at the Alden Press, Oxford

Contents

Membership of the Special Committee on Drugs and Drug Dependence

Professor Griffith Edwards (Chairman),
Addiction Research Unit,
Institute of Psychiatry,
London.

Dr Philip Boyd,
Emeritus Consultant Psychiatrist,
Department of Child and Adolescent Psychiatry,
The Middlesex Hospital,
London.

Dr P. H. Connell, CBE,
Emeritus Physician,
The Bethlem Royal Hospital and the Maudsley Hospital,
London.

Dr John Booth Davies,
Director,
Addiction Research Group,
University of Strathclyde,
Glasgow.

Professor A. Ghodse,
Director,
Department of Addictive Behaviours,
St. George's Hospital and Medical School,
University of London.

Dr P. T. d'Orban,
Consultant Forensic Psychiatrist,
The Royal Free Hospital,
London.

Dr Martin Plant,
Senior Research Fellow,
Alcohol Research Group,
Department of Psychiatry,
University of Edinburgh.

Dr John Strang,
Director of the Drug Dependence Clinical Research
  and Treatment Unit,
The Bethlem Royal Hospital and the Maudsley Hospital,
London.

Observer
Dr Dorothy Black,
Senior Medical Officer,
Mental Health Division,
Department of Health and Social Security.

Acknowledgements

The Special Committee wishes to thank the secretarial staff of the College for their support, and in particular Deborah Hart.

The typing of the Report was seen through its various draft stages by Mrs Julia Polglaze and we wish to acknowledge her exceptional helpfulness.

A number of agencies provided assistance in the compilation of data, including the Department of Health and Social Security, the Scottish Home and Health Department, the Department of Transport, the Home Office, the Office of Population Censuses and Surveys, the General Register Office for Scotland, Hodder and Stoughton Educational, the Brewers' Society and the Tobacco Advisory Council.

Acknowledgements

Foreword

The use and abuse of habit-forming drugs is a topic of great and growing concern both for the nation's health and for the nation's budget. There is an urgent need for more public education on this matter, and one of the most important functions of any Royal College is to provide it. Reports on alcohol and on tobacco have already appeared from our own and from other Royal Colleges. This latest contribution covers the wider and more complex scene of drug problems as a whole.

Politicians of all parties agree that the financial support for the treatment of the nation's health must have limits. It therefore behoves us all to consider how best to reduce the enormous physical and social damage caused by drugs. In this report we discuss both "illicit" and "socially acceptable" drugs, as they raise similar questions and may be equally harmful. We make a number of recommendations, but our main purpose is to introduce and support a more informed, objective, and sophisticated debate on a matter which affects us all.

J. L. T. Birley
President

Introduction
Drugs—the need for informed debate

Society's relationship with drugs is a matter of ebb and flow, of shifting coexistence. New drugs arrive and old drugs go out of fashion. In the nineteenth century laudanum, an alcoholic solution of opium, could be bought over the counter at any corner grocer's shop and for decades it was every family's favourite remedy for minor aches and pains. William Ewart Gladstone was known to have taken laudanum in his coffee to steady his nerves before making a parliamentary speech. Today it would be an offence attracting a possible sentence of imprisonment for a shop-keeper to sell that once popular cure-all remedy, and the mere hint that the prime minister was sipping laudanum in the House of Commons canteen would probably be enough to bring down the Government. The bottles have gone from the shelf; the last century's concern with "infant doping", the "opium sot" and "Britain's shameful trade with China" have also disappeared. The public health campaigns of that era have been forgotten, as have the crowded public meetings convened by the Anti-Opium Society and the Women's Anti-Opium Urgency League. Equally forgotten are Mrs Winslow's Soothing Syrup or Atkinson's Infants' Preservative (popular laudanum-based preparations) and the fact that in the middle of the last century Britain was consuming each year on average the equivalent of over 150 standard doses of morphine per head of population.

Instead the world today is suddenly aware that Valium, a tranquillizer first marketed in this country only in the 1960s, has achieved such popularity that in Britain at one time it came top of the list for all National Health Service prescriptions. The anxieties used to be about "the stimulant use of opium" in the mill towns of the industrial revolution and there were rumours

1

that the working classes were putting opium in their beer. Today there is a concern about the use of minor tranquillizers by young mothers living in the tower blocks of modern industrial cities. The question has to be asked whether the use of these latter-day anodynes to relieve the anomie and isolation of urban life is much other than opium re-incarnate.

To respond to the misuse of drugs in terms of such a slogan as "the elimination of the drug menace" is therefore not well-judged. Use of one drug may give way to another; particular sectors of society may become more involved or less involved in drug taking; this or that aspect of the problem may be ameliorated or go sharply out of control. It is not only drugs and patterns of drug use which change but also the way in which people see the problem, the explanations which people give for such behaviour (moral, medical or sociological), and the remedies which are seen as appropriate. The news desks have long forgotten the epidemic of ether drinking which suddenly emerged in the 1890s, while today it is discovered that with equal abruptness a substance so seemingly innocent as model aeroplane cement contributes to "glue sniffing". The frontiers of the drug problem are always shifting. If the spectator of this scene can be sure of anything it is that society's encounter with drugs will appear to another generation as quaint and time-bound, while that later age grapples in turn with its own manifestations of the drug problem and with substances of which the 1980s have never heard.

To talk of "co-existence" is not to preach cynicism or a tired laissez-faire. The true message is very positive. It is the insistence that there exists a responsibility to evolve the best co-existence possible for the present moment, with everything that is done informed by a sense of history, by a keen appraisal of the facts, by a reflective awareness of current value systems, and by a mature and balanced judgment of what is or is not possible. Drug problems will not be beaten out of society by yet harsher laws, lectured out of society by yet more hours of "health education", or treated out of society by yet more drug experts. There is a place however for legislation and education and treatment.

The purpose of this book

The purpose of this book is to contribute toward an examination of the nature of society's present co-existence with drugs, and to explore in which ways co-existence may stand in need of adjustment. It is not a tract designed to impose expert remedies, but, on the contrary, a book in which it is hoped to involve its readers actively in a shared process of exploration.

That leads to the question of the reader for whom this book is written. Because it is our whole society, and not just a few with special responsibilities, which has to establish and adjust the co-existence, this book is intended for a general readership, for "our society" in the round. At the same time of course, it is hoped that what follows will be useful to those in health and social services who deal with drug takers and to people who meet these problems in the courts or through their work in the probation services or through their responsibilities as administrators or civil servants. But the real front line lies with the ordinary citizen, the family in any street, tomorrow's classroom, the youth club's meeting any evening, the disco, and the press coverage of the next drug story. It is that professional, general and multiple audience which this report invites to engage in active debate.

How that purpose is to be met

If anyone is to examine constructively society's co-existence with drugs, it is first essential to be acquainted with the facts. An important aim of this book is therefore to provide a factual presentation of information on drugs, the effects of drugs, who is using drugs, and who is doing what about drugs today in our society. It is also essential in a book of this kind to lay out these facts in language uncluttered by jargon, and not only to give information but also to correct mis-information. In this report it is intended to dispose of such stereotyped beliefs as the view that "the drug problem" implies only illicit substances like heroin, cocaine or cannabis. Much of the damage sustained by society results not from those drugs but from cigarette smoking and the misuse of alcohol. Prescribed drugs such as tranquillizers, sedatives and sleeping tablets and a variety of over-the-counter drugs must also lie within the focus of concern. The idea that drug problems involve only the younger section of the community must be refuted.

If this book is to achieve its purpose, if there is to be a start toward a truly constructive examination of the necessary co-existence with drugs, the important first step is to get the basic facts accurately in focus. Many discussions on drugs have been both too little informed and too passionate, and this book aims to provide a corrective. The first section of the book — "Background to Understanding" — is concerned with these factual issues, but in addition wherever in later chapters particular drugs are being discussed brief notes will be given on the necessary basic facts, often noting with equal importance what is not known.

With the factual groundwork established in the first section of the book, the second section — "Drugs and Society" — comprises a set of chapters which will examine and debate society's experiences with particular drugs or classes of drugs. In each instance consideration of a chemical substance is the starting point for exploration of the social and policy issues resulting from and exemplified by that particular drug. It is thus possible to understand a little more clearly some of the fears, prejudices, premises, models of understanding and value systems which are so often involved in society's reaction to drugs.

The third section of this book — "Responding to Drug Problems" — explores how knowledge of the facts and appraisal of the debates is to be brought to bear on issues such as treatment, prevention and the legal response; in other words, how we are best to adjust our co-existence with drugs to the knowledge, needs and values of our age. A final chapter offers a set of recommendations for debate.

Why now?

Any society at any time does well to understand the way in which it is responding to important and complex social issues. Within terms of that perspective, "now" is axiomatically the time to examine society's co-existence with the drug problems of the present. It is our job for our time. The publication of this book does not need to be justified by crying that this is an exceptionally threatening moment in this country's (or the world's) encounter with drugs, and it is not necessary to preach doom. However, every epoch in the evolution of society's co-existence with drugs has its particular features. In trying to characterise some of the special features of the present phase in history there are themes which are worth identifying, and they are not simply the obvious ones such as the growth in heroin or cannabis use over the last few decades.

One of these themes, for instance, is the many-faceted debate which is emerging on the role of the law as an instrument in the control of the use and misuse of drugs. Experts are uneasy about the health consequences of cannabis, but many people question the acceptability of criminalising the cannabis user. Everyone must be appalled by deaths caused by drunken driving, but the ordinary citizen may be none too willing to give permission to the police, who have powers of "stop and search" for drug offences, to wait with a breathalyzer outside the pub at closing time. The courts use "probation with condition of residence" to put a young heroin user into a Therapeutic Community, but they will not invoke the Mental Health Act to prevent the heroin user's father from drinking himself to death. A particular feature of this epoch may be a growing awareness of the extraordinary inconsistencies and double standards which have developed in relation to a number of different mind-acting substances.

Another emerging and somewhat allied theme relates to the sense of what is to be expected from Government. Is society best left to get on with its own drug use, and drug problems dealt with in terms of informal cultural responses? The 19th century did not after all make too bad a job of handling the massive availability of opium, and one may wonder whether the relentless progression of government interference has not gone too far and brought its own hazards. Who today wants to repeat the American Prohibition experience? And yet these last few years have seen a growing demand that the supply of alcohol should not be left just to the unfettered play of free market forces and the pursuit of profit, and there is a growing unease in many circles at the Government's reluctance to take firmer action over cigarette smoking. A little bit of "voluntary agreement" with the tobacco industry over advertising, continuing sports sponsorship and posters on every hoarding, do seem a strange response to a drug which is killing 100,000 people each year. People cannot be made moral by legislation, but legislation is a fundamental part of public health. Does public opinion now expect Government to become more interventionist over alcohol and smoking and perhaps less interventionist in relation to certain other drugs?

Yet another important contemporary theme relates to a re-examination of the role of treatment and rehabilitation and the implication of "medicalisation" and the underlying disease model of addiction. Who is a suitable case for treatment, and what do people really expect of the treaters?

At the beginning of the last century there were no specialised institutes for treatment of either alcohol or drugs problems. Today Britain has 30 specialised Treatment Units for alcohol problems within the NHS and there is a great emphasis on the need for GPs and primary health care teams to involve themselves in this work. Over the last 15 years more than 30 specialised NHS centres have been established for the treatment of drug problems. There are out-patient clinics for cigarette smokers. Voluntary organisations are now extremely active in dealing with drug and alcohol problems and private hospitals are moving increasingly into this field. The present epoch is one which is not only seeing these things happen, but is also beginning to question the meaning and implications of all this treatment activity. Why another clinic for alcohol problems, and why the reluctance to tax alcohol so as to stabilise its real price? Why another drug clinic or day centre or rehabilitation hostel, and how is this activity to be related to the backdrop of inner city decay and youth unemployment? What is a constructive and apt response and what is confusion or mere smoke screen? In this book it will be argued that there is an enormously important and continuing place for treatment, but that it is timely to re-think the nature and limits of what treatment can by itself achieve.

A final theme which can be identified as characterising the nature of our co-existence with drugs is that the present age is probably threatened by this problem more than in any previous epoch. Over recent years Britain and many other parts of the world have experienced sharp changes in the extent and pattern of drug use. The sharpness of some of these changes certainly contributes to a need to re-examine the nature of the co-existence. It is not surprising that societies faced with rapid, multiple, and complex changes in experience with mind-acting substances should manifest a degree of confusion, cry panic in some circumstances and under-react in others, tie the drug debate into available rhetorics on liberty or moral decline, or rush only for more treatment.

It is not for a moment claimed that this book offers all the answers. Its aim is to help to make the debate more informed and less confused, and it moves no closures.

Part I
Background to understanding

Chapter 1
Causes for concern

Over recent years drug misuse in Britain and in many other countries has become the focus of intense public and political concern. At one point British television channels ran three major programmes on drugs during a single week. Drugs and "the drug menace" regularly make newspaper headlines — another undergraduate dies of an overdose, another playboy is arrested on a cocaine charge, another schoolchild is found dead after sniffing glue. A cannabis haul with a street value of £1 million is seized at Heathrow. A bishop denounces the drugged corruption of the young, and a University debating society recommends the legalisation of cannabis. Diverse news stories suggest that heroin has become an intrinsic part of urban deprivation or alternatively that the drug problem centres on the affluent and over-privileged. Drug issues are now finding their way into party political rhetoric. The Government has spent £4 million on anti-heroin publicity which has included a television campaign. Hoardings have been placarded with posters which announce that "heroin screws you up".

Is the current level of concern justified, or is it a panic instigated by the media and little more than the latest bandwagon for the scaremongers and opportunists? Is the anxiety attached to illicit drugs absurdly exaggerated in comparison to the worry which ought to be felt in relation to the continuing and large-scale damage caused by cigarette smoking and excessive drinking? Is it hypocritical to worry so much about illicit drugs when in 1985 the country was sedated or tranquillized by over 39 million prescriptions for mind acting drugs?

Drug taking has engendered not only anxiety but also confusion and lack of confidence as to where the line is to be held. Is it right

9

to object to our adolescent children using cannabis or is that the rear-guard posturing of the drinking generation? Can heroin touch *my* home or is it only the family riven with discord which is prone to drug misuse? If someone in my family starts to use drugs does that immediately imply that there has been something badly wrong with the support or the values which my home has offered? When a drug problem suddenly appears in a family more often than not no-one will know how to react, where to turn for help, or what to feel. Does treatment ever succeed or is addiction inexorable, and so far as heroin is concerned probably deadly? Are drug problems moral problems, social problems or disease problems? Is prevention a matter of building better cities, lecturing to schoolchildren, or strengthening the Drugs Squad? Can LSD really blow your mind? Is cannabis harmful? Is cocaine addictive?

Some of the recent and more exaggerated statements can certainly be dismissed as unduly alarmist. Drug pushers are not prowling around every school playground, cannabis does not lead inevitably to the use of heroin and one experience with heroin does not result in instant perversion of the soul. There has been too frequent an imbalance in levels of concern between illicit drugs on the one hand and alcohol and tobacco on the other. At the same time it would be dangerous and misleading to tell families and the general public, acutely worried about the spread of drug misuse, that they have been deceived and that their fears are silly and imaginary. Even the most cursory inspection of the facts reveals the astonishing change in this country's involvement with illicit drugs which has taken place over the last quarter of a century. The total number of addicts to opiates and cocaine on the Home Office Register in 1960 was 437, while by 1985 that total had risen to 8,819. In 1960 there was just one addict under the age of 21 known to the Home Office, whereas in 1985 that figure stood at 428. The types of drugs most commonly involved changed radically over the same years. There were only 94 notified cases of heroin addiction in 1960, but in 1985, of 8,819 notifications under the Misuse of Drugs Act, 8,089 subjects were using heroin. In 1960, there were no organized black-markets in heroin and no discernible importation of illicit opiates, while today's picture is that of a vastly profitable and complex black-market. Glue sniffing was unknown in 1960 but by 1985 it had emerged as an endemic problem in many urban areas. There were 235 offences involving cannabis in 1960 but 17,559 such convictions in 1985.

A more detailed presentation of figures on different types of drug misuse will be given in later chapters of this book. However, the preliminary data which have just been quoted persuasively indicate that Britain has experienced a profound change in the scale and nature of its drug problems over a comparatively brief span of time. The country has moved from a situation where heroin dependence was rare, and most usually associated with medical prescribing and the treatment of painful illness, to a situation where young people smoke or inject heroin in significant and worrying numbers. Not so long ago in this country any type of illicit drug misuse was unusual and exotic, amounting to little more than an occasional titillating scandal. Today illicit drug misuse is commonplace. Anxiety may sometimes have been exaggerated but it would be foolish to deny that society is being forced very rapidly to adjust to a new, nasty and tangible threat. Today every young person will grow up and move through life in a world where drugs of many different types are widely and often invitingly available.

Adjustment to change is always difficult and the threat of the unknown more worrying than familiar dangers. The level of anxiety and confusion which many people have experienced in relation to drugs is an important fact and rather than scornfully dismiss such reactions they should be understood, appreciated and put into perspective. They are important as a force which will shape public and political opinion, and which will colour every relevant debate.

Identifying the dimensions of anxiety

Different types of drug problem may give rise to different degrees and kinds of anxiety at different times and among different sectors of society. No one statement as to why people are worried about drugs can be valid. The reason why the Women's Movement is concerned about overprescribing of minor tranquillizers has a different basis from that of parental concern over drug use at a Pop Festival.

Some factors are drug- and situation-specific while others cross-cut between the different concerns. The headings given below are an attempt to identify some of the major strands in this web of reactions.

12 Drug scenes

Corruption or destruction of the individual

The public are worried about drugs because they believe that in a broad sense drug use can lead to trouble, and that it can then lead into more and more trouble. A drug problem first comes to many families as a totally unexpected visitation, trailing anxiety and anger, probation officers and court appearances. Apprehension centres strongly on the risks to younger people, on "what will happen to the children", on "what happens when they stay out late", on "bad company", on "what happens when they go to university".

Part of the fear relates to the immediate impact when the problem is first discovered—the worry, the questioning, the disgrace, the official procedures. It is these social consequences rather than the threat to public health which first cause concern. There are however deeper worries which lie below the surface of the initial parental reaction. Although the word "corruption" may seem too emotive, it is fear of corruption which is most commonly and immediately associated with the idea of "drug addiction". There is the fear that the drug user will become the "drug addict", that this means that the victim will be lost to the ordinary world, and become a liar, a thief, an outcast, and someone hell-bent on obtaining drugs at all costs.

At times, drug addiction can completely overwhelm the individual and cause years of distraught suffering both to him and his family, but the outcome is not always so extreme. Most adolescents who sniff glue grow out of that behaviour and do not follow such a self-destructive pathway. Most cannabis users are not on a road to corruption. Even a proportion of heroin use may be experimental and a passing phase.

Besides fear of corruption there may also be fears for the physical and mental health and indeed for the survival of the person who gets caught up in drug taking. It is the deaths which make the newspaper headlines. Glue sniffing can suddenly and appallingly kill a teenager. In 1985 there were 114 such deaths reported in the UK. Deaths due to use of heroin and other major illicit drugs numbered 464 in 1985. Each one of those happenings is a life wasted and a family bereaved. Fortunately the great majority of heroin users are not going to be killed by their addiction. To put the matter in perspective it has to be pointed out that about 1,500 young people between the ages of 15 and 24 are killed on the roads each year.

Fear that drugs will corrupt society

There is a general belief in many urban communities that society is in decline. The streets are getting nastier and mugging is commonplace. Old people are afraid to go out, and stay behind locked doors. A spate of reports on child abuse has hit the news. Drugs seem to slot into that gloomy picture as one more symptom of cities in decay. Drug problems can be viewed as both a result of society falling apart and a contributory cause of that decay.

Take again as a starting point the worst fear, that of drugs as a "threat to the very fabric of society". Few people would see Britain as beset by that extreme degree of danger but the fact that drugs have the potential to cause great damage to a society's wellbeing should not be overlooked. The most extreme instances of such social blight can be found today in certain Latin American countries where the illicit production of cocaine has become a dominant factor in the national economies. In Bolivia, for example, a schoolteacher earns an average of 40 dollars per month, while a labourer who is helping in the extraction of cocaine from the raw leaves will earn 20 dollars for one night's work. The total cash profit to Bolivia each year from the illicit sale of coca products is running at about 750,000,000 dollars. Concern has been voiced about the international growth in what is now being called "Narcoterrorism". Large-scale drug dealers may engage in terrorist acts against governments and assassinate politicians whom they see as a threat to the drug trade; terrorist organisations themselves may diversify to take a profitable interest in drugs. The entrenched influence of the Mafia in Italy, in the USA, and even more widely provides a familiar example of the corruption which can be associated with the power and riches of drug dealing. The Chinese Triad gangs provide yet another instance of the drugs-crime connection.

Danger to society of an extreme degree is still remote from the British experience. There is, however, evidence over recent years that the connection between more serious, organised and violent crime and drug importation has become closer. "Villains" who would once have been unwilling to have anything to do with drugs may now find the profits irresistible and bank robberies can provide cash for the drug business. Such criminal connections are by their nature veiled and obscure, and it is the shadowy threat which so easily gives rise to the thrilling exaggeration. Given the experience of other countries, any strengthening of professional criminal interest in drugs must however be a serious concern for the UK.

The potential connection between petty crime and drug taking also deserves scrutiny. Again to quote earlier experience, mugging and burglary in the 1960s became a plague in many American cities as heroin addicts engaged in acquisitive crime so as to pay for their drug habits. The drug problem was identified as the prime force fuelling the concurrent crime epidemic, despite powerful evidence that there was no simple causal connection. Drugs and the law-and-order issue therefore became inextricable in public debate and political response. The effort made by the Nixon administration to expand treatment facilities for addiction was intended as a strategy to undercut the crime wave.

In Britain the connection between acquisitive crime and drug use is not yet so close as it has been in the USA. This may be because heroin is cheap or because the welfare system in Britain helps pay for the drugs, but that some connection between drug taking and petty crime already exists (and that it has potential for growth) cannot be doubted—this issue is discussed further in Chapter 17 (p. 204).

The fear of society being corrupted by drugs goes beyond this tangible two-way issue of the relationship between drug use and crime to a more nebulous and pervasive fear that drugs threaten the moral fibre of society and undermine its values. Drugs are symbolically associated with permissiveness, the hippy life-style, long hair, punks, rock music and disdain for authority. This book will present the argument that drugs have, indeed, often become potently symbolic. In the 1960s cannabis and LSD were flaunted as part of the message of flower-power. The Beatles sang of "Lucy in the Sky with Diamonds". In ensuing chapters it will be argued that although such symbolism can be important the image may often have to be differentiated from the surrounding reality. Drug use, the pills and purple hearts of the motorcycle gang, cannabis use on the campuses, and LSD at pop festivals did not directly and causally lead to the changes in values and behaviour of the post-war decades but they were intertwined with those changes.

Always new drug worries on the horizon
As already mentioned in the introduction to this book, a particular feature of the drug problem which makes co-existence so difficult is the seemingly ever-changing nature of the threat. Patterns of

drug use undergo permutation and suddenly new drugs appear. A heroin epidemic in the late 1960s was followed a few years later by an outbreak of methamphetamine misuse and then quite suddenly barbiturates began to set a street problem. Cocaine use in the USA has caught that country badly off-guard and a new technique of cocaine inhalation (free-basing) has spread from coast to coast within a few years. Free-base cocaine, including "crack", has now made its appearance in the UK. The latest type of drug problem now on the horizon is that of the so-called "designer drugs", which are easily and cheaply prepared variants of more classic substances.

The unpredictable nature of drug problems relates not only to the type of drugs which may give rise to epidemics but also to the kind of populations which may prove vulnerable. One of today's fundamental assumptions is that drug problems are youth problems but this would have seemed absurd in 1950. The possibility of an association between conditions of urban deprivation and drug use is a concern which has arisen in Britain much more recently. Similarly, it has up to now been assumed in the UK that ethnic minorities are not particularly prone to drug misuse, except perhaps for cannabis smoking among people of West Indian origin. In view of the American experience it would be unwise to be too sanguine, and the fact that black communities in Britain are not as yet as badly affected by heroin may be a very fragile cause for comfort.

Yet another reason for wariness is the liability of established patterns of drug use to reveal sudden and unexpected adverse health consequences. The rediscovery over the last few years that a pregnant mother's excessive drinking can cause foetal damage or her smoking result in an under-weight baby, the discovery that cigarettes can cause cancer, and the extremely recent realisation that minor tranquillizers can give rise to severe and prolonged withdrawal symptoms, all provide instances of new hazards emerging with familiar and widely accepted types of drug use. An intensely topical health concern lies in the demonstration that the AIDS virus is spread by infected and shared needles and syringes, and is therefore a serious hazard to those involved in intravenous drug misuse. Intravenous drug misusers represent the most significant potential source for transmission of this virus to the heterosexual community.

The need for a better informed debate

It may be useful, at this point, to recapitulate and clarify the central argument of this chapter. Many people are confused and worried about drugs. Given the pace of change in the country's drug problems, it is not surprising that there has been difficulty in coming to terms with the unfamiliar and still evolving threats posed to individuals and society. The situation is not helped by cries of panic but nor can anxiety be allayed by patronising blandness.

The central purpose of this book is to support a more informed and objective debate on the nature, dimensions and causes of the country's drug problems in the belief that open debate is the best way of getting anxiety into perspective and of finding a way forward.

There must be a willingness to acknowledge that the debate can be conducted within terms of a number of alternative frameworks. The nature of debate itself is something which often needs to be understood when issues as socially contentious as drug misuse are being debated. The discussants themselves need to be sensitive and reflective about the assumptions and value-systems they bring with them. For instance, debate might be conducted equally well within a medical perspective, a social problems perspective, or a moral perspective. The debate may usefully concern the clash of these perspectives, but it would be harmful, for example, to introduce a seemingly medical definition of the debate with health appearing to be the highest priority if health is really only the stalking horse for social control or moralism. Although there is good evidence that excessive maternal drinking can cause or contribute to foetal abnormality, it is a misuse of that evidence to preach hell-fire to every woman who takes a glass of wine during pregnancy.

A willingness to examine multiple levels of understanding must also be an important feature of this debate. For example, drugs and drug dependence can be examined and debated legitimately in terms of what happens at receptor sites on the nerve cell or, alternatively, in terms of macro-economic influences which impinge on the planting of vineyards on Italian hillsides. It is necessary to look at the characteristics of the individual who is drawn into drug misuse but it is vital to avoid individualising the nature of the drug problem too narrowly. It is important to look at social and cultural as well as individual factors which predispose to drug misuse, at the social processes and competing factions which define the nature of the problems, and at the forces and perceptions which shape society's response. Society is the "case for study", as well as the patient.

There are, of course, many other characteristics of any debate which properly lays claim to being informed, and which pertain as much to drug misuse as to any other fruitful discourse. A thoughtful debate on drugs must have a sense of history, and of Britain's place within the world context of drug problems.

Chapter 2
Drugs that act on the mind

Drugs, as discussed in the context of this book, are chemicals which influence the mind. It is useful to have a basic classification of these substances, and this is provided in the first section of this chapter. Drugs may be taken into the body by different routes and the significance of choice of route will be discussed — what, for instance, are the implications of chewing rather than smoking tobacco? The factors which influence the actions of a drug on an individual will also be examined. It will be argued that a mechanistic "chemical which inexorably impinges on the brain" approach is an inadequate model for understanding the complexities of the drug and person interaction.

This chapter is a prelude to the more detailed "case histories" on different drugs provided in Section II of the book. It will aim to deal with general principles rather than detail, but a certain minimum of duplication with material in later chapters is inevitable for clarity of presentation.

A simple classification

There is an astonishing variety of drugs which can influence mental function. They range from such familiar substances as alcohol to exotics such as fly agaric. They may be derived from plant material or be the products of the laboratory. Some have a legitimate place in medicine while others may be used only illicitly for a "trip" or a "high". One drug calms the mind, another causes excitement, while yet another may offer infinitely complex mental experiences which defy easy description. Drugs vary in their harmfulness. Frequently the same substance will have a scientific name and a trade name, and it will probably be given different trade names in different countries.

18

Through all this complexity it is possible to construct a simple way of ordering and classifying drugs which is based on the fact that any drug is likely to belong to a recognisable family or type. A particular drug may have some special characteristics of its own but its general properties are likely to be those of its class.

Without going into too much technical detail it is useful to outline the scientific basis for this family segmentation. For drugs to be placed in the same group a number of different criteria have to be met. First, these drugs will have closely similar subjective and physiological effects on the human being, although they may differ in potency. Second, it may be the case that all drugs within one class attach themselves to the same type of microscopic "receptor sites" in the brain—for example, opiate drugs impinge on opiate receptors. Third, drugs which belong to the same family will produce broadly the same type of withdrawal state (p. 34). A fourth criterion is "cross tolerance", which implies that one drug will effectively substitute for another in the same group and so relieve the withdrawal symptoms which can occur with that other drug.

Five general types and some additional drugs

Most drugs can be placed in one of the five following categories: Opiates, Depressants, Stimulants, Hallucinogens and Minor Tranquillizers. There are however a number of important substances of a rather individual nature that do not fit easily into this classification and they will be considered separately.

Opiates (or opioids)

These drugs include a number of different chemical substances which can be extracted direct from the opium poppy (e.g. morphine and codeine), a "semi-synthetic" drug (heroin or diacetylmorphine) which is produced by chemical modification of the morphine nucleus, and a host of entirely synthetic substances such as methadone, meperidine (pethidine or demorol), dipipanone (diconal), dextromoramide and dihydrocodeine. Opiates have important uses in medicine—pain relief, suppression of cough, treatment of acute heart failure and symptomatic treatment of diarrhoea. They all tend to produce pleasant mood states characterised by euphoric detachment rather than simply a dulled sedation, and in varying degree they have a capacity to produce dependence which can cause a characteristic withdrawal state (see p. 57).

General depressants
This term is used to describe a group of drugs which have in common the ability to decrease the activity of the brain and thus cause sedation, sleepiness and relief of anxiety. Members of this family include alcohol, the barbiturates, chloral, paraldehyde and chlormethiazole. Paradoxically, these depressant drugs can appear to produce stimulation and excitement as a result of disinhibition, hence the popular misconception that alcohol is a stimulant. There is a characteristic withdrawal state (p. 157).

Minor tranquillizers (benzodiazepines)
Until recently many texts would have included the benzo-diazepines in the general depressant class of drugs because they produce much the same type and range of sedative-hypnotic effects. However, there is mounting evidence that the benzo-diazepines can result in a radically different type of dependence from that of the traditional depressants. For this, as well as certain other technical reasons, it seems sensible to give the benzodiazepines their own heading. They include such familiar drugs as chlordiazepoxide (Librium), diazepam (Valium), lorazepam (Ativan) and nitrazepam (Mogadon), as well as a host of other substances used for sedation, anxiety relief and muscle relaxation.

Stimulants
These drugs elevate mood, increase wakefulness, and give an enhanced sense of mental and physical energy. It is their ability to produce pleasurable stimulation and excitement which gives them their potential for misuse, and this category includes cocaine, the amphetamines and many other synthetics (e.g. phenmetrazine, diethylpropion, and other minor stimulants). Cocaine still has some use as a local anaesthetic and the amphetamines were once employed in medical practice but it is now recognised that their dangers far outweigh any advantages. Khat is a shrub whose leaves and twigs provide a mild stimulant widely used in certain parts of the Middle East, while caffeine is similarly used world-wide. It must be emphasised that dependence on major stimulants can be of devastating severity.

Hallucinogens (psychedelics or psychotomimetics)
These drugs can produce a spectrum of strange, intense and transcendental effects which give them their "recreational" popularity. They can also give rise to hallucinations (hence their name) and intense short-term mental disturbance. Included in this group is a wide variety of plant products such as peyote, mescaline, "magic mushrooms" containing psilocybin, and a large range of synthetics with LSD (lysergic acid diethylamide) as the prototype. Some had a traditional use in religious ritual while LSD for a time enjoyed a vogue as an adjunct to psychotherapy. Today, there are no orthodox medical indications for use of these drugs. Hallucinogens do not give rise to dependence in any true sense but nonetheless their use can be intensely hazardous.

Drugs that do not conform with the general classification
As already mentioned there are some drugs which do not fit into the five-part classification.

Cannabis
This is the inclusive name given to the products of the Indian Hemp plant. The principal active ingredient is delta-9 tetra-hydrocannabinol (THC). The reason why cannabis does not fit easily into the standard classification is that it can have actions both of a general depressant and hallucinogenic type.

Nicotine
This is another drug capable of producing complex effects. It has both stimulant and sedative properties.

Volatile inhalants
Under this heading can be placed many different industrial solvents, anaesthetic gases, glues, lacquers, lighter fuels and so on. This class of substances can produce rather mixed and complicated effects including sedative, anaesthetic and hallucinogenic experiences.

There are many other chemicals which have been reported at times as giving rise to some degree of misuse or dependence. Phencyclidine ("angel dust") originally introduced as a veterinary anaesthetic, has given rise to widespread misuse in the USA. It can cause intoxication, delirium and psychotic states. Amyl nitrite, a drug taken by inhalation and which is intended for the treatment of angina, has at times enjoyed a minor vogue among young people as a substance capable of producing a quick euphoric effect. The occasional patient will over-use adrenaline injections or ephedrine tablets prescribed for asthma, and rare cases have been reported of certain antidepressant drugs being misused.

There is at present acute concern about the possible spread of so-called "designer drugs" from North America to other parts of the world. This general term is used to describe a class of highly potent synthetic substances which mimic some of the properties of known drugs but which may also display new and very dangerous side-effects. Their clandestine manufacture is easily accomplished and they are likely to pose difficult problems of control.

A collector could go on extending the tail-end of this list almost endlessly. For practical purposes the conclusions are simple and two-fold. First, the great majority of the drugs to be dealt with in this book fit into one of the five major categories or constitute one of the major listed exceptions. Second, vigilance is needed in terms of health and social concern if we are to recognise in good time both newly emerging drug problems and unusual cases.

Routes of drug administration

The route by which a drug is taken into the body can be important for a number of reasons. Methods of administration vary in the rapidity with which a drug gets to the brain, in the likely blood or brain level achieved, in the risks of dependence, and in the danger of over-dose and certain types of physical damage. Some drugs can be taken in several different ways while for others only one method of administration is likely to be applicable. The principal routes are as follows:

Ingestion
Many drugs can be eaten or drunk — alcohol, laudanum (opium in alcoholic solution), bhang (a drink made from cannabis), and every variety of pill or capsule provides examples. The oral route is a slow way of getting the drug into the body compared with other methods and it is likely to carry lower risks of dependence.

Sucking or chewing
Cocaine has traditionally been used in the Andes by placing a wad of leaves inside the cheek, and a similar technique was employed

by the person who chewed his wad of tobacco. Tobacco is again being sold commercially in little packets like tea bags intended for sucking. Chewing provides a way of absorbing the drug through the lining of the mouth and it has the cost-effective advantage of not exposing the substance to destructive digestion in the stomach.

Inhalation

Inhalation is a rapid way of getting a drug into the blood stream through the lungs. Within 9 or 10 seconds of drawing on a cigarette a dose of nicotine reaches the brain. Some drugs are inhaled by smoking the raw materials (tobacco or cannabis), others are inhaled directly (volatile solvents), while still others rely on heat turning a solid into an inhalable gas by sublimation. An instance of the latter technique is seen in "chasing the dragon", when heroin is heated on a piece of tin foil and the upward-curling smoke rapidly inhaled. The so-called "free-basing" of cocaine provides a similar example.

Sniffing

Here the drug is absorbed through the lining of the nose. Tobacco snuff, sniffed cocaine and sniffed heroin illustrate this technique.

Intravenous injection

In objective terms this method is likely to be the most cost-effective manner of administering a drug as well as potentially the most dangerous. None of the drug is digested, burnt or otherwise wasted, and it is rapidly carried through the bloodstream from the injection site to the brain. There are great dangers of accidental overdose and all manner of dirt and infection can be introduced (hazards which are further discussed on p. 193). Intravenous injection is a particularly rapid way of establishing dependence on a drug. Heroin and other opiates are often taken by the intravenous route, cocaine can be used in this way, and barbiturate, amphetamine sulphate and other tablets or capsules which are not intended by the manufacturer for such administration can be ground up, mixed with water, and put into a syringe.

Other modes of injection

Some users, particularly at an early stage of their drug-using career, may prefer to inject a drug into their muscles or under the skin ("skin popping"). The same technique will have to be used if the surface veins have been blocked by the clotting and inflammation brought about by repeated injections.

Taking more than one drug at a time

There are patterns of drug taking which can involve the use of more than one drug either concurrently or in rapid sequence. There are, for example, a number of circumstances in which a stimulant and a depressant or opiate may be combined. Coffee is often taken with brandy, barbiturates and amphetamines used to be combined in pills known as "purple hearts", and the user of intravenous heroin may put cocaine into the same syringe. Such pharmacological pairings seem to result in a more pleasurable subjective effect than that obtained by the use of one type of drug alone. The stimulant effect of one drug can counteract the unwanted drowsiness induced by another.

Besides these fairly stable patterns of double use an opportunistic pattern consisting of varied and even chaotic sequential or concomitant use of almost any drug has frequently been observed. This type of multiple drug taking is referred to as "poly-drug misuse". It is typical of young urban drug-takers in many parts of the world today and might be seen as the ultimate common path when earlier indigenous patterns of drug use are overwhelmed by urbanisation and Westernisation. Heroin, cocaine, the over-spill of tranquillizers and sedatives, alcohol and tobacco, cannabis and hallucinogens will be used on the basis of availability and catch-as-catch can. The consequences are likely to be particularly untoward, and poly-drug misuse once established sets immensely difficult problems for treatment, prevention and control. There may be special dangers of overdose if, say, barbiturate use is combined with alcohol.

A drug's actions depend on more than the drug

It is a general truth that the effect that a drug will have on a given individual depends on several other factors besides its actual chemistry and this has a great bearing on many of the issues which will be discussed in later sections of this book. It is a mistake to think of drug actions on the brain only in terms of a direct cause and effect. A drug's actions are influenced to a large degree by personal characteristics of the individual, by the immediate setting and expectations, and by larger cultural influences which propose how the drug-taking is to be experienced.

As an example of individual differences in response to the same drug, people are commonly observed to respond differently to coffee. One person stays awake half the night after drinking a cup in the evening while his neighbour at the supper table drinks black coffee with impunity. Younger people and older people may be specially sensitive to the effects of a drug, and the mentally unstable, mentally ill or brain damaged person can react unpredictably. The influence of tolerance on the response to drugs is discussed later (p. 34).

Beyond these intrinsic individual differences which mediate and modify the drug response, there is also an inner ring of influences relating to environmental circumstances. If a person is told that LSD will give him richly mystical insights and there is soft lighting, silk cushions and Indian music, he may well be a candidate for transcendental experiences; while if someone has his beer spiked with LSD the onset of unexpected and unexplained distortions of perception may make him think that he is going mad.

The inner ring of the immediate environment merges with an outer ring of cultural influence. In India a farmer may give cannabis to his ox to make it work harder in the fields, while in Chelsea people smoke pot to relax and feel "laid-back". Drinking on the terraces may be associated with football hooliganism, but it would be far too simple to argue that drinking causes hooliganism; the drug effect is mediated through a cultural expectation that drinking in young men leads to, or indeed licenses, hooliganism.

These issues are therefore of more than mere academic importance. When the allure of drugs, their adverse effects, or the policies to mitigate those effects are considered, it is necessary to see the drug-brain interaction not as a simple chemical event but as a matter of considerable complexity involving the drug, the particular person, and the messages and teachings which come from the environment and which powerfully influence the nature and meaning of the drug experience.

Chapter 3
What is misuse?

If any debate is to be productive it is important at the outset to clarify the way in which key terms are to be used. "Drug misuse" is a term which will be employed throughout this book and it is vital therefore to define the meaning which it will be given. Such clarification is not just a matter of semantics. Implicit in such words as drug abuse, drug problem or drug misuse are complex and potentially value-laden ideas. The whole debate on drugs is at risk of being confused or distorted if the thinking behind such concepts is left vague.

A phrase which has recently come into favour in the UK is "the problem drug taker". This usefully emphasises that the focus of concern must be wider than the actual dependence on a drug. Prevention and treatment must be concerned with a wide range of possible social, physical and psychological causes and consequences of drug taking rather than just with the advanced case of addiction. This current phase may usefully help in a reorientation but otherwise begs many questions. What counts as a "problem"?

One man's meat

What one person stigmatises as the misuse of a drug someone else may see as innocent use. Here is a statement which paraphrases the views of an articulate young cannabis user:

> "All right, I smoke dope. It doesn't do me any harm. I've got a right to make my own choice—maybe you smoke cigarettes or drink beer. I don't see anything wrong in smoking dope, if you know what you're doing, use it sensibly. I don't call that 'a drug problem'. The only 'problem' comes from the State's persecution of cannabis users".

It is generally true that people tend to see their own drug use or the favoured substance of their peer group as "no problem", while at the same time viewing other peoples' drug taking as problematical. The cocaine user may not see cocaine as a problem — only perhaps heroin. The settled citizen who is taking quantities of tranquillizers and sleeping pills sees the "drug problem" as something a long way from home.

A despairing conclusion might be that all is in the eye of the beholder, and that we should therefore give up looking for an objective definition of the word "misuse". The young cannabis user who has just been quoted would dispose of that phrase as neither more nor less than a term of opprobrium applied by the state persecutors to other people's drug habits. However, beyond all this relativism it is possible to discern a set of premises which in almost anyone's judgement might constitute criteria for separating "use" from "misuse".

The search for objective criteria

If we identify these underlying criteria it should be possible, rationally, to test on which side of the use-misuse divide any particular type or pattern of drug taking may be deemed to fall. An attempt to list criteria which appear to be implicit in most approaches to this definition can be made as follows.

Actual harm to the individual
One element in the definition of misuse is the issue of harm. Misuse may be deemed to have occurred if an individual's drug taking has tangibly damaged physical or mental health or impaired that person's social functioning. It should be stressed that in terms of this element it is not necessary to wait for damage to be major or disastrous before seeing cause for concern. Drinking which is causing a hangover is misuse of alcohol.

Potential harm to the individual
A type or method of drug taking which puts the user's health or social well-being at risk of harm may be considered misuse even if overt harm has not as yet occurred. There is a parallel with driving — driving a motor car fast on the wrong side of the road around a blind corner constitutes dangerous driving whether or not the driver comes to actual harm at that moment. Intravenous

use of ground-up sleeping tablets is drug misuse whether or not the next injection happens to kill or cripple.

Actual or potential harm to other individuals
If a cigarette smoker puffs tobacco smoke in the faces of other people and exposes them to the potential risks of passive smoking, then the smoker's behaviour may be rated misuse. Taking a more extreme example, someone who commits an assault on another person while experiencing an LSD-induced psychotic state has as much misused that drug as a person who kills himself while in the same condition.

Harm to the interests of the community or state
This concept extends and goes beyond the simple idea of harm to individuals. In this instance the harm is to the public good. If individuals use heroin this cannot be viewed as an act which impinges on no one but themselves or their immediate family. Heroin use has economic, social and legal implications for the whole nation. The public has a right to express a view if the drug taking of certain individuals renders them incapable of contributing to the public purse while treatment of the consequences is consuming public resources. Society may also cry "misuse" if the individual's drug taking is seen as leading to wider social problems, luring others into drug involvement, or supporting criminal activity. But although the "public good" concept certainly needs to be acknowledged, society must be warned about certain rather facile assumptions that lurk in this area. It is for instance very unwise to assume that all young drug takers would be gainfully employed if only they stopped using drugs; many would simply take their place at the end of the youth unemployment queue. Furthermore, a significant proportion of young heroin users are already part of the work force.

Objectivity on whose authority?

The above analysis of the word "misuse" offers some explicit tests which can be applied in any particular circumstances. It would be pleasing if matters could be settled so simply, but that articulate young cannabis smoker will offer no such easy passage.

He will point out a set of difficulties in seemingly neat logic. For instance, he will insist that what at first appears to be harm consequent on drug misuse may be harm stemming from society's repressive reaction to the drug user and the consequent stigmatization and alienation which is engendered. Perhaps the heroin user dies in the public lavatory with a needle in his arm not so much because of the intrinsic danger of the drug but because he was put in prison for being in possession of heroin, released from gaol into a world of squats and homelessness, and then refused a supply of pure heroin from a clinic and left to buy dirty heroin of unreliable potency on the streets. If that argument makes the reader angry or uncomfortable (it is in some ways specious) there is more to follow. Who, for instance, arbitrates on "potential risk"? Who funds and who interprets the research which says that cannabis *may* cause psychosis? What is the probable risk of cannabis smoking leading to harm as compared with social drinking getting out of control?

Before these awkward contentions are dismissed as mere rhetoric, society would do well to heed the fact that they are exactly the type of arguments which are likely to be seriously and genuinely advanced by many people of good-will who question official attitudes to drugs and the boundaries which are set between "use" and "misuse". It will be necessary to look again at this particular topic later in this book when considering the debates which have evolved around specific drugs.

A working definition

Rather than retreating from the debate it is best to admit that the neat objective criteria which this chapter has offered are indeed tinged with subjectivity and arbitrariness. Use and misuse form a rather uncertain continuum. The proposed criteria are however likely to provide a reasonably helpful framework within which to discuss a range of individual drugs and drug-related issues. No doubt to the strong disapproval of that young cannabis user one further clause will be ventured at this stage. Any use of a drug which is outside the law may be regarded as *de facto* misuse, be it drinking alcohol to an extent which takes one over the legal limit, lighting up a cigarette in a no smoking area, being in possession of heroin, or cultivating, possessing or supplying cannabis.

In summary, the term "misuse" will be employed in this book with the following meaning:

Drug misuse is any taking of a drug which harms or threatens to harm the physical or mental health or social well-being of an individual, of other individuals, or of society at large, or which is illegal.

Within this formulation can be placed the dangerous use of licit substances such as alcohol and tobacco, the deleterious use of prescribed medicines and the taking of illicit drugs.

Chapter 4
The meaning of dependence

This chapter focuses on the meaning of just one phrase — "drug dependence". If that seems too academic it must be emphasised that as with the term "drug misuse", it is best to know what is being talked about before getting into any debate. Close exploration of the meaning of the word "dependence" can in fact lead to a very interesting journey.

The term "drug dependence" was recommended by the World Health Organization (WHO) in 1964 with the following proposed meaning:

"A state, psychic and sometimes also physical resulting from the interaction between a living organism and a drug, characterized by behavioural and other responses that always include a compulsion to take the drug on a continuous or periodic basis in order to experience its psychic effects, and sometimes to avoid the discomfort of its absence. Tolerance may or may not be present. A person may be dependent on more than one drug".

This dry form of words, drafted in a committee room in Geneva, represented a bold break with the received wisdom of previous years. WHO's purpose was to find a concept which would supplant the old idea of "addiction" which over the decades had become too narrow and too extreme in its connotations. There was a danger at that time that unless a drug habit conformed to the picture of morphine addiction it would be down-graded in importance and regarded as not quite a real addiction. Alcoholism, for instance, under the old terminology was viewed as an "habituation". WHO's 1964 approach proposed that each drug or family of drugs should be seen as giving rise to a particular type of dependence pattern, each being different but each valid in its own right. Morphine was no longer the template. "Dependence on alcohol" was now to be a full member of the club.

What people say about the dependence experience

Before seeking to analyse the meaning of the dependence idea it is worth noting that this come-lately concept stands in direct line with various other attempts to capture in words the following types of experiences:

> "I got to the stage when all I thought about was drink. I knew I'd got to get the boy a pair of jeans, I'd go down to the market and choose a pair, and then I'd say to myself why waste money, that's the price of a bottle of whisky".

> "You are a wonderful cook. No, I'm not going to have any salad thank you. Perhaps some of that delicious pudding later. Do you mind if I smoke?"

> "Right, I was a junkie. You know what that means? I walked the walk, I talked the talk. When I wasn't fixing I was scoring. Sick every morning".

> "Personally, I don't believe that one can be addicted to cannabis. But I found it far harder to stop than I ever expected".

> "Well, at the time I had this doctor who'd give me another lot of sleeping pills or tranquillizers as soon as I went into his consulting room, I got so I was taking too many. When in the end he said 'that's your limit' and tried to cut me down, I'd go round to other doctors and say I'm up from the country, got bad nerves, can you help me out? I felt terrible when I went into hospital and had to come off".

There is a common thread in what people are talking about although the experience is complex and difficult to capture in formal definitions. It would be doing those varied witnesses an injustice if what they are seeking to describe were to be dismissed as "just weak will" or "just excuses" or as "that's the way I feel about peppermint creams".

The historical background

The attempt to find words and concepts to capture those sorts of experience probably started at the end of the 18th or beginning of the 19th century. Drunkenness began in certain medical circles to be seen as a "disease" rather than a "vice", but there was still no special scientific terminology. The term "addiction" began occasionally to be used in the earlier part of the 19th century, but only in an imprecise fashion. People were more likely to see the issue in terms of the "opium sot" than the "opium addict" and it was common to refer to the "bad", the "stimulant" or the "luxurious" use of opium. It was only in the last quarter of the 19th century that the beginning of a scientific vocabulary emerged in this context, and in Britain the word "inebriety" came to the fore as an umbrella term rather similar in implications to the present day "dependence". Thus, in 1892, the "Inebriates Legislation Committee" of the British Medical Association pressed for "provision for the care and detention of inebriates in opium, morphine, chloral, chloroform, ether, cocaine or any other narcotic".

It was only at the onset of the present century and particularly in the years closely following the Great War that the word "addiction" came to replace "inebriety" and to hold sway in the English language and in Anglo-Saxon thinking.

"Addiction" thus became an accepted medical and scientific term, but in another sense it was always a word which carried trailing implications of evil, dark undertones of possession and an aura of moral decay. It is to be hoped that "dependence" has not become similarly tainted and that it is possible to approach the question of "what is dependence" with moralism set aside. There can be no doubt that *dependence* is now the accepted term scientifically, although *addiction* is still the term commonly used by the public. In this book the word "dependence" will usually be used, but not exclusively. For instance, the word "addict" can be preferable to the circumlocution "drug dependent person".

What is dependence?

This is not an easy question. What is the central nature of the condition about which those witnesses give so many hints and murmurs—craving and withdrawal symptoms, a sense of compulsion, alcohol more important than a pair of jeans? Is it simply a *physical* state or is it ultimately *psychological*? Or is it something to be explained by the sociologists? The answer has to be that it is a complex phenomenon which can truly be understood only as a meeting point of physical, psychological and social processes. In order to explain this statement these processes must be described in some detail.

Physical

Different types of dependence-inducing drug have different effects on the brain, but as a general rule biological systems react in such a way as to counter the effects of repeated drug administration. The person who regularly drinks eight pints of beer in an evening will not be obviously inebriated after such an intake (although he would be a menace behind the driving wheel and should be warned that such drinking carries many dangers). The ordinary pre-operative dose for an opiate would be about 10 mg and this would be enough to make most people drowsy: a heroin addict who has a well-established habit may have built up to a dose of 100 mg or more in one injection, an intake which would kill the ordinary pre-operative patient. Such *tolerance* may result from the drug being more rapidly cleared from the body (metabolic tolerance) or may reflect the direct ability of the brain cells to adapt (neuro-adaptation); the latter is usually by far the most important element in the build-up of tolerance. Some drugs (such as pentazocine) give rise to relatively little tolerance. Whatever the underlying causes the ultimate implication of tolerance is that a progressively increasing dose will be required to obtain the same effect.

The price to be paid for neuro-adaptation is a *rebound* when the drug is stopped and hence *withdrawal symptoms*. The withdrawal symptoms will tend to be the opposite of those produced by the drug itself. Thus withdrawal from a depressant drug will give rise to brain excitation. The excitation resulting from withdrawal of alcohol for instance, can cause hallucinations (DTs) or fits. Withdrawal of a stimulant such as amphetamine or cocaine will result in sleepiness, depression and a sense of let-down. Similarly, the characteristic withdrawal state associated with heroin and other opiates can be understood as the opposite picture to the direct effects on the nervous system of that class of drug, namely psychological distress as well as a host of physical symptoms such as diarrhoea, running nose and goose pimples.

For some dependence-inducing drugs, physiological withdrawal symptoms may be relatively slight (nicotine provides an example), while for other substances, such as the depressants and opiates, the withdrawal experience can range from mild to devastating in its intensity. The reality of these types of physiological disturbance is not to be doubted and here it is only possible to touch on the complexity of the issues involved. Tolerance and withdrawal are, for example, in many ways related, but do not always go hand-in-hand. There is no one underlying physiological mechanism which will account for all the phenomena which can occur here — physical dependence may involve changes in transmitter substances (chemical messengers), alterations in the permeability of nerve cell membranes, or interactions with the body's own natural production of opiate-like substances.

Whatever the subtlety and complexity of such disturbances one is left with the fact that many dependence-producing drugs can produce profound physiological malfunctions on their withdrawal. Physical withdrawal syndromes are not, however, the *essence* of dependence. It is possible to have dependence without withdrawal and withdrawal without dependence. The true significance (and limits in significance) of the physical element in dependence will become clear when the other two elements, psychological and social, are examined.

Psychological
Psychological factors are involved in the genesis and maintenance of dependence in several ways. Dependence-inducing drugs have the ability to act as reinforcers of drug-seeking activity. A monkey which is able to secure its own injection of cocaine in an experimental situation will press a bar in its cage several thousand times so as to get a further shot of the drug. Dependence is in this sense a *learnt* (operantly conditioned) behaviour. Other forms of learning can also affect dependence. The recurrent experience of withdrawal symptoms followed each time by relief of withdrawal by further drug taking can serve as additional and potent reinforcement for drugs such as the opiates. Secondary learning factors in relation to stimuli in the environment can trigger withdrawal symptoms or craving. The person who has developed a high degree of alcohol dependence reveals the force and reality of this psychological influence when he reports that after weeks of abstinence he still has to take a circuitous route

so as to avoid walking past bars or liquor stores. Such cues make him feel "very uncomfortable". Similarly, an injecting drug user may relate that in the early months of abstinence the sight of a needle or syringe brings on the actual physiological disturbance of a withdrawal state. Still at this psychological level of explanation, the importance of the way in which the drug user comes to think about himself and his drug taking may be very relevant. A patient who sees himself as addicted to cigarettes can set up a self-fulfilling prophecy that he is in the grip of an ineradicable compulsion. Such thoughts (or cognitions) merge with far more complex and perhaps unconscious mental processes at the psychodynamic and emotional level of psychological functioning.

Social

The psychological and social aspects of dependence are not completely separate. The individual learns the role of "addict", or "junkie", and may find that it is rewarding in giving him a personal sense of identity—being an addict is being someone. The jargon becomes part of the image. Dependence may be further reinforced by the positive experiences which come from being a member of a drug-using group, a sub-culture with shared attitudes to drug taking and to wider aspects of life. The slog and "hassle" of ensuring one's drug supply can itself become meaningful; it is something to do, the framework for the day, a job in its own right.

Dependence—the whole picture

Having tried to identify the three major elements in dependence it is important to stress that such divisions are somewhat academic. In reality what has to be assessed is the degree to which this or that element is contributing to the total field of interaction which keeps the dependence process spinning in any individual case. Such a vision of the nature of dependence is the only basis on which to respond to an individual in trouble, plan treatment, set up prevention programmes, or design national policies on a large scale. Such simplifications as "it's all in the drug" or "it's all psychological" or "it's all in the life style" will not serve society well.

Dependence syndromes

A 1981 report from the World Health Organization described recent thinking on the nature of dependence in the following terms which are close to those just presented:

> "The view that dependence is a clustering of phenomena (cognitive, behavioural and physiological) implies that multiple criteria are necessary for its assessment".

The report also outlined an identikit picture of the main features which, with variations, can be found to make up the "dependence syndromes" of most types of drug. An advantage of this WHO "syndrome" approach is that its elements rightly mix and cut across the physical, psychological and social dimensions. These features were described as including:

> "—a subjective awareness of compulsion to use a drug or drugs, usually during attempts to stop or moderate drug use;
> —a desire to stop drug use in the face of continued use;
> —a relatively stereotyped drug-taking habit i.e. a narrowing in the repertoire of drug-taking behaviour;
> —evidence of neuroadaptation (tolerance and withdrawal symptoms);
> —use of the drug to relieve or avoid withdrawal symptoms;
> —the salience of drug-seeking behaviour relative to other important priorities;
> —a rapid reinstatement of the syndrome after a period of abstinence".

This set of seven points provides a useful check-list if one remembers not only the considerable variability between the pictures produced by different drugs but also the fact that any individual's dependence will have to be placed somewhere along a very wide range of possible severity. One person may be just getting into cigarette smoking and still feel that his smoking is a rather casual and unimportant habit. Another may have reached the stage when he or she needs to light up a cigarette before getting out of bed in the morning (and certainly at supper before the pudding). In extreme cases dependence on say heroin, cocaine or alcohol may represent a condition of awesome severity, a disorder which dominates and destroys the individual. But even with those drugs dependence can show wide variation in intensity. It would therefore be as wrong to stereotype dependence as always overwhelming as it would be to dismiss it as trivial—the idea of range and the possibility of shift over time is essential to a true understanding of the phenomenon.

Drug misuse and drug dependence— how they do or do not go together

The meaning of the term *drug misuse* was discussed in Chapter 2 and that of *drug dependence* in this chapter. How are the two concepts related? The following three statements together seek to answer that question:-

(1) **Drug misuse can occur in the entire absence of dependence**. A dangerous drug, such as LSD, can be misused and give rise to serious problems although it has no great dependence potential. It must also be noted that many drugs with a severe dependence potential can give rise to misuse even when they have not been employed by an individual in such a way as to give rise to dependence. It is possible, for example, to develop alcoholic cirrhosis of the liver or to crash a car when drunk, without ever having reached the stage of alcohol dependence. *Misuse therefore matters in its own right*; it is not some kind of "poor relation" to dependence.

(2) **Drug dependence can occur without drug misuse**. This is another important fact which needs to be underlined. Dependence is not necessarily harmful in all circumstances and with all drugs. For instance, the traditional Eastern opium smoker may have been heavily dependent on his drug but, provided he had the money to support his habit comfortably, he might set himself and his family no problems for many years, and do himself no harm. He was perhaps a user rather than a misuser of opium.

(3) **Drug misuse and drug dependence often go hand-in-hand**. This further statement corrects any false romanticism about the innocent joys of the opium saloon. The opium smoker,

if heavily dependent, frequently neglected his business and social responsibilities as well as impairing his own health. By the same token some heroin takers may continue to inject the drug into their veins for many years without apparent harm and there are reports of stabilised or well-adjusted heroin users. However, much more often there is manifest damage or threat of damage, and so the appropriate word is "misuse". Hoping to get away with dependency on alcohol, barbiturate, cocaine or opiate, without incurring the pains and problems which mark the territory of *misuse*, is usually a quest for cloud-cuckoo land.

Chapter 5
Why do people misuse drugs?

The heading to this chapter represents a real question which is widely asked by people in the community. For instance, it is often raised by worried parents when a son or daughter is found to be taking drugs. Beyond this personal concern the question is also asked at a broader level. Why is this country experiencing a worsening drug problem? The answers must bear on policy decisions and on matters of prevention.

Certainly there is no single answer to this persistent question. Some people would like to believe that drug misuse is caused by "permissiveness"; others that it is due to the stress of modern life; still others that the cause lies in inner-city deprivation and the adverse social milieu. The truth is more difficult. The causes of drug misuse are multiple, varied and inter-related. To understand both the individual's and society's drug taking it is necessary to analyse the possible contributions of a number of influences. In this chapter these potential influences will be examined under a sequence of headings. It will start with the significance of what drugs actually and immediately do to and for the individual—their perceived "usefulness". The next issue will be the influence of a drug's availability on the likelihood and level of its use or misuse. Somewhat related to this point is the role of the drug pusher. From questions relating to aspects of the drug and its supply, the chapter proceeds to an examination of factors within the individual and, in particular, the vulnerability of the young. It then moves on to the influence of concentric layers of the environment; the family, the peer group, and the wider society. The need to integrate these levels of understanding is stressed.

The usefulness of drugs

One explanation for drug taking is that drug takers derive pleasure or benefit from the experience which a chemical provides — a thrill, a risk, a "high", or the relief of pain or anxiety. That type of reasoning may be too simple but it contains a measure of truth.

Unpleasant feelings and experiences are often alleviated in the short term by drugs, hence of course the medical use of tranquillizers. For some adolescents who are going through a period of personal anxiety, experimentation with drugs might be seen in part as a form of self-medication. The types of psychological distress which may provide an invitation to drug taking extend beyond such readily diagnosable states as "anxiety" or "depression" and are often far more amorphous — boredom or a sense of emptiness for instance, frustration, a lack of sense of purpose, half-suppressed anger, impairment of self-esteem. Drugs can be taken as an immediate short cut to pleasure and happiness and for spurious thrills.

At times drugs have also been used for other and more specific functional purposes. Long-distance truck drivers have used amphetamines as a means of keeping awake and people who are over-weight have been given these drugs for slimming. In some countries alcohol is the cheapest source of calories. Hallucinogens have been used as a doorway to mystical experience, as described in Aldous Huxley's *Doors of Perception*.

The personal usefulness of a drug must however be seen in terms of more than just its chemical impact on the brain. Taking a drink, a pill, a sniff of glue or an injection of heroin, can have a psychodynamic significance; the daughter of the alcohol-dependent mother may drink to identify with or punish that parent; the young heroin taker may be injecting his drug as a way of expressing his sense of worthlessness and despair or as an escape from his difficulty in human relationships. Drugs can also have a group or social value as will be discussed later.

Availability of the drug

It is a general truth that any factors which increase the availability of a drug will augment the likelihood of its use and misuse. The peasant farmer in Thailand who is growing opium poppies is more likely to use opium for his toothache than the farmer who is only growing vegetables. Similarly, the medical doctor in a Western country who has access to opiate drugs is more likely to become dependent on heroin or pethidine than the accountant living next door. Brewery workers are prone to drink too much of their own beer.

The examples given above illustrate the relevance of availability in its most obvious form, but the issues involved are usually more subtle. Availability in the wider sense depends not only on physical access to the product but also on the personal attitudes and social precepts which may or may not stand in the way of using that substance. Different opium growing villages experience different levels of opium misuse.

The availability of some drugs can be a reflection of medical prescribing or over-prescribing, whether of minor tranquillizers, sleeping pills, stimulants or opiates. With other drugs availability can be rooted in the black-market structure. The quest for understanding then leads back to the socio-economic situation of poor Third World countries producing opium or cocaine as well as the ramifications of the illicit international trade and the dealing systems which ultimately make these drugs available at the street corner. In many circumstances the availability of legal substances such as nicotine and alcohol is influenced by price and spending power (p. 174), and to an extent the same applies to illicit drugs.

Availability is thus the background to many subtle, personal, and cultural influences on drug taking. It would be dangerous to consider its relevance to policies on prevention only in terms of a mechanistic type of explanation. Clearly the explanations are likely to be multiple and interactive rather than single. Publicans have a high rate of cirrhosis of the liver, but why did that particular barman decide to take up that trade?

Pushers

The "evil drug pusher" has been a favourite demon in stories of drug taking. He is pictured as lurking at the edges of the school playground and even perhaps slipping heroin into the proferred bags of sweets. Illicit drugs are certainly sold and distributed through a structured system of importers and large-scale and small-scale dealers (many of the latter are themselves drug users), but the demon drug-pusher as an alien figure waiting in the shadows to corrupt the nation's youth is a figment of imagination.

Young people who start to take heroin will seldom do so because a drug pedlar has sought to deprave them but because they are mixing in a group in which heroin is available, because they are casually offered the drug by a friend, and because a variety of social and personal factors has increased the likelihood that they will accept such an offer. Much the same could be said about the first use of a cigarette or any other type of drug taking. Nevertheless there must be concern about the individual in the peer group who proselytises on behalf of drugs, who always has some for sale to friends, and who provides the contact between that drug-using circle and the outside dealer.

Aspects of the individual

Are people who misuse drugs "normal" or is there always a primary and underlying disorder of personality? The possible existence of an "addictive type of personality" has been much debated and researched. The best evidence is that no single underlying trait or unique constellation of personality features can be identified as predisposing to drug misuse. Some people will drink heavily because they are extrovert and like to engage in a lot of whatever is happening, while someone else in a corner of the same bar may be drinking heavily in lonely introverted reverie.

Almost any aspect of personality which makes it less easy for an individual to find ordinary rewards in life and ordinary happiness or to fit in with his peer group (and so provokes anxiety and tension) may predispose to drug taking as a short-term answer to such problems. Some of the possible feelings which might be relevant have been mentioned earlier in this chapter in relation to the functional usefulness of drugs.

If one dimension of character disturbance relates to non-specific aspects of personal distress, another dimension relates to a propensity to rule-breaking, to disregard for social expectations, and to a willingness to engage in deviant behaviour. However, it is too easy a leap from postulating that such personality characteristics may sometimes have a bearing on the genesis of drug taking to the all-embracing assumption that drug misuse must be a variant of so called "sociopathy" or "psychopathy".

While this leap is easy it is also dangerous. Many people who are misusing heroin may be found to have some characteristics which would fit them for a diagnosis of sociopathy; many other heroin users in that same patch of city will fail to exhibit these characteristics. Furthermore, what is being stigmatised as an underlying personality disorder causing drug misuse may on more sensitive exploration be understood as maladjusted behaviour resulting from involvement in the chaotic and deviant world of the drug user—that young woman is stealing and engaging in prostitution not because of an initial underlying psychopathy but because she needs to do this to pay for her heroin. What passes as sociopathy in the eyes of the middle-class investigator, who is looking at the inner-city drug sub-culture as an outsider, can sometimes more accurately be interpreted as an adaptive set of rules and behaviour for survival in an environment which is alien to that investigator's own background.

A final aspect of the possible contribution of individual factors to the genesis of drug taking relates not to personality disorder but to mental illness. Is there, for instance, a higher proportion of people with schizophrenia or manic-depressive illness among drug misusers than is to be found in the general population? The answer depends in part on how you define these underlying illnesses. Certain American sources have reported a rather high rate of depression among opiate users. It seems improbable, however, that gross mental illness is ever likely to make more than a marginal contribution to the totality of drug misuse which to date is certainly the British experience.

A general proposition relating to the influence of personality factors on drug taking is sometimes described within what is called the two-factor theory. This proposes that the more the environment invites drug taking, the less likely is it that the person who takes that drug will be found to be in any way different from the generality of the population. No one is seriously proposing that psychopathy is an explanation for cigarette smoking. But this theory also suggests that when there is a heavy loading of personal abnormality very little additional pressure will be needed from the environment to tip the individual toward drug taking. That there is truth in this limb of the argument can be illustrated by those individuals who are most intensively and self-destructively involved in heroin taking, as, for example, the addict who has thrombosed or blocked all his limb veins and still persists in trying to inject into his neck. Not even his drug-using friends countenance this dangerous practice; they regard him as a tragic and burnt-out case, a liability. It is not too difficult to believe that it is at this sad end of the spectrum that severe personality problems will be found to cluster.

The question of age

Cutting across all the personal and social factors which have been discussed above is that of age. Is "the drug problem" simply a "youth problem"?

The eruption of illicit drug misuse which has occurred in many countries over the last decades has predominantly involved adolescents and young adults. Where opiate or similarly dangerous drug use develops there often seems to have been a progression from the use of so-called "gateway" drugs (tobacco, alcohol, cannabis), in the mid-teenage years, to experimentation with perhaps amphetamines or sedatives a little later, while by the late teens or early twenties this is followed by the first use of heroin or other injectable drugs. Of course such a progression may stop short anywhere along the line. In many settings it would be unusual to find a person who was initiated into heroin use after the age of 25, especially if he or she had not had prior experience with these "gateway" substances.

To that extent, and within the "drug epidemic" perspective, the upswing in drug misuse can therefore be viewed as a youth problem. There has also been an increase in smoking and drinking among the young age group. These statements have to be balanced, however, by an awareness that much self-damaging drug taking is an adult activity — the misuse of psychotropics, the bulk of cigarette smoking and excessive drinking all exemplify this fact. Alcohol problems among the elderly have recently been recognised as a clinical concern. To point a finger at the young while ignoring the drug taking of their elders is false and hypocritical.

If it is accepted that within these balanced terms there is still truth in the assertion that the young are particularly vulnerable to drug misuse, one then has to explore the reasons for this relationship.

The answer lies partly in adolescence being generally and properly an age of experiment, adventure, risk-taking and challenge to authority. It is a time of urgent quest for self-identity and for the winning of approval from a peer group outside one's home. It is also frequently a time of much pain and inner perplexity, and for coming to terms with sexuality and disappointments in love. These late teenage years may be a time for moving from both home and school and of facing the demands of university, the first job or indeed unemployment. The shift from adolescence to adulthood is inherently a difficult business. It is a stage of development through which most young people will pass successfully but every aspect of this process of transition carries some risk of the possible lure of drugs and drug-centred groups.

Families

Families can influence the likelihood of drug taking both in terms of protecting against or alternatively increasing the risk involved. The children of cigarette smokers are at greater risk of growing up to be smokers than are children who have grown up in a non-smoking home. A family which is unhappy and unsupportive puts its young members at increased risk of many problems, including drug taking. A broken home can expose a child to similar problems. Conversely, a family which offers both affection and firm expectations is one which will be relatively, but not absolutely, protected against dangerous adolescent experimentation with drugs. It is necessary to say "not absolutely" because other interacting factors may so conspire that a singularly happy and loving family suddenly finds that a late teenage son or daughter is injecting heroin.

To state once more the general truth that a well-integrated family offers a good start in life may seem platitudinous. However, in the context of drug problems and the prevention of such problems this well-worn statement is not a platitude. It is not possible to wave a magic wand or legislate for family happiness, but understanding the genesis of drug problems means re-discovering in particular form the relevance of certain fundamental truths, whether it is the integration of the family, the quality of schooling or the implications of rewarding employment and social opportunity.

A very different aspect of family influence is the possible role of genetics in predisposition to drug taking. So far as alcohol is concerned there is evidence that genetic loading may contribute in some cases to the individual becoming an excessive drinker. Even so the contribution to drinking made by genetic factors is never likely to be more than a small part of the total explanation. In relation to drugs other than alcohol, there is no evidence available which persuasively answers this question. There is, of course, a danger in a ready acceptance of an "hereditary taint" when it would be more accurate but more disturbing to look at the actual structure and dynamics of that family or the conditions of the city in which the family lives.

Peer groups and sub-cultures

Drug taking is frequently a group activity, be it glue sniffing or a round of drinks. The group proposes that the drug should be taken, aids in its supply, and gives moral support and approval to its use. The drug-taking activity is invested with meaning by a group consensus which goes far beyond the significance of any direct chemical impact on the brain. Cannabis is smoked by Rastafarians in a seemingly religious context; the same drug will be seen as evidence of liberal thinking among some student groups, while its use among a group of adolescents may symbolise toughness and daring.

Beyond the immediate group influence is the potential bearing of a *sub-culture*. By this is meant a social network of shared beliefs, values, and practices which are in some ways distinct from those of the surrounding and larger society. Drug taking epitomises the tangible reality of this concept. For instance, a young executive is free-basing cocaine with his friends in a penthouse flat not simply because this immediate group thinks that cocaine is fun. He and they are also influenced by and responding to the wider sub-cultural ethic of a particular sector of society which believes that cocaine symbolises success, sophistication, and the "penthouse" life. Cocaine is as much a symbol of exuberant affluence as the expensive sun-tan.

Different drugs are embedded in very different sub-cultures. Down the road from those cocaine using executives there may exist a heroin-taking sub-culture. For this social network injecting of opiates and other drugs, talking about drugs in a "junky" argot, "scoring skag", all provide a shared meaning to life which links city with city. The other side of town a punk group may be using amphetamines because they believe that punks ought to take amphetamines.

Society and culture

In analysing the multiple causes of drug-taking the logical next step beyond the individual, the group, and the sub-cultural influences must be the outer ring of the wider environment — the influence of society and culture at large.

Some cultures are permissive toward alcohol, and particularly those regions which are engaged in wine-growing: France, Italy or Chile provide examples. Many aspects of everyday life in those countries are likely to encourage drinking, not only in terms of the ready availability of relatively cheap alcohol sold in every café, taverna or bodega, but also because the social norms subtly approve or encourage drinking. It is as socially approved in such countries to have a glass of wine at mid-morning as it is to ask for a cup of coffee. In contrast in traditional Chinese culture drinking is something to be engaged in only moderately, and drunkenness is tantamount to "loss of face".

Drinking thus provides classic examples of the power and relevance of socio-cultural influences in determining norms and patterns of a particular drug's use and consequent levels of harm. Can similarly large-scale environmental influences be seen as having an impact on levels of drug use within a society? Many Western countries are pro-drug societies with lax attitudes to drunkenness, with advertisements for cigarettes on every hoarding, with pop stars who are directly or indirectly advocating the splendours of cannabis or LSD, and with a population which expects the medical profession to provide a pill for every ill. It has to be asked whether in that kind of social climate warnings about the evils of adolescent drug taking can carry much weight. Perhaps it is rather too self-comforting for adults to believe that grown-up attitudes towards chemical pleasures are a world away from the attitudes formed by the young.

Under this broad environmental heading the realities of what life can provide have to be considered as much as the beliefs and attitudes which society puts on offer. In sections of a society where there is poor housing, poor education and uncertain job opportunities and where many people are living in isolation and outside any intimately supportive social structure, all kinds of medico-social problems are likely to be rife, as for instance child abuse, delinquency or suicide. It is not surprising therefore that, if serious drug problems start to spread nationally, certain cities or city tracts will be more vulnerable to such an epidemic than more privileged localities. Causality is not always straightforward. It is not necessarily poor quality housing or unemployment which are directly influential, but more probably the indirect influence of breakdown in social and family support, and the social climate which prevails.

As was stressed at the beginning of this chapter, all-inclusive explanations of drug-taking are a deception and this is equally true of "social deprivation" as *the* cause of drug problems. At certain times and in some parts of a country such an explanation may have force, but even in the most run-down city ghetto only a minority of young people will be using heroin. Furthermore, it is all too likely that heroin will be found to have made its entry in the neighbouring suburb of privileged mansions and swimming pools. One explanation is never the whole answer.

Putting explanations together

This chapter has placed much emphasis on the need to search for multiple and interactive causes of drug misuse rather than on easy universal explanations. The phrase "multiple and interactive" can however appear a little too academic. Let us briefly try to make this phrase more real by looking at the history of a 22 year-old heroin user:

Tom had been brought up on a West Country farm. His father was an excessive drinker and was frequently brutal when drunk. His mother "had bad nerves" and "took Valium by the handful". Tom was described by his school-masters as "a loner". At 16 he ran away to London, worked as a kitchen porter, was rapidly introduced to alcohol through the dregs in other peoples's glasses and was introduced to cannabis at the discos he frequented. He lived in squats or slept rough. Before long he embarked on a series of chaotic sexual adventures and was working as a prostitute although he would never have given himself this designation. An older man introduced him to heavy use of cocaine and paid for his drug; he moved from discos to nightclubs. That affair broke down and in a mood of depression he began to use heroin. The heroin came from Afghanistan.

"Why", this chapter argues, is a necessary but not an easy question. Taking an extreme case as that above may make a point but it can also be misleading. Why, today, is some doctor giving a patient repeated Valium prescriptions which have extended continuously over a two-year period? Why indeed is the doctor himself smoking 40 cigarettes a day? These questions are as pertinent at the undramatic as at the dramatic end of the spectrum. Whatever the drug, and whoever the drug taker, the complexity has to be met rather than denied.

Part II
Drugs and society

Chapter 6
Opiates

Ask the average person in the street what he or she means by drugs or drug addiction and it is likely that the automatic answer will be in terms of heroin. Heroin is portrayed as being in some mystical sense the ultimate drug evil. Britain is unusual in the world community in allowing heroin to be used for legitimate medical purposes such as pain relief and care of the terminally ill. Furthermore, this country stands virtually alone in it being legally permissible in certain circumstances (p. 204) for British doctors to prescribe heroin in the treatment of addiction. In nearly every other country the addictive potential of heroin is viewed as so dangerous that medical practitioners are totally banned from prescribing it.

This chapter focuses on the opiates, and heroin firmly finds its place within that class of substances. The discussion which follows will trace the extended history of Britain's involvement with opiates over the centuries and the twists and turns in that remarkable story. Because society has had such a long acquaintance with opiates, the way in which it has grappled with this particular group of drugs highlights many important general themes, and so more attention has been given to historical issues than has been thought necessary with many other drugs mentioned in this book.

The chapter starts with some notes on the major opiates which to a lesser or greater degree are subject to misuse in Britain today, together with a brief discussion of their dependence potential and lethality. This builds on the short section on the pharmacology of these substances in Chapter 2. The discussion will then move on to a consideration of various aspects of society's long involvement with the derivatives of the poppy and their chemical imitators.

53

What are the opiates?

Without going into too much technical detail it may be helpful to list some of the commoner opiate drugs which anyone may read about in the newspapers.

Opium is obtained by scarifying the seed pods of the poppy; the resulting exudate is scraped off as a gummy paste. Opium in this form is rarely used in Britain today, as the black-market usually sees this product converted chemically into the more profitable and less bulky heroin.

Morphine. Opium comprises more than 20 separate alkaloids (alkaline drugs) of which the most important is morphine. The morphine thus obtained is about 10 times more powerful on a weight for weight basis than raw opium itself, and has become the standard opiate against which all others are measured.

Codeine is another of the alkaloids found in opium and is widely used for the relief of mild to moderate pain, as a treatment for diarrhoea and vomiting, and as a cough suppressant. It is available in numerous over-the-counter preparations, often in combination with other pain-killers such as aspirin or with stimulant drugs such as ephedrine and caffeine.

Heroin (diacetylmorphine) is a chemically obtained derivative of morphine and in the body it is converted back again to the parent substance. In equivalent doses heroin is about two-and-a-half times as potent as morphine.

Dipipanone has been widely misused in Britain in the last decade. It is marketed in combination with the anti-nausea drug cyclizine as Diconal. Although the tablet is designed for oral use only, a large number of drug users found that it was easy to obtain from some doctors who lacked care or scruples, and they would then crush and dissolve the tablet for injection. Diconal was regarded by many drug users as being as attractive as heroin and it commanded a similar black-market price. In 1984 an amendment to the Misuse of Drugs Act was passed which prohibited doctors from prescribing dipipanone to drug addicts unless a special licence for such prescribing had been obtained by the doctor from the Home Office (see p. 204). This placed Diconal in the same category as heroin and cocaine, and since this date the prescribing of Diconal to opiate addicts has virtually ceased.

Pethidine is another entirely synthetic opiate-like drug which comes in tablets and ampoule form. Its sole medicinal use is as a pain-killer. Its addictive potential has sometimes been under-estimated and patients have become addicted in the course of treatment for painful illness, while individuals in the health professions have themselves become addicted as a result of self-prescribing. However, pethidine has not become a popular "street" drug in Britain.

Dextromoramide has been an increasingly popular drug among drug users and is known under its brand name of Palfium. It is manufactured as tablets, ampoules and suppositories, but it is the tablets which are most usually available on the black-market. Although the tablets are prepared for oral use, the black-market purchaser will frequently crush and inject this material.

Methadone is seen as the opiate of choice by prescribing drug clinics in the treatment of drug addicts (see p. 188). Probably its main merit from the point of view of these clinics is its unexciting characteristics in oral form, with a slow onset and long duration of action over 24 hours, permitting once daily intake. Methadone, prepared as an uninjectable linctus, provides a competent means of controlling withdrawal symptoms while the opiate addict gradually reduces the dose to zero. The black-market appeal of this form of the drug is considerably less than that of the other major opiates, although methadone in tablet or ampoule form has some small popularity on the black-market.

Opiate antagonists are drugs which occupy the opiate receptor sites in the brain yet do not induce euphoria (a sense of mental well-being). In an individual who is not physically dependent they will merely block or reverse the effect of a recently-taken opiate, and will have no effect if no opiate has been taken. As such they can be life-saving when given to the unconscious patient who has taken an opiate overdose. In an opiate addict who has become physically dependent an antagonist will also block any opiate effect and will consequently precipitate a sudden full-blown opiate withdrawal syndrome. The only commercially available opiate antagonist in use today in the UK is naloxone (marketed as Narcan) which is available in ampoule form for emergency injection as treatment of suspected opiate overdose. This drug appears to have no abuse potential and no black-market value. Naltrexone (see p. 189) is a new opiate antagonist which is not yet available in the UK but is currently being studied. It is manufactured as a tablet for oral use (unlike the injection-only naloxone) and has a long duration of effect of well over 24 hours (unlike the three or four hours effect of naloxone). Once product safety and efficacy have been established for naltrexone, it may be that this drug will have a future place in helping the recently detoxified patient remain off drugs.

Mixed agonist/antagonists are drugs which occupy the opiate receptor sites in the brain and exert effects which are partly morphine-like (agonist effects) whilst in other sites they will block these effects (antagonist effects). One example of this group of drugs is pentazocine which may be prescribed for the relief of moderate to severe pain.

Buprenorphine is a relatively recent agonist-antagonist which is available on prescription for the relief of mild to moderate pain. In the last year or two, there have been reports of increasing misuse of this drug by opiate addicts who crush and inject the tablets to obtain a heroin-like effect. Buprenorphine is not currently covered by the Misuse of Drugs Act, nor by international conventions.

Opiates: effects, dependence potential and lethality

Opiates exert their main effects on the central nervous system (CNS) and on the gastro-intestinal tract. It is the former site of action which accounts for the misuse potential and dependence liability of this group of drugs. CNS effects include pain relief and euphoria. When taken by a rapid-delivery system (such as intravenously or by smoking heroin), the sense of euphoria is intense and this "rush" has sometimes been likened to sexual orgasm.

It is important to consider the pain relief as covering emotional as well as physical pain. Not only do opiates relieve the pain of a broken leg or the ache of a chronic ulcer, but they also numb the misery of a broken relationship and dull the distress of an unhappy marriage, isolation, poor housing and unemployment. Such drugged relief of emotional and social adversities can of course only be superficial and spurious; the underlying problems remain unresolved and are screened only temporarily by the haze of opiates. It is the combination of pain relief and euphoria which make the opiates particularly valuable in the management of patients with painful and incurable conditions.

Opiates are drugs with dependence (addiction) potential, and the person who has become dependent will show drug tolerance, causing a need to increase the dose required to obtain the same effect, a characteristic set of withdrawal symptoms, and a manifest craving to go on taking the drug. Different members of this class of drugs possess varying degrees of dependence potential but it would be totally misleading to see the risk of dependence as rooted solely in the chemical structure of the drug. The risk depends also on the personality of the user and his subjective experience of the drug, on the way the drug is used, and on the surrounding circumstances.

Heroin carries an exceptionally high risk of dependence and it is interesting therefore that even this dangerous substance can be seen to illustrate the fact that there is no drug in which casual use leads inexorably to fully-established dependence. It is certainly true that for most heroin users their dependence crept up on them unaware while they deceived themselves into thinking that they were in control of the drug. The spread of heroin taken by smoking in the last decade was accompanied by a mistaken belief that physical dependence was a feature only of injected use, and many heroin smokers were surprised by the power of the compulsion once their habit was established.

Nevertheless there are instances of young people taking heroin on a casual or weekend basis without apparently going on to develop dependence. Anyone attempting to do this is, of course, courting extreme danger of dependence and all its untoward consequences.

The use of heroin and other opiates can threaten life in several different ways. These drugs are frequently taken by intravenous injection with all the attendant dangers of infection—AIDS, hepatitis, septicaemia and so on. Deaths can also result from an acute out-pouring of fluid into the lungs (pulmonary oedema). The special danger attached to many opiates is the possibility of death associated with overdose and the depression of breathing if the user miscalculates the dose, buys a black-market drug of unusual potency or forgets that tolerance to the drug will be diminished after a period of abstinence.

Opiates and society

The history of the opiates starts with opium use in ancient civilisations and goes on to the heroin epidemics of modern cities and the shadowy threat of new and yet more dangerous opiate-like drugs.

The long history of opium

Opiates are very definitely not new to mankind. Sumerian tablets believed to be 6,000 years old refer to the use of opium as a pain-killer and sedative. Its medical use was described by the Greeks in the 3rd century BC and it was then frequently mentioned in the writings of Greek and Roman authors. Its use probably spread to India and thence to China in the 7th and 8th centuries AD through Arabian traders.

In China, use of opium was restricted to its application as a medicine until hedonistic smoking of the drug became fashionable in the 17th century. Throughout these centuries China's opium consumption was of an imported product, and it is ironic that China's home-grown opium industry only developed following the determined promotion of opium by the British and against the better judgement of the Chinese authorities. In 1720, the Emperor prohibited the sale and smoking of opium as the first of a number of interventions aimed at curbing this developing habit. The British were the main providers of this opium through the East India Company who saw the Chinese market as a major outlet for their crop. The quantities of opium and sums of money involved were enormous and the Chinese addict population was believed eventually to have been in excess of 15 million.

Under the banner of "free enterprise" Britain insisted on the right to trade in opium across national boundaries and engaged in the Opium Wars of 1839–42 and 1856–58 to establish this trading right. Despite humiliating losses (which included the ceding of Hong Kong, the payment of £60 million and the removal of trade restrictions), China continued with attempts to curb opiate use by its people. Determined opium consumers were beheaded and their families sent into slavery, but despite this the opium trade continued to boom. The problem of opium smoking in China was dealt with effectively and virtually eradicated only when the Communist regime came to power.

Opium in Britain
Opium was widely used in Britain as a medicine from the 16th century onwards. It held a central place in the limited armamentarium of the physician. In the 1660s the famous English physician Thomas Sydenham pointed out that "medicine would be a cripple without it; and whosoever understands it well, will do more with it alone than he could hope to do from any single medicine". It was undoubtedly Thomas Sydenham who popularised the alcoholic tincture of opium which became widely known as laudanum. It is difficult today to imagine the important everyday place held by opium in those times, but it must be realised that it was seen as an almost universal panacea; an aspirin or Valium of a former era.

In the early 19th century, opium use was generally viewed as acceptable and unremarkable. In 1821 Thomas De Quincey published his autobiographical *Confessions of an English Opium Eater* which promoted widespread debate. Use was not however restricted to creative hedonists such as the Lake Poets; the drug was also being taken on a regular basis by many people who used it as a household remedy or as a palliative for the hardships of life. The widespread acceptance of this drug in the Victorian era has already been alluded to in the Introduction to this book.

In the second half of the 19th century medical concern about opium use developed alongside the growing concern about alcohol problems and the emergence of the Temperance Movement. Until that time, excessive opiate and alcohol use were seen as personal excesses. During the latter part of the 19th century the "morphinist" and "morphinomaniac" came to be identified as a patient with a disease; a physical disease which included a disease of the will.

New technologies
Scientific advances brought technological changes which have altered the style and manner of opiate use in the world today.

In 1803 morphine was successfully isolated by chemists from the raw opium, and in the years that followed morphine gained an established place as an opiate preparation whose dose could be measured exactly. Amongst other benefits, morphine was initially claimed to be an effective cure for opium addiction. In the mid-19th century in the USA soldiers in the Civil War were issued with both morphine and the newly-invented hypodermic syringe for self-administration in the event of injury. As a result intravenous morphine use became so widespread that morphine addiction came to be known as the "soldier's disease", and at the end of the war 45,000 addicts returned home.

In 1874 a new opiate was manufactured in St Mary's Hospital, London. This was diacetylmorphine—later to become known as diamorphine or heroin. By 1898, the Bayer Pharmaceutical Company began commercial production of the drug which was used in its early years as a cure for morphine addiction. The story continues in the same vein. During World War II Germany developed methadone as a new "safe substitute" for heroin. Throughout the 20th century many synthetic opiates have been developed, often with the hope of finding a pain-killer which was free of dependence risk, but that hope has always been disappointed.

In the early to mid-1970s research provided the spectacular discovery that there are naturally-occurring substances in the body with morphine-like effects. There are hopes that this will open the way for a greater understanding of the mechanism of pain relief, opiate misuse and opiate dependence, and so eventually lead to the development of a new range of drugs operating in an entirely different way.

The establishment of controls
At the turn of the century, opiate misuse had come to be seen in this country as a matter for some, but certainly not agonised, concern. The widespread use of opium as a household remedy was on the wane and doctors were beginning to come across sporadic instances of morphine or heroin dependence. At the same time, America was seeking to introduce international narcotics controls and put pressure on Britain to become a signatory to the first Opium Convention in the Hague in 1912. Along with other signatories the United Kingdom was obliged to prepare permanent drug control legislation which eventually resulted in the first Dangerous Drugs Act in 1920.

Those regulations restricted a doctor to dispensing controlled drugs only "so far as may be necessary for the exercise of his profession". The meaning of this phrase was open to conflicting legal interpretations; the Home Office believed that the Act precluded doctors from prescribing opiates to opiate-dependent patients. Doctors who were giving heroin or morphine on a maintenance basis to such patients were reluctant to accept this view, although they were beginning to face prosecution. A committee was therefore set up by the Ministry of Health under the highly prestigious chairmanship of Sir Humphrey Rolleston, the President of the Royal College of Physicians.

Rolleston's historic report, issued in 1926, found conclusively for the doctors. It ruled that the prescribing of heroin and morphine to an opiate addict might constitute "legitimate medical treatment" for the following types of patient:

"(a) those who are undergoing treatment for the cure of addiction by the gradual withdrawal method;

(b) persons for whom, after every effort has been made for the cure of addiction, the drug cannot be completely withdrawn either because (i) complete withdrawal produces symptoms which cannot be satisfactorily treated under the ordinary conditions of private practice; or (ii) the patient, while capable of leading a useful and fairly normal life so long as he takes a certain non-progressive quantity, usually small, of the drug of addiction, ceases to be able to do so when the regular allowance is withdrawn".

The Rolleston Report had no statutory power but it came to be accepted as embodying what would today be called "guidelines for good medical practice". A doctor who in good faith prescribed an opiate to his dependent patient would be left unmolested by the police. Thus addiction to opiates remained centrally defined as a medical rather than a criminal issue. Meanwhile, on the other side of the Atlantic matters developed in a starkly opposite direction. After a brief experiment with prescribing clinics the Harrison Narcotics Act was interpreted as forbidding doctors to prescribe to addicts. The clinics were closed, doctors were prosecuted, and the dependence problem driven underground.

Following the Rolleston Report Britain appeared to settle down to many years of easy and peaceful co-existence with the opiates. The days when tincture of opium was on sale at the grocer's shop seemed long ago. According to the unofficial Home Office index there were never more than about 400–600 addicts in the country; there was no black-market (the doctors wrote out the prescriptions) and no drug subculture. Morphine or pethidine were the drugs most usually involved rather than heroin. Somehow this approach came to be known as the "British System".

It was in fact never a carefully thought out system but more an informal way of working, but this did not prevent certain American commentators in the 1950s and 1960s from advocating the British System (and the legalisation of opiate prescribing to addicts) as the answer to America's rising tide of opiate problems. These commentators wrongly presumed that the British approach *caused* the UK's low prevalence of opiate problems and the absence of an organised black-market. The correct interpretation should more probably have been the other way round: Britain was in fact able to operate this relaxed and predominantly medical response to opiate problems because underlying social and historical forces had resulted in the country having a very much smaller opiate problem than the USA. Talk of transposing one country's approach to a very different national context without any understanding of the background complexities was flattering but naïve.

The British System breaks down

Paradoxically, as the Americans were writing their favourable reports on the British approach, Britain's long-standing peaceful co-existence with opiate problems was beginning to break down. Another phase in the long-standing, ever-evolving history of this country's relationship with these drugs was about to start.

During the 1960s the prevalence and nature of opiate problems in the UK began to change. (Some very preliminary data were given in an earlier chapter, p. 10). By 1968 the total of known opiate addicts had risen to 2,782, of whom over three-quarters were using heroin, compared with well under a quarter who had been using heroin before 1960. The new addicts were younger and usually male. It was not until 1960 that the Home Office became aware for the first time of an opiate addict under the age of 20, but by 1968 there were 764 opiate addicts under 20, virtually all of whom were dependent on heroin. While the numbers of opiate addicts who had been introduced to opiates in the course of medical treatment had remained stable, large increases were seen in the number of individuals who had become dependent as a direct result of irresponsible prescribing by a few unprincipled doctors who took advantage of their professional position, and by others who also unwittingly over-prescribed. A drug-using sub-culture grew in London and for the first time the word "junkie" passed into the coinage of this country's language. A burgeoning black market of illicit heroin then developed.

Amid these changes, the Second Brain Committee was convened. Its report (1965) made recommendations in three areas. The prescribing of heroin and cocaine to drug addicts should be restricted to specially licensed doctors. Special clinics should be set up to treat heroin and cocaine addicts and these would be staffed by the specially licensed doctors who could prescribe heroin and cocaine. Lastly, there should be compulsory notification of heroin and cocaine addicts to a central register.

These three proposals formed the basis for the new Dangerous Drugs Act (1967) and for the Drug Dependence Units which were set up in 1968. A fourth proposal concerning the compulsory detention of addicts in treatment centres for the purpose of treament and withdrawal from drugs was never adopted. Drug addiction *per se* was not, and still is not, grounds for compulsory detention.

The birth of the British drug clinics

Drug clinics were born with the brief of taking over the management of the two or three thousand opiate addicts from the private and non-specialist doctors who had previously been dealing with this group. Their present work is described in more detail in Chapter 16.

From their inception, clinics wrestled with the twin problems of needing to prescribe sufficient supplies of drugs so that patients did not turn back to the black-market, while at the same time not prescribing such large amounts that there was a surplus to be sold on the streets. Between 60% and 80% of the patients taken on in 1968 were receiving heroin as all or part of their prescription from the clinics. The policy, based on this difficult "not too little not too much" balancing act and aiming both at under-cutting the black-market and serving the needs of the individual patients, seemed at first to pay dividends. Large numbers of addicts were brought into treatment by the lure of prescribed heroin; there was not too much leakage from the clinics to the black-market; over-prescribing private doctors had been curbed by the new Act; only trivial amounts of imported black-market heroin were circulating; and it looked as if the number of addicts known to the Home Office might begin to plateau. Controlled prescribing might have replaced every individual doctor's right to prescribe to addicts as he thought best but the spirit of Rolleston lived on.

Although the rate of growth in numbers of notified opiate addicts somewhat slowed down, the figures in the 1970s continued in fact to drift slowly upwards. By the end of that decade the annual caseload of the clinics had increased from their late 1960s figure of about 2,000 to a late 1970s figure of about 5,000. However, the underlying picture was probably more disturbing. A large number of heroin users existed in the community but chose not to present to the drug clinics. By the end of the 1970s the situation was once more beginning to slip out of control and the notification rate for cases known to the Home Office began to accelerate upwards. By 1985 the number of opiate addicts known to the Home Office had reached a record 8,819 and that figure should perhaps be multiplied by a factor of about five to give a realistic total for the country.

What has caused this worsening picture to develop? One explanation offered is that the recent up-turn in notification has been caused by the expansion of a flourishing black-market which has blossomed as a reaction to the tight-fisted prescribing policies which the clinics have themselves increasingly adopted. When the clinics first opened the great majority of new patients were being prescribed heroin or methadone in injectable form and on a fairly long-term basis. Today prescribing by these clinics of any type of injectable drug is unusual, and most commonly the new patient will be given only a relatively short-term prescription of oral methadone. This policy change has come about not because of any official directive but because experienced clinicians have come to believe that this conservative prescribing is good (and better) practice.

Those who support the "tight fisted clinics" line of explanation would thus argue that Britain is in worsening difficulties with heroin because the clinic doctors have abandoned an essential function which these treatment centres were originally intended to serve—the prescribing of drugs to addicts with sufficient open-handedness to satisfy the patients demand or "need" for drugs, to tempt patients away from black-market dealing, and to undercut and weaken the black-market.

Such an argument is not well supported by a more careful analysis of the evolutions in the heroin problem. It seems likely that the worsening situation with opiates owes much more to the influence of large changes in the international heroin supply scene than to clinic policies. Large quantities of cheap heroin have been arriving over recent years not only in Britain but also in most other countries in continental Europe. The geographical origins of the drug have successively included the countries of the Golden Triangle, Iran, and now particularly the Indian sub-continent. To understand the upswing in British heroin problems the market economics of the heroin trade and the economic and social situation in countries from which the drug originates have to be examined. The possibility also exists that unemployment and urban deprivation in the consumer countries may stimulate the demand for heroin. The lesson of history is very clearly that the causes of fluctuations in the extent of opiate use in this or any other country are likely to be many and interacting. To give too much credit to the clinics either for improvement in the heroin situation over one short period or worsening over another would be to ignore the large and important background influences which have been in play.

Chasing the dragon
A major change in the method of heroin use occurred in the late 1970s. In the 1960s and the first half of the 1970s, heroin had almost always been taken by injection. In the late 1970s, with the arrival of new types of black-market heroin, there emerged a fashion of taking the drug by snorting (like snuff) and subsequently by smoking, known as "chasing the dragon".

Chasing the dragon involves heating black-market smoking heroin on tin foil above a flame and inhaling the dragon's tail of smoke as it comes off the tin foil. Not all heroin can be smoked, and this was a feature of the new heroin arriving from South West Asia. It is probable that this new and much more acceptable way of taking the drug (without injecting) has contributed to the speed with which this behaviour has spread. Nevertheless, the emergence of heroin smoking as a popular route of administration is not universal across Britain and although there are some parts of the country where over half of the heroin users are taking the drug by smoking, there are other parts of the country where injecting still appears to be paramount.

Economics

The black-market in opiates is now dominated by illicitly manufactured heroin which is illegally imported and sold in this country. A black-market also exists for diverted supplies of legitimately manufactured opiates such as Diconal, Palfium, methadone and heroin ampoules which have been obtained by diversion from legitimate prescribing or have been obtained by chemist or hospital pharmacy burglaries. However, these sources pale into insignificance compared with today's black-market in imported heroin. The spectacular increase in the size of the heroin market is reflected in the vast quantities of heroin now seized by customs, which have increased from just a few kilograms of heroin per year in the early 1970s to a figure of 334.2 kilograms in 1985.

Sadly, this increase in seizures appears to reflect more the increasing scale of the market than an increase in the effectiveness of customs activity. As the availability on the streets and the geographical spread of heroin has increased in recent years, the street price of the black-market drug has fallen and is currently about £60 per gram, while the purity of this black-market gram has increased over the same period to its present average of 40–50%. If controls began to bite there should be a resulting increase in the street price and a decrease in the purity of the product, neither of which are yet evident. The purities found in the UK are far in excess of those at street level in America.

The opium growers in the country of origin are likely to be impoverished peasant farmers who see a means of bettering themselves, their families and their community by growing this relatively high value crop. The local farmer will hope to get from £20–£100 per kilogram of raw opium. From this original kilogram, about 1/10 of a kilogram of heroin can be manufactured. Within the last decade there has been a major change in the chain of production of heroin with the emergence of local opium-refining laboratories near the production fields, so that the product is shipped in the form of high-purity heroin rather than as raw opium or morphine. This emergence of local heroin-producing laboratories has brought casualties in its wake. Opium-producing countries such as Pakistan now have large numbers of heroin addicts in their indigenous population where previously only the use of raw opium was widespread.

Although the profit to the local farmer may appear large when compared with any alternative crop, it is small compared with that further along the distribution chain. One kilogram of heroin at the Pakistan/Afghan border will typically cost about £4,000. With no further preparation this same heroin will be worth over £20,000 once it has reached Britain; and once it has been broken down into ounce-sized units it will sell for a total of between £30,000–£40,000. By the time it eventually reaches the individual user at the bottom of the distribution pyramid (at which point it is likely to be sold in wraps or bags of fractions of a gram), the original kilogram will sell for over £100,000.

The selling of heroin is a commercial business. In common with all other businesses different types of people are involved at different levels in the enterprise. The importer will be working in kilograms of the drug which will be imported from the country of origin either directly to the country of consumption or through other countries in an attempt to avoid the inquisitive interest of Customs and Excise. The heroin at this stage is at its peak purity. From this point on it may be diluted or "cut" with fillers designed to increase the physical bulk of the product and thus create greater income.

Whatever changes may be brought about in the country of consumption, the heroin business (along with cocaine and marihuana) has established a global economy which shows little sign of dwindling. World production of heroin is believed to be still rising steadily, as illustrated by continued increases in the world seizures of this drug (which for example doubled from 6 tons in 1982 to 12 tons in 1983). There are now countries whose economic survival seems to depend on the production of heroin or other illicit drugs, and any talk of crop eradication or crop substitution must take note of the overall difficulties of the local population in such Third World countries.

Designer drugs—yet another development on the horizon
It would be unwise ever to assume that the story of the twists and turns in society's involvement with opiates has reached some final state of equilibrium. A disturbing development in America has been the emergence of black-market synthetic opiate-like

drugs—the so-called "designer drugs" (p. 22). As yet these drugs have not made any inroads into the British black-market, but the possibility of their arrival is a cause for considerable concern. In America, black-market manufacturers have been exploiting a loophole in the legislation by altering the chemical structure of pre-existing drugs and creating immensely powerful new opiate-like substances. Unfortunately there have been appalling accidents with these drugs in America where small quantities of contaminants have resulted in damage to the brain with a clinical picture similar to that of advanced Parkinson's Disease.

Conclusions?
Humility in the face of history

History demonstrates that for a very long time society has been profoundly grateful for the medicinal powers of the opiates and seemingly for a much shorter period it has been gravely troubled by the problems of their misuse. New drugs and new methods of deployment have brought new dangers, and there appears to be no end to this dangerous road. The use and misuse of opiates has long had an international dimension, whether in terms of the British in the 19th century trying to force opium onto the Chinese, or of heroin from the East flooding into Europe today. Periods of stability are followed by breakdown and instability. Opiates have been used for so many centuries that their story is particularly rich and complex, and perhaps only that of alcohol could rival it. Other drugs have developed or are evolving their own histories, some short and some long.

The long history of the opiates is perhaps just another example of the vast challenge faced by mankind to integrate the complexity of human ingenuity with the resources of nature so that these may be used beneficially and not destructively. Just as De Quincey described in his *Confessions* 150 years ago, the opiates tempt man with the "Elixir of Life". But that is truly an illusion; there is no such easy access to Paradise.

Chapter 7
Alcohol

In 1985 the annual figure in Britain for the number of people convicted of drunken driving was close to 100,000; in 1960 the total had been less than 9,000. The numbers of cars on the road, changes in police practice and alterations in the relevant legislation may all have influenced the statistics but the fact that there has been an astonishing increase in this serious and threatening aspect of the nation's drinking problem cannot be doubted. Between 90,000 and 100,000 people are convicted each year in the UK for public drunkenness.

In addition about 14,500 patients are admitted each year to psychiatric hospitals in Britain for alcohol dependence and alcohol psychosis, of whom a third are first admissions. Alcohol misuse is also responsible for at least three quarters of the two-and-a-half thousand deaths from chronic liver disease and cirrhosis recorded in Britain each year.

Such statistics only give a limited indication of the real extent of alcohol-related problems. Over a quarter of road accidents in Britain involve people who are over the permitted blood alcohol level. Alcohol misuse has been identified as a major factor in head injuries, drownings, crimes, accidents, and a wide range of other problems such as football hooliganism, absenteeism and inefficiency at work. In addition, alcohol dependence frequently causes brain damage and a wide range of other serious and irreversible conditions. Prolonged heavy drinking is associated with cancer and with suicide.

Economists have suggested that alcohol misuse annually costs about £1,600 million in England and Wales alone. Estimates such as this are inevitably incomplete. Many of the costs and benefits associated with alcohol either have not been or cannot be assessed.

Unhappiness and pain, together with enjoyment, are not easily put into an equation.

If the statistics just quoted were more widely known and honestly accepted they might help to dispel the pervasive and complacent belief that alcohol misuse is not really a drug problem, and correct the extraordinary lack of balance between social and governmental concern over heroin and other illicit drugs and the neglect offered to the much greater havoc wrought by alcohol and by cigarette smoking. One reason for including alcohol in a book on drugs is to emphasise that alcohol is a drug among drugs, with alcohol problems constituting a vast part of the nation's total drug problems. Furthermore, people who misuse illegal drugs often misuse alcohol, and vice versa.

The causes and consequences of excessive drinking cannot be discussed here at great length. Those issues received full attention in a recent Royal College of Psychiatrists publication *Alcohol: Our Favourite Drug*. In this chapter the discussion on alcohol will concentrate on examining the relevance of what has been learnt about drink to an understanding of drugs. The parallels are many and their study is illuminating.

Alcohol has a lot to do with alcohol problems

To understand the health and social significance of this seemingly epigrammatic heading it is only necessary to turn to Fig. 1. This graph illustrates a general finding which would be relevant to a wider time-base by means of an analysis relating to the years 1970–1982. The line which traces the per capita consumption for alcohol shows a steady increase in drinking from 1970 to 1979. Other lines further show that over this same period drunkenness arrests, admission to mental illness hospitals and cirrhosis mortality all increased in parallel. When the alcohol consumption graph began to make a moderate dip downwards after 1979, the three indicators of alcohol-related problems began either to go downwards or level off. Simple inspection of the way in which these four lines are behaving suggests that alcohol consumption and alcohol problems march hand-in-hand and that impression is confirmed by formal statistical testing. The correlation co-efficients which are given in brackets in the legend to the graph are measures of statistical associations and confirm that consumption is strongly associated with each of the three "problem" measures.

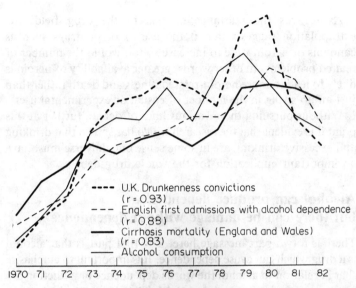

Figure 1. Alcohol consumption, drunkenness convictions, alcohol admissions and cirrhosis mortality 1970–82 (all per person aged 15 or over). Correlation between the given parameter and alcohol consumption is the statistic r. (Reprinted with permission from Kendell (1984) courtesy of Pergamon Journals Ltd.)

These findings are not peculiar to the UK. In other countries rising levels of consumption have been accompanied by a proliferation of alcohol-related harm. There is a clear link between the general level of national alcohol consumption and the level of alcohol misuse. Countries in which per capita alcohol consumption is high generally have much higher rates of liver cirrhosis mortality than do countries in which alcohol consumption is low.

The association between alcohol consumption and levels of alcohol misuse was highlighted in 1956 by a French demographer, Ledermann. Although there is a generally clear relationship between the "normal" level of drinking and the level of problems, the precise pattern of this link varies from time to time and from place to place. No one would go so far as to claim a strict "natural law" which determines the precise relationship between these variables. But a mass of observations derived from many different countries amply confirms the contention that, give or take a little, more drinking means more drinking problems; or, in other words, alcohol has a lot to do with alcohol misuse.

As regards the relevance of this to the drug field, the extrapolation suggests that if the use of other drugs such as cannabis or heroin were to increase so too would the number of related problems. In other words, greater availability of heroin is likely to lead to more heroin-related illness and death rather than just an up-swing in the number of casual or experimental users.

Without pursuing these various lines of debate further at this point it is evident that the research which has shown that drinking and excessive drinking are in some sense one universe must have an important implication for the whole drug debate.

Alcohol can produce dependence but there can be damage without dependence

There is a two-part message here. The first part is that alcohol is a drug which can cause dependence. It is important to emphasise that in relation to alcohol the words dependence or addiction are not being used as figures of speech; dependence on alcohol can reach a stage which is compulsive and appallingly destructive. It would be a serious mistake to regard alcohol as only some kind of milk-and-water drug in comparison to heroin. Given the circumstances, the person, and the necessary exposure to alcohol, the alcohol dependence syndrome can achieve an intensity which dominates and destroys that person's life.

The dependent drinker, like the dependent heroin user, seeks to ward off unpleasant withdrawal symptoms by continued use. Withdrawal from alcohol can be more dangerous than that from heroin. Dependence on alcohol can of course exist in many degrees of severity and it is misleading to picture this condition only in its most extreme forms. Such a narrow view will lead to under-recognition of the early case.

The lesson for drug problems to be learnt from alcohol dependence is that as recently as the 1950s the World Health Organization was issuing documents which suggested that alcohol did not quite have the credentials truly to be classed as an addictive drug. Such an approach offered a message which grossly under-estimated the real threat of alcohol as a potentially dependence-inducing substance. If that sort of misjudgement could be made in relation to a drug with which Western society has had some thousands of years experience, how much easier may it be to under-estimate the dependence potential of drugs which have come lately onto the scene? The roll-call of such mistakes certainly includes heroin, barbiturates and the minor tranquillizers, and there are now hints that the dependence risk from cannabis may have been under-estimated. Alcohol has demonstrated the immense caution which is needed in predicting the dependence potential of any drug.

The second part of the message which alcohol dependence has for the drug field is paradoxical, because in assessing the total health and social impact of a drug's misuse it is unwise to put dependence too much at the centre of the stage. Alcohol dependence results from prolonged heavy drinking. However, many alcohol-related problems occur in people who are in no way dependent. It is possible to experience or to inflict severe harm through inappropriate or unwise drinking on a single occasion. Drunken driving, for example, mainly involves people (and their victims) who are not alcohol dependent. The risks of incurring some alcohol-related complications may exist with levels of drinking which would pass as "social" (brain damage may come into this category). What needs to be understood is that alcohol (with or without concurrent dependence) can cause and contribute to a vast array of mental, physical and social problems, chronically or acutely, to a major or minor degree.

The true nature and extent of the price which society pays for its use of alcohol is only to be fully understood by a perspective which takes *all* alcohol-related problems seriously into account rather than by focusing only on the obvious case and the extreme end of the dependence spectrum. Exactly the same message applies in the drug field. Prevention, treatment, policies and public statements should not be exclusively focused on the extreme case of heroin dependence but should take account of the whole spectrum of drug-related problems which individuals and society in general are encountering.

Blaming alcohol

It has been emphasised that alcohol misuse can cause or contribute to all manner of health and social ills and there is ample evidence to support that statement. Historical analysis of society's engagement with alcohol also shows that at times it has become a popular rhetoric to blame it unreservedly for every evil that besets the individual, the family, and the State. Alcohol is made the whipping-boy, while the many underlying problems which breed and exacerbate alcohol problems are ignored or excused. Slum drinking has been made responsible for the slums and for pauperism, crime, irreligion, the breakdown of family life and even the threat of revolution. Such blaming of alcohol is a convenient strategy, and excuses the need to look at the social and economic factors which led to those slums and their attendant ills.

There are numerous historical examples of such blaming strategies in relation to alcohol. The Temperance Movement sometimes fell into the trap of seeing the urban problems of the industrial revolution entirely in this light. The following quotation is from an American document of 1832:

> "That ardent spirit makes three-fourths of our criminals is the united testimony of judges and lawyers in this country and in England . . .. Almost all cases of murder have occurred under the influence of alcohol . . .. Those guilty of burglary, larceny, counterfeiting, riots, etc. are almost uniformly ascertained to have destroyed their moral sensibilities and emboldened themselves for the violation of their country's laws by the inebriating cup".

The alluring belief that alcohol should be scape-goated as the root of all evil reached its zenith with the American enactment of prohibition. This comment together with the very apt accompanying quotation comes from Professor Harry Levine, who has done much to illuminate the history of that era:

> "In 1919, on the day that national Constitutional prohibition went into effect in the United States, the famous preacher Billy Sunday repeated before 10,000 people and a huge radio audience the central fantasy at the heart of the temperance and prohibition crusades:
>
> > 'The reign of tears is over. The slums will soon be a memory. We will turn our prisons into factories and our jails into storehouses and corncribs. Men will walk upright now, women will smile and the children will laugh. Hell will be forever rent'."

Billy Sunday and his listeners were to be sadly disappointed. Anyone who supposes that heroin is the actual cause of inner city problems (drug dealers were blamed for the 1985 Birmingham riots by that City's Chief Constable), that cannabis causes the disaffection of the young, that excessive prescribing of psychotropics is the cause of the social submission of women, has fallen victim to some variant of the Billy Sunday message. There are many invitations today to see drugs as the root cause of those social problems which, in fact, underlie the drug problems but which are so awkward or seemingly intractable that people would rather avert their eyes.

Alcohol problems medicalised

When in 1884 the President of the Society for the Study and Cure of Inebriety, Dr Norman Kerr, gave his address at its inaugural meeting in London he had no doubt that "inebriety" was largely a disease, and a physical disease at that:

> "I have not attempted to dogmatize on disputed points as to whether inebriety is a sin, a vice, a crime, or a disease. In my humble judgement it is sometimes all four, but oftener a disease than anything else, and even when anything else, generally a disease as well . . . in all indulgences in intoxicants there is a physical influence in operation, a physiological neurotic effect, the tendency of which is to create an appetite for more of the intoxicating agent. By whatever name you designate it, I am persuaded that inebriety is mostly physical, and for the most part has a physical origin".

For ideas on addictions, Kerr's speech was in every sense a keynote address. It is worthwhile therefore to follow his thoughts a little further and identify what he saw as the immediate social consequences of this disease formulation of inebriety:

> "We shall be satisfied if we succeed in impressing on the public mind that inebriates are not necessarily scoundrels— that to treat the dipsomaniac as a criminal is not to cure but to confirm his inebriety, not to reform him but to make him worse—that the moral, social, political, economical, and spiritual mischiefs arising from intemperance are the result

of the operation of natural law, of the physiological and
pathological action of an irritant narcotic poison on the brain
. . .''

At the beginning of the 19th century, the idea that drunkenness
was very much the business of the medical profession would have
seemed bizarre, and as already mentioned in Chapter 4 there was
no such concept as "addiction" popularly available. By the time
Dr Norman Kerr gave that inaugural address the study and cure
of inebriety had become a medical growth industry. There were
doctors in many countries who claimed to speak as experts on
the subject, and treatment institutions were founded. In
sociological terms the medical "ownership" of "alcoholism" was
being established, and what legitimised this bid for ownership was
the concept of inebriety as disease. Disease is the doctor's business.

Debate on the disease status of alcoholism has continued to this
day. Alcoholics Anonymous has been profoundly influential in
reinforcing this disease view and it was a position which was
adopted unreservedly in the years after the Second World War
by the whole "Alcoholism Movement" in America. The 19th
century disease concept was re-discovered and promulgated as
dogma.

In retrospect it can be seen that what does or does not count
as a disease is arbitrary, and that "disease" is itself a socially-
determined concept. The intentions of the disease formulation
were humane, and as the quotation from Kerr shows one of the
aims was to lift the burden of guilt and moral condemnation, and
route the "dipsomaniac" to treatment rather than the gaol cell.
To dismiss the benign social achievements of the disease concept
would therefore be ungenerous and it is a way of looking at
alcohol dependence which has been and continues to be personally
helpful to many drinkers.

But there are losses as well as gains from this "medicalisation",
whether such a process is applied to alcohol or to drug problems,
and the analogies which bear on the drug field should be
examined. Medical and physical explanations make an important
contribution to the understanding of drug dependence, but it will
lead to disastrous misunderstanding if it is ever supposed in this
arena that "the action of a narcotic poison on the brain" can
explain drug taking and drug problems in all their complexity,
"moral, social, political, economical and spiritual". Such a

simple-minded and narrowly biological vision of problems which in their origin and nature are essentially the interactive meeting point of many different processes and influences will, if accepted, lead to responses and policies which are radically misconceived.

Explanations of drug taking require a profound awareness of many dimensions other than the physical or strictly medical ones, and society should therefore avoid inappropriate expectations of its medical resources to carry the burden of responsibility for "curing" what is society's problem by massive investment in treatment. As will be argued in Chapter 16, while provision of adequate and appropriate treatment services is a vital part of society's total response to drug problems, what doctors can offer has limits. Medical doctors also have an important but at the same time limited contribution to make in the prevention of drug problems.

In summary, what the alcohol example seems to suggest is that in relation to the whole range of substance problems the question to be asked is what different professions can and cannot explain, and what they are or are not able to contribute to the field of action. This issue has been discussed here in relation to medicalisation but exactly the same questioning should be applied dispassionately to the sociologists, the psychologists, the economists, or to any other group which claims monopolistic authority in "the study and cure of inebriety".

Informal social controls

There is another instance in which the drug field can profitably borrow from thinking that has developed in the field of alcohol studies. It is one where sociological and anthropological work has been particularly fruitful.

In some cultures alcohol has led to mayhem, and this has especially been the case where drink has been introduced to a society with no previous experience of this substance. The damage which was done to many American-Indian groups by their sudden introduction to liquor—to "firewater"—illustrates the rapid and disastrous establishment of a habit of drinking to the point of intoxication.

This sad story might be contrasted with instances of certain other cultural attitudes and behaviour. In orthodox Jewish society people seldom get drunk. Similarly, the Chinese are famous for the moderation of their drinking habits whether they are living in China or in any of the many Chinese communities around the world. Alcohol is prohibited in Islam.

These and many other examples could be quoted which seem either to prove that alcohol is a lethal drug with which society should not be entrusted, or to show that it is a substance that can be safely controlled by the dictates of manners and custom. In fact, what these contrasting examples reveal is that the safety of a drug does not reside simply in the drug itself, but to a large extent in the informal social controls which are exerted by society. The drug analogies are obvious. Opium may be integrated into village life in remote areas of Thailand (opium as the only available "aspirin") while coca has been chewed for centuries in the high Andes.

The question should be asked as to what forces weaken this essential fabric of informal control. Rapid socio-economic change at a pace to which the individual and society cannot accomodate is one such factor. Informal controls may also be shattered by a rapid influx of drugs with which a society's or a person's defences cannot cope, or old informal controls may be broken down by new techniques—injection of heroin replacing opium smoking, for instance. Proscriptions and prescriptions are inculcated and observed almost without awareness, and they are often more potent than the statute book. It is necessary, however, to examine how formal policies may strengthen this immensely important but often rather invisible asset of informal controls.

Entrenchment

The use of alcohol is strongly entrenched in many societies. It is by far the most widely used psychoactive drug in the United Kingdom. Over 90% of adults in Britain and over 60% of those in Northern Ireland drink alcohol at least occasionally. The per capita consumption of alcohol in the United Kingdom almost doubled between 1950 and 1977, although it has recently slightly declined due to the impact of the recession on spending power. Three quarters of a million people in Britain work in the drink trade and each year the Exchequer derives a massive tax income from the sales of alcoholic drinks. The production and export trades have been rewarded by the Queen's Award to British Industry. Alcohol is a commodity which is increasingly advertised, promoted and sold by international conglomerates. The trade interests are powerful and have their advocates in Parliament.

The lesson which is to be learned from the story of alcohol is that once the use of a drug is widely accepted it may be difficult to take effective steps to control its misuse. Public opinion in Britain generally supports a status quo which tragically involves a horrifying level of alcohol misuse. Draconian policies such as large price increases or advertising bans appear to be unpopular, even if other policies such as stiffer penalties for drunken driving do have widespread support. Powerful vested interests and perhaps more significantly public sentiment combine to reduce the importance of health as a factor in determining national policy on alcohol.

This situation is epitomised by the fact that successive governments since 1979 have declined to publish a report on *Alcohol Policies in the United Kingdom* which was produced by the Central Policy Review Staff, otherwise known as the "Think Tank". This document, which has since been published in pirated edition in Sweden, stated that treatment and education by themselves cannot be expected to counter alcohol misuse. It concluded that such misuse is unlikely to be checked unless the overall level of national alcohol consumption was also restrained by appropriate price controls.

The only official Government response to this debate has been a discussion paper, *Drinking Sensibly*, which was published in 1981. This rejected the view advanced by the "Think Tank" report as follows:

"And it has to be faced that Government controls capable of effectively influencing the minority who misuse alcohol could not be established without affecting the choices available to the majority of the population who drink sensibly. Also, while the misuse of alcohol may cause serious health and social problems, the production of, and trade in, alcoholic drinks, form an important part of our economy in terms of jobs, exports, investment and a source of revenue for the Government—all of which could be adversely affected by any measures designed to restrict consumption".

In fact there is little evidence that any of the main political parties seriously dispute this view. Ultimately, the level of alcohol misuse that exists in the United Kingdom is a political rather than a medical issue.

The history of policies on alcohol shows that once the use of a particular drug becomes socially, economically and politically entrenched, concerns for health are not going to be accorded much credit. If public and political will does not support action on drug problems not much more will be seen than a few token gestures. Britain's response to alcohol and tobacco is very uncertainly supported by such a will. The wish to deal with the costly and destructive problems set by misuse of alcohol only comes at occasional moments of crisis, but the active will is not there to follow it through.

Chapter 8
Tobacco

"Among 1,000 young adult males in England and Wales who smoke cigarettes, on average, about 1 will be murdered, 6 will be killed on the roads, and 250 will be killed before their time by Tobacco" (Royal College of Physicians, *Health or Smoking*, 1983).

Tobacco kills and cripples on a massive scale. Every year at least 100,000 people die prematurely in the United Kingdom due to the effects of smoking. Cigarettes are a prime cause of cancer of the lung and of chronic bronchitis and emphysema. They contribute substantially to heart disease. There is a relationship between cigarette smoking and peptic ulcer. Smoking by women during pregnancy is associated with reduced birth weight and an increased risk of spontaneous abortion. The recent marketing of little bags of tobacco—'Skol bandits'—which can be placed in the mouth and sucked has introduced a new health danger. This habit is associated with cancer of the mouth's lining.

How has society come to be exposed to such frightening risks, and in what ways has it responded to this threat? These are the questions which will be explored in this chapter. The issues raised by alcohol and tobacco (the two favoured "recreational" drugs) have much in common, and society's ambivalent grappling with the health danger posed by smoking could be used to illustrate many of the themes which have already been discussed in relation to alcohol. Rather than tread the same ground over again the focus will be on tobacco as an instance of society haplessly discovering that it has accepted the entrenchment of a highly addictive drug whose use carries lethal consequences on a scale to make the cholera epidemics of a previous century look puny. The use of this drug, although legal, is responsible for more health damage

81

in the United Kingdom than are all other drugs (including alcohol) combined. The Royal College of Physicians estimated that the cost to the National Health Service in 1981 of tobacco-related illnesses was £155,000,000. That only a short chapter is devoted to tobacco must not be interpreted as under-rating the menace of the tobacco problem relative to other drugs.

Tobacco—
three hundred years of acceptance

The tobacco plant and its potent component, nicotine, were named after Jean Nicot. He was a French ambassador to Portugal during the sixteenth century who eulogised what he believed to be the medicinal merits of this plant.

Tobacco had long been used by people in South America. The tobacco habit spread rapidly in Europe and soon became widely established. Pipe smoking was originally the common form of use and one can trace the appearance of the elegant clay pipe in European painting. The chewing of tobacco also became widespread and in the 18th century snuff taking won acceptance as a genteel habit.

Whatever the method by which tobacco is taken, the user is essentially employing a technique for extracting nicotine from the leaf material and securing its absorption into the blood-stream and so to the brain, where it will have its main impact. What might be regarded as a technical breakthrough occurred when cigarettes first made their appearance in the 1850s, cigars dating from somewhat earlier. The seemingly simple innovation of wrapping appropriately packed tobacco in a paper tube provided a method for delivering nicotine to the central nervous system which is almost as rapid and efficient as an intravenous injection. Each pull on a cigarette and drawing of smoke into the lungs shoots a dose of nicotine into the blood stream, and within 10–15 seconds this dose will have reached the brain. There are none of the practical difficulties inherent in pipe smoking to impede a heavy intake, and the relative mildness of the cigarette means that with practice its smoke can be drawn deeply into the lungs. Cigarettes burn tobacco at a high temperature, which adds to the danger of the inhaled products.

There have been many refinements in the curing and preparation of cigarette tobacco since early days, and the

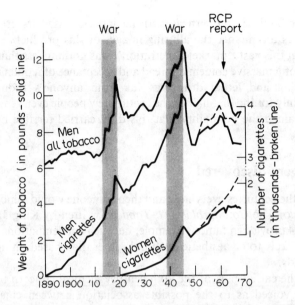

Figure 1. Tobacco consumption in the United Kingdom from 1890–1968 (Reprinted from Royal College of Physicians report, 1971.)

technology of modern cigarette production is complex. During the nineteenth century cigarettes gained in popularity at the expense of other tobacco products. Fig. 1 gives data on tobacco sales reproduced from a Royal College of Physicians report in 1971. The figure shows the rise in cigarette smoking which occurred among women from about 1920 onwards and it was cigarettes which introduced women to the tobacco habit on a large scale for the first time.

So cigarettes became an integral part of 20th century life, a pleasurable commodity, a drug, and a symbol. In the First World War, General Pershing sent a telegram from France to the authorities in Washington: "Tobacco is as indispensable as the daily ration; we must have thousands of tons of it without delay". The Turkish cigarette and the elegant cigarette holder became symbols of sophistication. Nations were typified by the cigarettes they smoked; Camels in America, Gauloises in France, Wills Woodbine in England. In the movies the curling cigarette smoke mingled with romance. Meanwhile governments became economically dependent on the resulting tax revenue, the tobacco industry waxed fat, tobacconists sold cigarettes at every street corner, and the modern advertising industry used its creative energies to enhance the alluring images of this product.

That this vast "market penetration" was nothing less than the story of a massive epidemic spread and acceptance of a potentially crippling and lethal drug was far from anyone's thoughts. Certainly for the first half of the century few people even remotely entertained the possibility that this drug carried terrible health risks.

Dangers discovered

Over the centuries every now and then someone would denounce tobacco. The *Counterblaste to Tobacco* written by King James in 1664 provides a famous example; but such condemnations were more likely to be aesthetic or moral rather than based on health grounds.

In the earlier part of the 20th century medical concern began to be voiced as to the possible association between cigarette smoking and cancer of the lung, but no one could adduce any proof. What had become evident was that lung-cancer mortality (whatever its cause) was alarmingly on the up-swing. Deaths from this disease rose among men from 10 per million living in 1901–1910 to 84 in 1931–1940, and between 1941 and 1949 this had further escalated to 198. A previously rare cancer had become one of the commonest types of malignancy.

Attempts were made to explain and dismiss these figures in terms of changed post-mortem practice or the advent of mass X-ray leading to greater detection, and atmospheric pollution was blamed. Meanwhile a disastrous health threat was clearly emerging. To the Public Health and research world, identification of the causes of this cancer epidemic had become an urgent necessity.

A highly important research report was presented in 1950, when Richard Doll and Bradford Hill published a short paper in the *British Medical Journal* entitled "Smoking and Cancer of the Lung". No one piece of work by itself is likely to clinch a demonstration of cause-and-effect in such a complex field, but the results which Doll and Hill reported in this epidemiological study suggested that for patients aged over 45 heavy smoking carried an increase in cancer risk which went hand-in-hand with the quantity smoked. From that publication onwards the evidence that cigarette smoking can cause cancer and other forms of lung disease and heart disease has accumulated with overwhelming persuasiveness.

The symbolism of the cigarette began to be confused. According to the advertising hoardings it still reflected all those glamorous and socially attractive qualities which had helped win for cigarettes their exciting and familiar place in 20th century imagery. But at the same time a sort of gallows humour emerged and cigarettes became "cancer sticks" or "a nail in the coffin". Suddenly every packet provided a Government health warning.

This confusion of images aptly mirrored the contradictions in society's responses when suddenly faced with the discovery that a favoured "recreational drug" was causing death and illness on a grand scale.

As stated earlier, one of the central themes of this chapter is an exploration of society's response to cigarettes once the dangers became evident. It is also necessary to look at the response of the individual smoker, industry and advertising, the anti-smoking campaigners, and Government. Although cigarette smoking is the case in point many of the same issues are relevant to alcohol and to psychotropic drugs, and there are analogies in relation to the social and economic base of illicit drugs; cocaine, for instance, in the economic structure of certain South American countries.

After 1950 —
personal response to manifest danger

In looking first at how the individual citizen responded to the news that cigarettes were dangerous, it is evident that many have stopped smoking and many who would in a previous decade have started the habit have not taken it up. Most of those who do smoke are ambivalent toward their habit. The proportion of males who smoke fell from 52% in 1972 to approximately 38% in 1982. The corresponding proportion of female smokers has also fallen and is now roughly one third. Between 1973 and 1985 the annual number of manufactured cigarettes sold in the UK declined from 137,000 million to 97,750 million. Among both sexes smoking is inversely related to socio-economic status. Only 20% of professional people smoke compared with over 40% of unskilled manual workers. However, among those who continued to smoke, average weekly cigarette consumption, although lower in

1982 than in 1976, was as high or higher than it was in 1972.

A recent survey by the Office of Population Censuses and Surveys concluded that threequarters of smokers agreed that smoking cost more than it was worth, and that many smokers as well as non-smokers favoured banning smoking from all public places. In addition a substantial minority of smokers favour restricting tobacco advertising and the sponsorship of the arts and sport by tobacco companies. The majority of adult cigarette smokers are in fact what are termed "dissonant" smokers. They are unhappy about their smoking, would like to give up, but often cannot do so despite many efforts.

The reason why cigarette smokers so often fail to stop, despite awareness of the dangers, is, of course, that nicotine is a strongly dependence-inducing drug, and cigarettes offer a splendid technique for delivering nicotine to the brain in a way that builds up dependence very quickly. What is seen here is an example of the thrusting drive toward continued "drug seeking" over and above other personal considerations once a strong dependence is established. Cigarette smoking provides a vital illustration of the reality and malign significance of the drug dependent state in which the rationality and freedom of individual choice is impaired.

Industry and advertising—brazening it out

Peter Taylor in his book *Smoke Ring: The Politics of Tobacco* has described the position in these terms:

> "Every year the tobacco industry spends around 2 billion dollars globally to ensure that cigarettes are associated with glamour, success, and sophistication, instead of lung cancer, bronchitis and heart disease".

The response of the tobacco industry to the news that cigarettes are dangerous has involved a number of strategies, including a determination to keep on going as if nothing had happened, with an almost bland detachment from the consequences in death and suffering. The tobacco companies continue vigorously to market and promote cigarettes. Sometimes the industry cynically denies the dangers, at others it takes an agnostic line and professes that danger is none of its business. With a ban imposed on direct television advertising the tobacco industry has moved heavily into sports and arts sponsorship, ensuring massive prime-time exposure for highly visible trade names and logos which circumvent the advertising restrictions.

To this extent tobacco represents the ultimate nightmare of drug misuse, that of an intrinsically malignant form of drug dependence which is firmly established and which is defended by influence, wealth and vested interest. Probably about 100 members in the House of Commons can be counted on to support the tobacco interests. Efforts have also been made to set up a form of science sponsorship with the industry funding a body which ironically is named the "Health Promotion Research Trust". This agency provides support for research into health topics. The manufacturers of a widely discredited product clearly use the resulting publicity to obtain a vicarious respectability.

If one response by industry and advertising has been to sit firm and bluff things out, other techniques have certainly included winning friends and influence, and enhancing the image even further. Tobacco industry money has gone toward FOREST, an organisation which fights for the so-called rights of the smoker and the line of argument is that the attack on smoking is an attack on basic freedoms. It would be interesting to know if the tobacco industry would apply such an argument to heroin or cocaine.

However, the industry has to some extent bowed to the pressures which come from health interests, and has put resources and technology into the design of cigarettes to make them safer and yet still acceptable to the smoker; for example, lower tar cigarettes, filter cigarettes and "New Smoking Material". Nevertheless there has been strong opposition from industry to the acceptance of *mandatory* controls. Its preference has been for "voluntary agreements" with Government, such as voluntary controls on advertising.

Since 1950, the manufacturers have done their best to ensure that cigarettes retain a friendly public image despite the fact that this product is responsible for the greatest contemporary preventable cause of death; indeed, several brands bear the Royal Coat of Arms.

The health lobbies

A number of different organisations have made important contributions to the growing health awareness on the dangers of tobacco. The original report of the Royal College of Physicians in 1962 was immensely influential and a series of subsequent reports have up-dated the message. The British Medical Association has been active in this field and has consistently argued for a complete ban on cigarette advertising.

A major contribution to increasing public and political awareness of the inherent dangers of tobacco has been made by ASH (Action on Smoking and Health). This is a campaigning body which was established in 1971 by the Royal College of Physicians. ASH, with its Scottish and Ulster counterparts, is largely funded by government money. It has succeeded in co-ordinating voluntary action against smoking and has provided a focus for articulate opposition to the tobacco lobby. The effectiveness of ASH is underlined by the subsequent formation of FOREST. The now abolished Health Education Council and the Scottish Health Education Group also conducted important anti-smoking campaigns.

This amalgam of positive influences has contributed to a profound change in the climate of opinion. Today not every sitting-room boasts an ashtray and to light up a cigarette when no one else is smoking can prove a little awkward. The family doctor probably does not smoke. There are more no-smoking areas in public places and no-smoking seats on public transport. Cinemas and restaurants are more conscious of the nuisance to clients. Life Insurance companies enquire about smoking habits. This subtle change in the groundswell of public opinion, which is manifest in dozens of different little ways is highly important. It supports the non-smoker and encourages the smoker to cut down or quit. Hopefully it also carries a message to Government.

Government action and inaction

The vital question now is whether this change in climate can be expected to affect the quality of Government response. Up to the present the Government has certainly taken some positive steps but the general impression is one of half-heartedness, contradictoriness and lack of co-ordination. Government policy is essentially non-interventionist.

The reasons for the weakness of the Government's response are not difficult to identify. The annual tax taken from tobacco is currently at a level of about £5,000 million. The tobacco manufacturing industry in the UK provides direct employment for about 30,000 people and many others derive indirect economic or employment benefit. The Government provides much more money to subsidise the expansion of cigarette production than it gives to health education. Even the Department of Health is ambivalent. In giving evidence to a Parliamentary Committee in 1977 a DHSS official declared that:

"From the Department's angle the health costs which would be saved if people ceased to smoke are not as great as the benefit [welfare] costs which go on [those people] living longer because they have not smoked".

Robbed of jargon those words mean that it is good policy to practice euthanasia by cigarette smoking if this saves on the costs of old age pensions.

What happens in the next decade?

When the use of a dependence inducing drug becomes entrenched in society the discovery of its dangers will signal the difficult beginning of remedial action. Very clearly, however, the story traced in this chapter shows that such information, no matter how persuasive, is not by itself going to turn matters around. Millions more people may die while vested interests defend their positions, governments display pusillanimous ambivalence, and individual smokers struggle with their addiction. This seems to be the essential story of the response to cigarette smoking so far.

If over the next decade there is to be further worthwhile progress it will require more definite Government leadership than has so far been evident. A statutory ban on advertising and sports sponsorship is overdue. Warnings on cigarette packets should be larger, more varied and with greater verbal impact. Health education should be far more systematically attempted and strongly supported; and of course it should be vigorously evaluated.

The most crucial and at the same time the most difficult issue which must be tackled is that of how the Government's financial dependence on tobacco revenue should be alleviated. The difficulties are of immense size and ramification, but inter-departmental examination of this question should be undertaken at once. The Department of Trade and Industry, the Department of Employment and the Treasury as well as the Department of Health and Social Security should all co-operate in identifying a strategy and implementing a policy.

Essentially the cigarette story is that of the appalling consequences for society when the problems of human dependence on a drug become compounded by national dependence on the money obtained by that drug's sale and taxation, together with the dependence on the jobs created by the drug's production, distribution and marketing. Recovering from that sort of dependence will require commitment and determination from the whole nation.

Chapter 9
Cocaine

Over recent years the USA has experienced a "cocaine epidemic" and it has been estimated that more than 20 million Americans have tried this drug. A telephone help line set up in New Jersey to provide immediate assistance for cocaine users has been reported as dealing with some 750 calls each day from drug takers themselves or from worried family members.

The drug has come into the United States from coca growing countries in Latin America. So plentiful have been these supplies that cocaine is no longer a luxury commodity, is relatively cheap, and has constituted the latest and most intensely worrying drug epidemic abruptly to have affected the USA. Its addictive potential and the disruptive effects of heavy use on the individual's life are now well recognised.

The cocaine problem is not as yet nearly so serious in Britain as on the other side of the Atlantic; for one reason it is still relatively expensive in this country. However, there is evidence that cocaine has begun to make its appearance here; in 1980 police and customs seizures totalled 40.2 kg and in 1985 85.4 kg. Although there are occasional reports of it reaching users at street level its price means that use is usually restricted to the relatively wealthy. The American experience of an explosive increase in the use of cocaine over a few years should be a fair warning of the seriousness with which Britain should be viewing the potential threat of this drug. American drug problems do not inevitably serve as a prelude to similar outbreaks in Europe, but most often they do. An attitude of "it can't happen here" or a belief that cocaine can be dismissed as some kind of fun-drug of high society would be dangerously complacent. As has often happened before with fashions in drug use, America has set the trend which may later be followed by Britain.

91

Both in the USA and now to an extent in Britain the spread and acceptance of cocaine has been fostered by an association with images of a monied and successful life-style. Reference has already been made in Chapter 5 to the seductive lure of such imagery. The typical user has been portrayed as the young executive, the media professional, the lawyer or stockbroker, rather than a member of any of the traditional drug sub-cultures. This glamorous image is compounded by the totally erroneous idea that cocaine is non-addictive, and with extreme naivety it has often been asserted that whatever health dangers exist can be avoided by the practiced user. Publications have circulated which rapturously extol the supposed virtues of this drug and even suggest that it should be legalised. Paradoxically, it is not so many years ago that cocaine was widely viewed as nasty and dangerous, as a drug of the underworld, the gambler, or the "junkie" type of addict. What is equally surprising is that although cocaine and the amphetamines have closely similar effects on the central nervous system, today's trendy user of cocaine would see his chosen drug in an entirely different light from the rather down-market image he gives to "speed".

So similar are the pharmacological properties of both cocaine and the amphetamines that having dealt with the actions of amphetamines in another chapter of this book, it would hardly be necessary to provide a separate chapter on cocaine if these drugs were being considered in pharmacological terms alone. One stimulant drug is much like another in its impact on the brain. This chapter will therefore give a brief note on pharmacological aspects of cocaine and its methods of use and will then focus on the strange disjunction between a drug's reality and its image. Mention will be made of the destabilising effect of cocaine on the economics of producer countries.

Pharmacology and the way the drug is taken

Cocaine is an alkaloid which is to be found in the leaves of the coca bush, a shrub indigenous to large parts of South America. The properties of coca were well-known to the Incas. Cocaine hydrochloride was first employed in medical practice toward the end of the last century when its properties as a local anaesthetic were exploited. It still has some possible use as an anaesthetic, for instance in minor surgery to the eye, although to a considerable extent synthetic drugs such as amethocaine have now supplanted cocaine in topical anaesthetic use.

In coca-growing regions the drug is taken by placing a wad of leaves together with a little lime in a corner of the cheek. Cocaine is thus released only slowly and in low dosage, and there is a rather flat curve for the cocaine level in the blood with no sudden peak. The cocaine chewer does not therefore obtain anything approaching a "high", but is intentionally seeking a mild stimulant effect that will, for instance, help him to endure the hardships of life as a labourer in the Andean highlands.

In its indigenous use cocaine is also employed as a household cure-all; and the ritual of chewing and the offer of leaves to a friend have social significance. A pedlar sells or barters the coca, travelling from village to village. Thus in different ways the coca habit is embedded in the traditional social and economic life of these remote parts of the world.

As mentioned it is the hydrochloride of this drug which has been employed in medical practice, and until comparatively recently it was likely to be this form of the drug that was misused in the Western and developed world. The hydrochloride is a white crystalline substance which is readily soluble in water, and as such easily injectable. In the late 1960s and early 1970s it was frequently employed by heroin addicts as a drug which when injected together with heroin (often in the same syringe), would allegedly improve the "buzz" and remove the unwanted lassitude produced by heroin alone. The latter-day cocaine user in the USA and the UK is however much more likely to "snort" the drug up the nose where it is readily absorbed by the nasal lining and quickly passes into the blood-stream. Much higher blood levels are obtained than by chewing, and a peak effect on mood will be obtained within three to four minutes.

The most recent vogue is for "free-base" cocaine by which is meant the alkaloid freed from the hydrochloride attachment. This form of the drug also includes the substance colloquially known as "crack". The property of the free base that makes it attractive to the user is its high degree of volatility, which allows it to be smoked with the possibility of a greatly enhanced rate of absorption. The drug will be carried by the bloodstream from lungs to brain in a matter of seconds, so the person using the free-base is able to administer and experience cocaine in a way which closely mimics the sudden impact of an injected drug, without having to engage in injecting. The experience with free-base is typically described by the user as "lifting your head", as a sudden and over-whelming surge of excitement and pleasure. For reasons which are discussed later free-basing carries particularly appalling risks of dependence.

Over the last few years a crude extraction product, cocaine sulphate, has begun to make its appearance in towns and cities in such countries as Peru and Bolivia. Cocaine sulphate can also be smoked and therefore is another example of "technology" leading to the possibility of a new and more troublesome pattern of use.

Cocaine—the plight of producer countries

The spread of coca paste smoking has been the first sign that producer countries were themselves experiencing trouble with cocaine. Certainly the idyllic image of cocaine as a drug with which traditional coca-producing countries happily co-existed in terms of the seemingly benign chewing of the leaves has been entirely over-taken by events.

Over the last few years countries in the Andean region have suddenly been forced to realise that they themselves have become the victims of their own cocaine production. Not only are illicit entrepreneurs making enormous fortunes by exporting cocaine to the USA but the overspill from this production is affecting the indigenous population. The drug is so cheap and universally available in some areas that even young children have become addicted. The economic implications may at first suggest added wealth for poor communities but in reality many aspects of their economic and social development are distorted. At worst the profits go to finance assassination, to direct attack on legitimate governments, and towards international crime and terrorism.

The false image of the "recreational drug"

The image of cocaine as a drug with no dependence potential and lacking serious dangers is grossly misleading. It is potentially a highly addictive drug and its use can cause severe complications and even death. The reason why it is possible for users to go on believing in the benign image of cocaine as a "recreational" drug is the fact that, as with heroin or any other addictive drug (see p. 57), the possibility exists of "walking along the brink". This is another instance of the general truth that no drug is absolutely addictive to all users in all circumstances.

Some individuals who are using cocaine in a controlled, intermittent and low-dose fashion may continue in this way without mishap for many years, and perhaps "for ever". When such a person sees a friend who has got into serious trouble with cocaine he persuades himself that his friend was foolish and that his trouble was unnecessary whereas he himself is wiser and can control the drug. Unfortunately, this sanguine attitude is based on dangerous rationalisation, for there is a very fair chance that only a few months later this currently self-confident and unworried user will have escalated into heavier and more dangerous use. The facts are such that no one can guarantee that this will not happen. This is an account given by a man in his 30s:

> "The business was going well, I was making a lot of money, there was a lot of cash around which the tax man didn't need to know about. In the evening I would usually go to a nightclub and that is where I was introduced to cocaine. At first it was a social thing. Everyone that year was sniffing coke. To begin with for me it was casual. Then I started to buy my own. I could keep drinking longer without getting boozed if I took coke. Looking back I suppose that a couple of years later it had become a bit of a habit, I was spending a lot of money on the stuff, sometimes bingeing on it, getting a bit paranoid. It was at that point I was introduced to free-basing and within about 6 months it was disaster, when I wasn't smoking I was preparing the next dose and cooking it up, morning to night, out of my mind, the business gone. A real dive into disaster".

One sees deployed here those same rationalisations and defence mechanisms that are used by the cigarette smoker—"it can't happen to me".

To deal with the probability of risk on an exact and statistical basis is more difficult, but one American survey estimated that about 30–40% of cocaine users would graduate to "misuse". What can very definitely happen is dependence, with the user's life dominated and disrupted by this drug. Dependence risks are greater with intravenous use and free-basing than with nasal use, but the latter is itself far from being risk-free. Experiments in which monkeys have been trained repeatedly to press a lever so that a dose of cocaine is automatically "self-injected" as a reward for so many presses, have yielded dramatic and horrifying results. A monkey given access in this way to unlimited cocaine will continue repeatedly to seek injections until it falls unconscious and then it will get up and start the process all over again. The relationship between the way animals behave in response to the availability of a particular drug in this type of experimental situation and the dependence potential of that drug for humans is generally found to be close. On this basis cocaine would be expected to set a considerable danger of dependence to humans attempting to use the drug recreationally, especially if the users are rich or the drug becomes cheaper.

As with the amphetamines and other stimulants cocaine does not readily produce florid withdrawal symptoms of the types which may occur with heroin or alcohol. A cocaine withdrawal syndrome has now been recognised and can give rise to feelings of great weakness and depression, but cocaine is probably dependence-inducing primarily because of directly positive and "reinforcing" effects which the drug has on the brain and on the mind.

When someone becomes very dependent on cocaine the adverse personal consequences can be appalling. There will be a strong compulsion to obtain the drug whatever the eventual consequences, such as bankruptcy, criminal involvement, or the break-up of the family. As in the experiences of the young man quoted above more and more time is likely to be spent in "runs" or binges of cocaine, and finally life may virtually be given over to cocaine use so that ordinary social functioning becomes impossible. It is this personal and social disruption which is the hallmark of cocaine dependence.

The false image of "no harm"

The direct social consequences of cocaine dependence on the user's life can be disastrous but there are also other complications. High dosages of cocaine (whether or not in the context of dependence) can cause mental disturbance and physical damage. These complications include the possibility of a florid psychosis with paranoid experiences, closely resembling the short-term psychotic disturbance which can occur with the amphetamines (see p. 99). A classical symptom of cocaine psychosis is the experience of imaginary "bugs" under the skin, with much itching, severe scratching and self-mutilation. Cocaine suppresses the appetite, so the heavy user is likely to experience weight loss and may suffer from various nutritional deficiencies. There can be complications relating to the route of administration. There are all the risks familiar to any sort of injected drug use. When the drug is sniffed there is the bizarre possibility of constriction of the blood vessels leading to perforation of the nasal septum, and the question has recently been raised of smoked cocaine base causing damage to the linings of the lungs. The "cutting agents" employed by the black-market dealer to dilute the cocaine before selling it also carry their own dangers of toxicity.

Certain of the more irresponsible writers of popular "drug manuals" in the USA have recently advocated that if someone finds cocaine too stimulating, he should combine his cocaine use with barbiturates or heroin, thus not only decreasing over-excitement but also achieving a "high" of enhanced quality. Without setting up a "natural progression" theory such as the old proposal that cannabis leads inexorably to heroin, there emerges the possibility of one drug leading to the use of another and of entry into a "drug world". As with the patient quoted above, heavy drinking and use of cocaine are quite often combined.

A further risk is the actual danger of the user killing himself. An overdose with cocaine may cause collapse or sudden death, and because different people can show different sensitivity to the effects of cocaine such accidents are unpredictable. The steep transient rise in blood pressure which can be caused by cocaine may cause bleeding within the brain and may result in a young person suffering a stroke. The drug can also cause convulsions, and on rare occasions a sequence of epileptic fits in quick succession which may endanger life.

When a user enjoying the pleasures of cocaine, shared with and morally supported by a circle of drug-using friends, is confronted by such evidence, he is all too likely to go on rationalising and denying the negative consequences even when these have begun to be experienced. Some of these risks are more common than others. Dependence on cocaine is relatively common, and hence also the type of cocaine-obsessed disruption of personal life which goes with dependence. Cocaine psychosis is far from rare and although the attack usually lasts only a few hours or days the potential threats to the individual's mental welfare are not to be dismissed. A perforated nasal septum may be only a rare and minor embarrassment, but there may be chronic damage to the nasal passages. Cocaine deaths are at present rare in Britain, but in areas of the USA where the use of this drug is on the increase, so also are the related deaths.

What answers?

In recent years cocaine has created severe problems both for the developing and developed countries, and dealing with this threat is a concern which they very much share in common. Efforts have been made both at crop substitution and at elimination of the production of the drug at its source, but so far the economic and political barriers to this type of prevention strategy have proved baffling.

The current and far too prevalent favourable image of cocaine in the developed world has been built up without any help from professional advertising. What would it have cost the manufacturers of a detergent, previously burdened with a negative image and failing commercially, to mount a campaign which successfully turned that image around to one of "the detergent of the executive classes"? There has been no advertising, except for the fringe publications which come from California and other parts of the United States, and which among other things have told the reader how to grow his own coca bushes. Media attention may of course indirectly do something to add to the glamorised image, but the larger message must surely be that within society there always is the capacity for a constant and spontaneous ebb and flow in drug fashion, with fantasies and images certainly not related to the hard realities. The core issue for prevention is how to establish a system of community education to combat those perverse images and which ensures that the devil does not have all the good tunes. This is the question to which there are still too few good answers.

Chapter 10
Amphetamines

The following is an extract from a research monograph on *Amphetamine Psychosis* published in 1958. This book was written by Dr Philip Connell, and in it he described his observations on 42 patients:

> ". . . the typical clinical picture is a paranoid psychotic reaction, with delusions and auditory hallucinations. Ideas of reference were present in twenty-five patients, delusions of persecution in thirty-four, auditory hallucinations in twenty-nine and visual hallucinations in twenty-one. Fear or terror was reported by sixteen patients . . . All grades of severity of disturbance are represented in this series, from vague ideas of reference and ideas of persecution to acute terror, fear of being killed by a gang, and seeing and hearing persecutors".

Paranoid psychosis, hallucinations, acute terror, pursuit by imaginary gangs, all sound like the heavy end of the spectrum for psychological disturbances. Yet the drug which caused this chaotic mental disorder in those patients could, at the time, be bought across the counter. As pep pill, nasal inhaler, or slimming tablet it had won widespread medical and popular acceptance. Amphetamines were to become part of the swinging 60s youth scene and the world of late night cafés.

Before tracing in detail the story of society's engagement with these drugs, it might help to describe briefly an example of the type of illness that Dr Connell reported. This case history dates from the same period:

"Jim, a builder's labourer aged 35, went into a pub near London's Victoria station at about 12 o'clock one Saturday lunch-time. He ordered himself a pint of cider and at that moment he was joined by a friend who suggested that he tried 'putting something in his drink that would give it no end of a kick'. That 'something' was the amphetamine-impregnated wadding from a nasal inhaler. It was dropped into the cider, stirred around, and drunk back. A further round or two were consumed but no more amphetamine added. At about one o'clock Jim noticed that insects were crawling all over his friend and he caused some offence by trying to brush them off. He left the pub on his own and wandered off to Hyde Park. There he was under the impression that the ground was covered with nuggets of gold and silver and he spent some hours wandering around the park picking up the metal foil from cigarette packets and stuffing this material into his pockets. As it grew dark he became aware that Red Indians were lurking in the shadows and waiting to rob him of his treasure. Acting on this delusion he caused a public disturbance and was picked up by the police. The police took him to hospital where he was admitted in a floridly psychotic and wildly agitated state. He recovered within about 2 days".

How did such a dangerous drug come to be so casually available? What will be considered in this chapter are first the circumstances in which the amphetamines became drugs of epidemic misuse, then the circumstances which have seemingly contributed to their declining popularity, and finally the very tentative lessons which can be drawn.

The drugs

Three particular forms of amphetamine substance are best known, namely "amphetamine" (Benzedrine), dextro amphetamine (Dexedrine) and methamphetamine (Methedrine). The amphetamines have an action which is "sympathomimetic", that is they stimulate the nervous system in some ways like adrenaline. Adrenaline occurs naturally within the human body and is secreted particularly at times of stress by the adrenal glands. The amphetamines have a profoundly stimulating and arousing effect on the central nervous system (CNS), and it is this which is an important factor for the illicit drug user.

During the 1960s the amphetamines often appeared in preparations combined with other drugs. Drinamyl, the so-called "purple heart" because of its shape and colour, was probably the best known, and this combination with a barbiturate gave it special risk of dependence. Bizarre combinations of amphetamine and thyroid were put on sale as a treatment for obesity. At the present time, however, only two amphetamine preparations are listed in the *British National Formulary*, namely Dexedrine and Durophet. The latter is a slow-release mixture of amphetamine and dextroamphetamine.

Realisation of the dangers associated with amphetamines led to the development of a number of other supposedly safer substances for use in the treatment of obesity. These include diethylpropion hydrochloride (Apisate, Tenuate Dospan), mazindol (Teronac), phentermine (Duromine), fenfluramine hydrochloride (Ponderax), methyl phenidate (Ritalin) and pemoline (Ronyl, Volital). All have broadly similar effects to the amphetamines. Some of these are marginally safer but none are free from risk of misuse and dependence. Phenmetrazine (Preludin) is a stimulant with properties similar to amphetamine and gave rise to epidemic misuse in Sweden during the 1950s and 1960s.

The amphetamines— discovery and the spread of acceptance

Amphetamine itself was first synthesised in 1887 and became widely available during the 1930s when it was found to be of benefit in the treatment of nasal congestion. The amphetamine inhaler rapidly became a popular decongestant both in the USA and the UK and could be purchased without prescription. The amphetamines have also been used in the treatment of hyperkinesis (hyperactivity) in children and the rare condition narcolepsy (episodes of uncontrollable sleeping). However, the amphetamines were most frequently employed in the treatment of mild depression, and for obesity in which their appetite-suppressant properties seemed useful.

When any drug touches three such wide markets as the treatment of a stuffy nose, nervous depression and obesity, it is likely to be a huge commercial success. It should be realised that at the time when amphetamines were being advocated for their anti-depressant properties there were no true anti-depressants available. Psychiatrists were eager to find "physical" treatments for mental illness and amphetamines were an inviting possibility. In consequence amphetamines and Drinamyl were widely prescribed for patients who were a bit miserable and "down in the dumps" or lacking in energy, but it soon became apparent that these drugs had little to offer in the treatment of severe depressive illness; they just added anxiety and agitation to the depression.

In relation to the treatment of obesity the market penetration achieved by the amphetamines was again remarkable. There are always many people worried about their weight and to them and their doctors the amphetamines appeared to be an ideal therapeutic agent. Not only did these tablets suppress appetite but they gave the patient a sense of energy, uplift and well-being. In the short term they did help in weight reduction but whether they offered any longer-term benefit was far more questionable. In any case it was exactly this sort of use which gave rise to the widespread medically-induced amphetamine dependence which will be discussed later. It is only fair to note that the doctors who were prescribing amphetamines did so in good faith and at the time were unaware of the dangers.

Alongside this medical use of amphetamine came their acceptance as "pep-pills" which would keep a person awake when driving or working a night-shift in the factory. They also came to be accepted as stimulants which would supposedly enhance energy, concentration and mental and physical performance. Amphetamines were widely prescribed to troops during the Second World War to enable them to keep functioning under conditions of fatigue and stress. Their use by sportsmen and women, although illegal, has been well publicised. A number of sporting achievements, ranging from the conquest of mountain peaks to the exploits of cyclists in the Tour de France, are known to have been aided by the use of amphetamines (most sporting bodies have of course now come to regard the practice of enhancing performance through drugs as either unethical, counter-productive, or both). Lorry drivers in the USA have used them to stay awake for long journeys without rest, hence their colloquial name "coast to coast" among these drivers. They have even been tried in the mash of battery hens to keep them awake, laying more eggs; and students have used them to facilitate all-night exam-swotting sessions.

By the 1950s the situation had been reached in which amphetamines were the stock of the bathroom cupboard, when doctors prescribed the drug on a very large scale for common conditions without any knowledge of the need for caution, and when the manufacturers sent sample packets of Drinamyl through the post to every house physician. Respectable citizens took a pill or two to help them with the weekend gardening. As so often happens with drugs, the borderline between "medical" and "recreational" use became very hazy.

Problems became apparent

There was no one instant when recognition suddenly dawned that doctors, patients and society at large had once more stumbled unwittingly into widespread and virtually uncontrolled acceptance of a dangerous drug. Different dangers became apparent at different times and the time-scale of these varied between countries.

For instance, the first reports that amphetamines could produce an acute short-lived psychotic illness came from Germany in the 1930s. Connell's 1958 monograph gave a far more detailed description of this reaction than had previously been available but even so the warnings which he then issued were not sufficiently heeded.

Rather separate from the discovery that amphetamines could cause psychotic illness came the awareness that this was a group of drugs with very serious dependence potential. The dependence problem affected two different social groups, on the one hand young people who were using the drug "recreationally", and on the other patients who had become dependent in the course of medical treatment for obesity or depression.

Epidemic misuse among the young

In the UK it was the misuse of amphetamines among young people in the 1960s which started to make the headlines. Although after 1957 these drugs had been officially obtainable only on prescription, amphetamines were nonetheless widely available in clubs and night spots, on college and university campuses and also in schools during the early and mid-1960s. Forged prescriptions, medically unnecessary "repeat" prescriptions, and thefts from chemists' shops were the common sources of supply for pharmaceutically-manufactured amphetamines. Amphetamine sulphate is a relatively easy chemical to manufacture illegally, and this also provided a source.

The availability of pep pills and purple hearts meshed neatly with the needs and images of the changing youth culture of the post-war generation. Extended education, relatively high wages, distinctive styles of music, and radical modes of dress and behaviour emerged. So too, for the first time on a large scale, did the phenomenon of gang sub-cultures, notably the Mods and Rockers, with the fights between these two groups receiving disproportionate coverage in the media. It has been suggested by several commentators that considerable public over-reaction was stimulated by inaccurate and sensational reporting, which exaggerated both the extent and the importance of these events. Amphetamine use was only one component in a wide repertoire of behaviours which contributed to the notoriety of these teenage groups, yet the drug aspect was always treated by the media as if it were the central feature of concern, and amphetamine misuse was widely linked by such coverage with youthful misbehaviour, aggression and crime. Prior to the widespread use of the amphetamines, drug-taking behaviour had never been associated particularly with the young. For the first time a particular set of teenage behaviours, some dangerous and anti-social and some merely inconvenient or startling, became associated with the illegal use of a particular chemical substance.

Much of this use of amphetamines by young people was casual, experimental and really quite innocent, and there was an element of "moral panic" in the public response. But among these young weekend or late-night amphetamine users there were some who developed dependence on the drug and who were caught up in a disruptive pattern of stimulant misuse, quite often to a point where psychotic episodes occurred.

The picture of amphetamine use among young people in the UK then took a dramatic turn for the worse in the late 1960s when an epidemic of methamphetamine injection occurred in and around London. It was the fact that this type of amphetamine could readily be taken in high dose by injection which caused such chaos. No one could now doubt the potential for the amphetamine class of drugs to pose a major threat. Besides the inherent risks of unsterile injection, this way of taking the drug led to florid psychotic disturbance and to an intense type of dependence characterised by a binge or "run" of methamphetamine injections lasting for several days, followed by a short break or "crash" and then the cycle started again. Many of the young users who were caught up in this epidemic were previous or concurrent takers of heroin, and injected methamphetamine seemed to be a very acceptable alternative to an opiate when the heroin addict found his supplies curtailed. Frequently the source of supply for methamphetamine was those same doctors who had previously been prescribing heroin with astonishing laxity.

Other countries experienced a similar epidemic spread of stimulant misuse. Phenmetrazine (Preludin) first became available in Sweden in the mid-1950s and by the 1960s this drug was very extensively misused, with the problem much abetted by over-generous prescribing. An epidemic of amphetamine misuse erupted in Japan shortly after the second World War (largely fed by stockpiles of the drug left behind by US forces), and injection became a widespread practice. Prevalence estimates varied, but in the 1950s the Japanese Pharmacists Association suggested that there were 1.5 million amphetamine misusers in that country.

Epidemic misuse of amphetamines had clearly got underway in the USA and Canada in the 1950s, with intravenous use being common. The finding that such epidemic outbreaks of amphetamine misuse usually occur in the context of general medical and public acceptance of these drugs was demonstrated by the US experience. In 1958 the licit production of amphetamine in the USA amounted to 3.5 billion tablets and 10 years later had mounted to 8 billion tablets. The situation in the US armed forces almost reached a level of farce, as revealed in an official report that showed that between 1966 and 1969 the US Army averaged 13.8 ten milligram amphetamine doses per person per year, the Air Force 17.5, and the Navy 21.1. As late as the 1970s amphetamines were a standard issue for US troops in Southeast Asia.

The settled middle-aged user

The prominent pattern of amphetamine misuse has therefore been that of the epidemic type just described. In such epidemics the usual source of supply is the over-spill of licit prescribing, often supported later by additional illicit manufacture and a good deal of theft or "leakage" from factories, warehouses, and pharmacies. The drug users who have contributed to this kind of epidemic have tended to be the young, and although the use pattern for many would be intermittent and rather harmless, the epidemic would easily turn to chaotic intravenous use which would then be frequently associated with psychotic experiences.

That summarises one type of "amphetamine problem" but it is important to realise that a second type of problem is likely to co-exist with this epidemic picture. Although less dramatic, this appeared among individuals who received amphetamines on prescription for *bona fide* medical reasons, but who then became dependent on them or experienced other adverse effects. As it emerged in the 1950s and 60s, this latter group had much in common with the therapeutic opiate dependents for whom the "British System" of drug controls was formulated by the Rolleston Committee in 1926. Those involved were mainly socially stable individuals whose drug problems were largely iatrogenic (of medical origin) and who were not regarded as constituting any serious form of social threat. Careful data gathered by a group of doctors in the Newcastle area and published in 1962 revealed that one in five women and one in four men who were prescribed amphetamines by their GPs were likely to become continued dependent users.

Amphetamine misuse—ebb and flow

There can be no doubt that in the 1980s the misuse of amphetamines in the UK and in many other countries has constituted less of a problem than it did 10 or 20 years ago. The problem is however far from beaten and in some ways is worsening again. In 1975 there were 1,501 convictions relating to amphetamines, and in 1985 2,946. Amphetamines are still freely available on the black-market, amphetamine sulphate has a quite widespread use as an injectable drug, and illicit "laboratories" are still uncovered. There can never be a guarantee that the situation in relation to these drugs will not again suddenly deteriorate.

With all due caution borne in mind it is still legitimate to ask how the partial change for the better had come about. Most pessimistically it could be argued that the country is only seeing the familiar shift and play between the popularity and availability of different classes of drugs, but without any real overall improvement. For instance, the fact that amphetamines are not more widely used might be related to an up-swing in cocaine. In Britain that connection is probably not particularly close and the present price of cocaine prevents it from taking over too widely from the amphetamines, although in the USA the evidence of cocaine substituting in this way may be more persuasive. In the UK the worry might be that as injected methamphetamine substituted for heroin in the late 1960s, so in the present decade the increasing availability of rather cheap black-market heroin may partially have damped down the interest in injected amphetamines. Such debate on the "hydrostatic" relationship between different drugs is speculative but the issue is important.

There is little doubt that in the UK the largest positive influence limiting amphetamine misuse has been the slow growth in medical awareness of the danger of these drugs, leading to changes in medical prescribing as well as a growing realisation among the general population that "pep pills" are none-too-wise a prop. Various reports and campaigns have influenced this situation but what is of great interest is that prescribing practice was changed by persuasion and voluntary agreement among doctors rather than by legislative curbs on the medical profession. In 1954 the annual report of the Ministry of Health advised that amphetamines were non-toxic, that dependence upon them was rare and that they produced no major ill-effects. By 1968, however, the *British Medical Journal* published a report on amphetamine prescribing by the British Medical Association's Committee on Medical Science, Education and Research, which concluded that amphetamines had few therapeutic uses and should be subject to strict voluntary control. It was recommended that these drugs should only be prescribed for those few conditions, such as narcolepsy, for which no alternative drugs were available.

Turning to the 1983 edition of the *British National Formulary*, there is an entry stating that:

> "The amphetamines have a limited field of usefulness and their use should be discouraged as they may cause dependence and psychotic states . . . . Amphetamines have no place in the management of depression or obesity".

Medical appraisal of these drugs had thus changed radically since the Ministry's over-sanguine pronouncement of 30 years earlier.

Within the general context of voluntary control an important and symbolic event was the "Ipswich Experiment". This was a voluntary curb on the prescription of amphetamines instigated initially by doctors in Ipswich in November, 1969. This action resulted in a dramatic decrease in the quantities of amphetamines stored by pharmacies and chemists vulnerable to theft, and also helped to reduce the extent of therapeutic dependence upon these drugs. The "Ipswich Experiment" was widely hailed as an unequivocal success although a similar experiment in Bristol was less striking.

Within the same voluntary framework, the manufacturers and the Pharmaceutical Society made a significant contribution in bringing epidemic misuse under control. After the outbreak of abuse with injected methamphetamine in 1968, the drug manufacturers had discussions with officials from the Ministry of Health and the British Medical Association and voluntarily withdrew supplies of the drug to chemists, and that "epidemic" ended as quickly as it had started. Even so some illicit drug users responded to this situation by switching to amphetamine sulphate. The Pharmaceutical Society then took the unusual step in 1969 of advising its members not to dispense amphetamine sulphate powder, following the discovery that some doctors, wittingly or otherwise, were reviving the black-market in illicit amphetamines. This action by the Pharmaceutical Society, far from leading to a clash with the medical profession, was widely applauded.

Although the importance of voluntary changes in medical prescribing and of voluntary actions taken by the manufacturers have been stressed there was also a change in the framework of the law. The Drugs (Prevention of Misuse) Act of 1964 specially focused on bringing amphetamines, LSD and methaqualone under strict legislative control, with penalties for possession, trafficking, and illicit manufacture. This legislation was later included in the 1967 Dangerous Drugs Act and consolidated in the 1971 Misuse of Drugs Act, with injectable amphetamines being placed in Class A and oral preparations in Class B. The days when amphetamine inhalers could be purchased over the counter now seemed historically distant.

Amphetamines—what lessons to be learnt?

The various chapters of this book which seek to trace out the story of society's involvement with different drugs inevitably reveal an interlocking of themes as well as highlighting some special issues relating to particular drugs. As regards amphetamines, one theme which evidently interlocks with concerns over certain other drugs is that the safety of new drugs affecting the mind needs to be assessed far more carefully and dispassionately. Initial enthusiasm for a new drug by the pharmaceutical industry and among medical practitioners can be a devastatingly unreliable guide to safety and to dependence potential. The amphetamines present a particularly clear instance of the epidemic misuse of a drug being fostered and fed by legitimate prescribing and manufacture and by the general attitudes of acceptance in society. The "why it occurred" question is every bit as important as "why it faded" and lessons from the amphetamine story very much overlap with what can be gleaned from experience with barbiturates and benzodiazepines. It would of course be too simple to blame everything on doctors and on the sources of supply. As already stated the rise of amphetamines was also facilitated by their meeting certain needs — needs of a treatment demand and of the demand of a new youth culture for a fun-drug which aptly was nick-named "speed".

As to why a flow was followed over some years by a relative ebb in the tide of amphetamines, some of the operative factors may have been substitution by other drugs, change in medical and general awareness, change in medical prescribing and a stricter legal framework of control. It is enormously difficult to go beyond that listing to make firm statements about the proportional importance of this or that factor in a very interactive process of change which took place over many years. There was no one master-stroke, no one moment of change and certainly as yet no complete victory.

It does seem reasonable, however, to draw three fairly confident conclusions from the fact that the seemingly remorseless rise in amphetamine problems was followed by a relative decline a few years later. Undoubtedly, one lesson is that the success of prevention policies needs to be monitored in terms of the ebb and flow of the whole drug ecology rather than focusing exclusively on one drug. In those terms heroin may be a very unfortunate substitute for amphetamines whereas if benzodiazepines have replaced "purple hearts" that may be some gain, despite the problems which benzodiazepines themselves undoubtedly pose. Secondly, it is probably fair to conclude that the amphetamine story suggests that both medical practice and medical fashion can have much to do with the genesis of drug problems, while at the same time pointing out that voluntary action by doctors and manufacturers can, in some circumstances, make powerful contributions to stemming an epidemic. Lastly, there would be few who would argue that both getting amphetamines off the counter and enacting a law which can deal with illicit manufacture and distribution were other than very necessary to support such efforts.

Perhaps the most important and humbling lesson to be learnt from this complex story is that even with the wisdom of hindsight, it is difficult to unravel the causes of the rise and fall of drug epidemics. Nevertheless, there must be some good cheer, however guarded, and some important lessons, however provisional, in the evidence that all drug epidemics do not climb for ever upwards.

Chapter 11
Hallucinogens

Can drugs which affect the mind induce states of consciousness which offer entry to a world of insights which are not otherwise easily or at all available? The title of Aldous Huxley's well-known book *The Doors of Perception* unequivocally carries the message that certain drugs have such powers. However, Huxley was far from being the first literary figure to assert that drugs provide a chemical short-cut to a hidden world of creativity and transcendental experience. There were nineteenth century British parallels in de Quincey's *Confessions of an Opium Eater* and Coleridge's opium dreams, while Baudelaire in France celebrated the mystical effects of cannabis and opium in *Les Paradis Artificiels*.

There is no need to search too hard for present-day equivalents of those beliefs. Alcoholism is not only associated with the image of the creative writer (Brendan Behan and Dylan Thomas provide examples) but many people probably use alcohol so as to be in touch with feelings which are not otherwise accessible. It is not only the poets but also the everyday drinker who believes that intoxication can at times add an edge and colouring transcending the ordinary world of experience. For most people alcohol is a rather bad drug for such purposes. Within the cult values of the 1960s cannabis was extolled as far exceeding alcohol in its ability to bring about such an "expansion of consciousness", doing so without a hangover or other untoward consequences of drunkenness.

This chapter deals with a group of substances known as the hallucinogens, with powers of this type which are far more dramatic than anything offered by other classes of drug. Many other names have been applied to this group, such as "psychotomimetics" and "psychedelics". An older and very apt term for them was "phantastica". Beyond all other drugs they have been used or portrayed as the keys to a world of extraordinary experience, and although cannabis has some properties which resemble those of the hallucinogens, they are not nearly so dramatic.

The issue to be explored here is whether these drugs can indeed provide a key to very special revelations, or whether those seeming insights are more often ephemeral, pretentious or bogus. Even if there were true revelations to be had, what would the risks be in terms of untoward consequences? The artificial paradise may turn rather too easily and too treacherously into an artificial hell.

This chapter will begin with a brief account of the more remote history of hallucinogens and then go on to describe the discovery of LSD and its emergence as a cult drug in the 1960s. Whether the focus is on distant or more recent times, the common and continuing trend to be explored under this first heading is the use of these drugs in pursuit of supposed positive experiences. In the past those experiences were once related to religion or mysticism, while later the same or similar drugs were used in pursuit of a secular self-awareness.

The evidence on the other side of the coin will then be examined and a look taken at the harm which may occur when the quest for insight results in untoward and even disastrous consequences. These dangers will be illustrated by special reference to LSD, while other major hallucinogens will be discussed more briefly. Finally, a comment will be made as to whether hallucinogens are astonishing gifts which offer magical knowledge of personal understanding or whether they are really no more than a dangerous snare and delusion.

Hallucinogens as keys to hidden experience

Knowledge and use of hallucinogenic substances goes back to antiquity. The mushroom *Amanita muscaria* (fly agaric) may have been the source of the legendary "soma" used in India some 3,500 years ago. It was considered to be divine and mention is made of it in the Hindu scriptures. Many other ancient cultures appear to have used plants and their extracts in religious ceremonials, but such substances were also employed as intoxicants in medicine, magic, witchcraft and crime. Hashish was well known to the ancient Egyptians and Chinese. Plants such as henbane and belladonna which contain hyoscyamine and atropine were used by the Greeks, Romans and Persians, and their use flourished in Europe in the Middle Ages.

The variety of hallucinogenic plants found in the Western Hemisphere is considerable, and more than one hundred and twenty different species are known today. Cohoba snuff was used by the indigenous people of the Caribbean. The mescal bean was used by the Indians in the region now known as Texas. In Northern Canada the Indians chewed the roots of a plant called sweet flag.

It has been in Mexico and in the Northern parts of South America that the richest natural sources of the hallucinogens have been found, and they have been used in that region for over 3,000 years. In particular, mention should be made of three groups, the psilocybe and related mushrooms, the peyote cactus, and ololiuqui or morning glory. At the time of the Spanish Conquest these plants were being widely used in a sacramental manner by the indigenous people but were considered diabolical and were suppressed by the Christian invaders. The Aztec name for the psilocybe mushroom means "Flesh of the Gods" and Aztec priests and elders administered these mushrooms in the course of their religious ceremonies. Such religious cults have persisted into this century and even today the Native American Church has a legal dispensation to use the "button" of the peyote cactus, which contains mescaline, as a sacrament in their services.

At first glance the use of hallucinogens in today's society might seem very dissimilar to their use in earlier times. They are now largely used hedonistically as a challenge to authority and as a rejection of established values rather than as having any religious or mystical qualities. But this is to forget that in the 1960s many pioneers of research in this field, and in the use of the new hallucinogens, did see potential either in a quasi religious context in which man could reach towards a higher spiritual plane, or in terms of exploring and enlarging psychological and social well-being. Cult figures emerged who preached this message and the young followed in their wake.

The modern history of these drugs started early this century with the extraction and chemical analysis of the active principles contained in certain plants. Following this line of exploration, Dr Albert Hofmann started in 1938 to investigate a fungus called

Claviceps purpurea which grows parasitically on rye and from which ergot is produced. Ergot poisoning had been responsible for epidemics of a condition long known as St. Anthony's Fire (ergotism) in which gangrene and convulsions can occur, but ergot and its derivatives also had a medical value.

Lysergic acid is a component of one of the principal alkaloids of ergot, and Hofmann was interested in its evaluation as a circulatory and respiratory stimulant. Lysergic acid diethylamide was the twenty-fifth lysergic acid derivative which Hofmann produced and was therefore labelled LSD 25. In 1943, he accidentally absorbed a small quantity of this substance in the laboratory and experienced two hours of a very unusual dream-like state. He was fascinated by this unexpected reaction and embarked on a series of self-experiments which he has described graphically in his writings. What proved especially remarkable about his findings, apart from the hallucinations themselves, was the minute dose of LSD needed to produce these effects. Compared with mescaline, already known to have hallucinogenic properties, LSD was 10,000 times more active.

Following the publication of Hofmann's findings the whole concept of hallucinatory drugs became extremely popular and attracted the attention of chemists, psychologists and psychiatrists as well as many lay people, including the young in school and college. It was against this background that Huxley's book, mentioned above, became a best seller. By the 1960s most of the active principles of hallucinogenic plants were isolated and synthesised, and a host of totally new synthetic hallucinogens were soon to be discovered in the course of chemical research.

The widespread experimentation with LSD and other hallucinogens which occurred among young people in those years developed at a time when the younger generation was claiming a new-found freedom to experiment with life. It was in the 1960s that adolescents began to define their own values for themselves and create their own sub-culture. Politically, with the advent of the nuclear age, events in the world at large seemed daunting, and many young people retreated to a world of fantasy and inner experience, in which they became absorbed. This was exemplified by the musical "Hair". At the same time psychiatry was revolutionised by the discovery of psychotropic drugs, and the whole concept of using chemical substances to alter mood, perception and thought processes was given added impetus.

So the quest was under way for a chemical key to inner discovery and a short cut to an idealised world of joy, peace and charismatic love. Of all the drugs that seemed to promise this magic the hallucinogens appeared to be supreme. Even if they were seen to carry an element of risk, this too appealed to youth. Enthusiasm for these drugs and their social, philosophical and religious implications also drew some of the more serious professional workers out of the measured sphere of scientific method into the same utopian clouds.

However, serious problems began to arise as a result of widespread and indiscriminate personal experimentation. It led, as Hofmann himself pointed out, "to all the accidents and catastrophes that have given LSD the reputation among many people of a Satanic drug".

Public reaction against the dangers of both the recreational and the so called therapeutic use of these drugs was severe. In 1966 first the California State Legislature and then the US Federal Government outlawed the manufacture, distribution and use of LSD, subsequently extending legislation to cover alternative hallucinogens. Soon afterwards similar legislation was introduced in Britain and LSD, psilocybin, mescaline and others were included in the Misuse of Drugs Act 1971. More were added to the list by subsequent amendments as or before they appeared on the street scene. As a result of this legislation and of public disquiet even reputable research was discouraged and abandoned, and in recent years these drugs have become just part and parcel of the street scene of illegal recreational substances.

In the section which follows, some of the evidence which contributed to this worried appraisal of the dangers will be examined. For the sake of simplicity LSD will be used as an example of these dangers and the adverse effects of LSD will be taken to illustrate the negative consequences which may result generally with this class of drugs. First a description will be given of the physical properties of the drug and of the wanted effects sought for, as well as how these may merge into a "bad trip". Other dangerous complications which have then to be considered are "flashback" phenomena, suicide or accident, and brief or longer-term psychotic reactions.

LSD—potential dangers

LSD is white and odourless and virtually invisible in effective doses. It is therefore diluted with other materials and presented illicitly in a large variety of tablets and capsules or as a drop on a piece of blotting paper. Colloquially it is usually known as "acid". It is nearly always taken by mouth. As small a dose as 10 micrograms will produce a noticeable euphoric effect, and a marked hallucinogenic experience, as described below, will result from doses ranging from 50 to 200 micrograms.

There is no physical dependence or withdrawal syndrome associated with regular LSD use, but people are certainly encountered for whom LSD taking has become an enormously important part of life. They may have "tripped" with the drug a hundred or more times, and so have become psychologically dependent, leading to a state of alienation and isolation colloquially described as "acid head".

There is paucity of reliable information on the prevalence and patterns of LSD or other hallucinogen use in the UK. These drugs have fluctuated in their popularity and availability, and at present only perhaps 1% or less of the general population have "ever used", while in certain circles rates of experimentation are higher and individuals will be found who have used these substances (mostly LSD) several or many times. Surveys of students, for instance, have shown rates for "ever used" of up to 8%. Rates in the USA are higher.

The psychological effect of LSD is extremely variable, depending on the experience, attitude and expectation of the taker as well as his personality, his current emotional state and the setting. This variability itself constitutes a danger: LSD is a very unpredictable drug. The "wanted" response known as a "trip" can range from increased stimulation of the senses and enjoyable fantasies to feelings of ecstasy. The perceptual distortions have often been described as pseudo-hallucinations rather than real hallucinations because the individual may remain aware at the time that they are distorted perceptions. Confusion of time, space, body image and boundaries can occur with what have been called synaesthesias or the blending of different sensory modalities (e.g. sight and sound). Most sensory experiences are heightened, mood rapidly varies and fluctuates, responses to other people may range from indifference to paranoia. Loss of thought control and concentration may occur and recent memory may fail, while very early life memories may emerge.

Allied to such events, individuals may believe that they are undergoing some form of cosmic and mystical experience. All kinds of bizarre and imaginative ideas have been reported in the course of the loosening of thought control, and associations such as those concerned with death, rebirth and reincarnation. These experiences will usually start within 30 to 40 minutes after the drug has been taken and reach their peak in about two to three hours, fluctuating in intensity and terminating within 12 hours.

The wanted and unwanted effects shade into each other imperceptibly: there is no clear boundary between an enjoyable fantasy and a rapid slide into terror and chaos, commonly termed a "bad trip". It is not clear why "bad trips" happen and they can occur in someone who has previously enjoyed taking LSD and is experienced with it. The size of the dose, while contributing to the bad effect, is not itself necessarily responsible. Some individuals are more susceptible than others to these experiences and it is this personal vulnerability to mental disequilibrium that makes LSD such a dangerous drug. Panic mounts as a sense of confusion and disintegration prevails and the individual loses all contact with reality, becomes paranoid and experiences frightening delusions and hallucinations.

In most cases the "bad trip" fades away as the action of the drug ceases, but in some individuals the disturbance either does not stop as expected or it recurs. The latter may happen on several occasions either soon after taking the LSD or months later. Such "flashbacks" as they are called are usually very unpleasant. They may be provoked by taking other drugs but their cause is unknown. They are not usually as severe as the original trips which they follow but may resemble them and they may recur repeatedly, gradually disappearing if the subject remains off drugs. They are usually highly disconcerting to the person concerned who may indeed begin to fear for his sanity; and the anxiety which they provoke can give rise to a sense of panic.

Among other serious hazards which are sometimes associated with taking LSD and other hallucinogens is sudden, dangerous, irrational and impulsive behaviour. Thus during a trip there is always the possibility of an individual making a serious misjudgement and taking some unforeseen action, even when in company, but particularly if alone. Serious accidents may result

to himself or others. Aggression may be released during an LSD
episode either towards other people or towards the individual
himself as self-mutilation or even suicide. On the whole such
events are fortunately rare, but the following case history
illustrates the possibility of very real tragedy:

> A young man who had smoked cannabis continuously for
> several years and had occasionally eaten magic mushrooms
> was induced by friends to try LSD. His first two experiences
> were full of excitement and he felt totally released from his
> own inhibitions and enjoyed the close company of his friends
> as they described the weird and fascinating sensations which
> they were sharing. However, by the end of the fifth trip, a
> few weeks later, he began to feel extremely anxious with a
> strong suspicion of other people and great sense of confusion.
> In a moment of frenzy, after struggling with a companion,
> he jumped from the balcony of a high-rise flat shouting that
> he needed to meet his creator, and he died instantly.

Following even a single trip an individual may emerge as anxious
and panicky, or mentally disturbed. A brief psychotic illness which
can closely resemble a florid schizophrenic episode but which
clears after a few days is a not uncommon reaction to LSD, but
the spectrum of possible reactions can include more prolonged
disturbance. Sometimes the drug appears to precipitate
schizophrenia in a pre-disposed individual, but whether LSD can
itself cause a very prolonged or chronic schizophrenia-like illness
is open to debate.

From this account it must be evident that LSD and the
hallucinogens in general are drugs with the potential to produce
quite appalling psychological consequences. The statistical risk
of any particular trip going wrong is relatively small but
nonetheless real, and the extraordinary unpredictability of these
drugs means that no-one can guarantee that any trip (even for
the experienced user) will be safe. The well recognised dangers
lie in the mental sphere or are the physical consequences of mental
disturbance. Although much has been written about possible brain
damage, chromosomal damage and congenital defects as a result
of repeatedly taking LSD, the evidence for such direct physical
damage is not convincing. No deaths have been reported as arising
directly from LSD overdose.

Some other hallucinogens

Before proceeding to any final assessment of these drugs it is useful
to give a brief note on some other members of the hallucinogen
group. There are in fact a host of plant or synthetic substances
which could be included and no attempt will be made here at
completeness. Only psilocybin, mescaline, and PCP will be
described.

Psilocybin and psilocin are found in the psilocybe and conocybe
mushrooms, originally identified in Central America but now
discovered as related species (magic mushrooms) in many other
parts of the world, including Europe. An interesting legal point
exists in regard to the magic mushroom in Britain in that it may
be possessed and eaten raw but it is illegal to make preparations
from it. The cult of the magic mushroom ("Liberty caps") has
found a good deal of favour in the UK in recent years, and in
rainy periods parties of young people will travel to various parts
of the country at weekends to go mushroom picking and
picnicking. Untoward events are rare on these occasions but the
practice is not without danger. Serious mistakes can be made in
identifying the particular species and much more poisonous
mushrooms or fungi may be eaten instead. Pleasurable fantasy
experiences with magic mushrooms may entice a young person
to experiment with more powerful hallucinogens. In addition,
hallucinations similar in intensity to those of LSD can sometimes
occur, and so can the occasional "bad trip". In rare cases transient
acute psychotic episodes have followed the ingestion of these
mushrooms. Psilocybin is said to be about thirty times stronger
than mescaline and two hundred times less potent than LSD.

Mescaline was the first hallucinogen to be synthesised and was
the "curtain raiser" to LSD. It was identified as the active
principle of the mescal button of the peyote cactus, growing in
Mexico and Peru. Mescaline itself was already being used
experimentally and recreationally by a few initiates before LSD
took its place in the 1950s. Mescaline and a number of other
chemically-related compounds (including one called DOM or
"STP") are generally comparable to LSD but some are more toxic
and the psychoactive effects less consistent and reliable.

PCP or phencyclidine (Angel Dust) continues to play a part
in the illicit drug scene in American and Canada. It is almost
unknown in Europe. It can be taken by mouth, smoked, snorted

or injected. As already outlined in Chapter 2 (p. 21) phencyclidine has both intoxicating (alcohol-like) properties as well as marked hallucinogenic potential and it is in many ways a drug with atypical effects. Physically it can cause severe neurological symptoms including speech disturbance, uncoordination and blurred vision. Convulsions, coma and respiratory arrest may also occur. Psychologically it may produce a very marked mental disturbance including acute psychosis, severe depression, violent aggression and suicide. Severe paranoia and feelings of extreme alienation have resulted in bizarre behaviour. Phencyclidine is in every sense an extremely dangerous drug.

The debate

Earlier in this chapter mention was made of the long history of the hallucinogens and their early use in the course of religious and mystical experience. The modern "rediscovery" of these drugs and their cult in the 1960s can be seen as part of a wave of cultural change which has placed emphasis on the value of self-knowledge and the reaching into inner mysteries. Although at the time much of this cult was an adventure by young people, there was also a more serious side to the concept of LSD use, in particular as an adjunct to psychotherapy.

Quite a number of committed psychiatrists in the USA and a few in Britain worked with the drug in the course of their treatment of patients, and were convinced of its efficacy in shortening the period of therapy. However, such opinions were not easy to substantiate and the great majority of psychiatrists and psychotherapists remained both doubtful and antagonistic to the idea. They suspected that the claims to success were spurious and they considered the attendant risks too great to justify such experimentation.

The protagonists however believed that, properly undertaken, the risks were not excessive and that all methods of psychological exploration have their dangers. This concept was echoed by many lay people who supported this approach and who would argue that the antagonists are representatives of a frightened and materialistic world that is essentially opposed not just to these drugs but to anything which breaks down the rigid boundaries of the materialist's "reality".

As it happened the indiscriminate use of LSD and other hallucinogens brought them into such disrepute that any potential therapeutic or creative use with LSD was abandoned along with its legal proscription as a dangerous and undesirable drug.

It has to be conceded that experience with hallucinogens has been meaningful to many people; to those who have used these drugs as part of their religion over many centuries, to the creative writer, to the casual individual who has tasted exciting fantasies, and indeed to the patients who appeared to benefit from them in psychotherapy. It is astonishing that a few micrograms of a chemical should open such windows, and society has not yet come fully to terms with this fact. At the same time it is extremely hard to judge the validity of the claims which people taking LSD have made for their intensely subjective experiences.

The debate on hallucinogens should not seek to deny their strange magic. However, the general case against them would seem to be overwhelming. Whatever the pleasure or even the arguable creative and therapeutic potential of drug-induced dreams, the resulting nightmares (the bad trips, flashbacks, psychotic illnesses and dangerous behaviour) are indeed too common, too unpredictable and too devastating to justify this form of experimentation with the human mind.

As possible shortcuts to insight and understanding these drugs have a certain allure but from what has been learnt about them they are too hazardous. Personal insight and understanding can perhaps only be reached safely not by instant chemical reaction but through the slow, often painful and difficult process of living and growing, which at times may be assisted by more conventional methods of psychotherapy.

Chapter 12
Cannabis

Every now and then an official committee manages to produce a report which turns upside-down all the usual expectations that government reports must for ever be boring and platitudinous. On such an occasion society is presented with an incisive or even disturbing analysis of a particular problem which provides an example of how important social issues should be analysed dispassionately. The tone of public debate is enriched. In hard days comfort can be drawn from the evidence of the qualities in our society that such a report provides.

The Wootton Report on Cannabis, issued in 1968, was undoubtedly a publication of that stature. Its distinction owed much to the chairman of its committee, Baroness Wootton, who is not only a social scientist of renown but a critic and commentator famous for her independence of mind. The background review of the literature was carried out by Sir Aubrey Lewis, whose name was a byword to generations of psychiatrists for unforgiving scientific exactness. The committee's membership represented a spectrum of scientific and public experience. Its provenance was the Advisory Committee on Drug Dependence (a government-appointed body which preceded the present Advisory Council), and Barbara Wootton's cannabis committee was a working group of the main Committee.

After a painstaking review of the evidence the Wootton Committee concluded that the dangers of moderate use of cannabis had been exaggerated, while emphasising that cannabis was not free from risk. The report explicitly recommended against legalisation of the drug but suggested that penalties for small-scale possession should be reduced.

It might have been expected that such a piece of writing with its few, well-reasoned, and clear conclusions would have been widely welcomed as a basis for temperate and informed debate. It is the essential argument of this chapter that such an expectation is naïve; the cannabis debate has not been very much concerned with the facts but has been the stage for a fundamental clash of values. Facts, science, objectivity, truth, dispassionate analysis have all been obscured in the resulting confrontation.

It is a sad reminder that a society which can on occasion produce a brilliant committee report is commonly the same society which will display a crass inability to respond constructively to the challenge of fresh thinking.

The following brief set of quotations show how the popular press greeted the publication of this report:

"NOW THE DRUGS ROLL IN . . .
Foreign 'dealers' flew into London the same morning the Wootton Report was published. In a matter of hours the capital became one of the easiest places in Europe to buy cannabis . . . Home Secretary James Callaghan should toss the Wootton Report where it belongs — into the nearest waste-paper basket."
(Simon Regan, *News of the World*, 12th January, 1969).

"CANNABIS REPORT 'CHARTER FOR JUNKIES'"
(Terence Shaw and David Toshak, *Daily Telegraph*, 9th January, 1969).

"RUSSIAN ROULETTE WITH A FULLY-LOADED REVOLVER — THAT'S POT"
(Brian Freemantle, *Daily Express*, 13th January, 1969).

"THE THIRD POISON"
(Julian Holland, Daily Mail, 9th January, 1969).

Two quotations from Hansard relating to the parliamentary debate on Wootton are also revealing. The following is an extract from a speech made by James Callaghan (the then Home Secretary):

"I think it came as a surprise, if not a shock, to most people, when that notorious advertisement appeared in the Times in

1967, to find that there is a lobby in favour of legalising cannabis . . . it is another aspect of the so-called permissive society, and I am glad if my decision has enabled the House to call a halt to the advancing tide of permissiveness''.

Mr Callaghan suggested that Baroness Wootton had been nobbled by the pro-pot lobby. The opposition spokesman Quintin Hogg, QC (later Lord Hailsham) took the view that a little bit of gossip with his friends was better than Sir Aubrey's critical scientific review:

"When I talk to members of my profession, and, often enough, to members of the medical profession, I find that, although they cannot always give figures which prove these facts, as has been the case all over the world, this drug is associated in their minds and professional experience with crime, violence and abnormality of one sort or another, but, most commonly of all, with a kind of degradation of the personality''.

These quotations from press and Parliament show just one side to the cannabis debate, that of the protagonists who, blind to the evidence, launch an attack on this drug not because of its toxicity but because they see it as symbol of permissiveness, long hair, and the questioning of majority values. On the opposite side are those who, treating the facts with equal disregard, perceive in the same drug the totem of liberal and humane thinking. Each side will take and distort selective pickings from the body of scientific evidence that suits their bias. Cannabis illustrates strikingly how symbolism becomes tangled with the objective appraisal of a drug's danger, but this type of confusion extends beyond this particular drug. Drugs are symbols, as has already been pointed out in an earlier chapter (p. 47). Extending the licensing hours of bars and public houses becomes a politico-moral issue related to dismantling the "nanny" State, or the liquor industry becomes a demonic representation of capitalism.

In this chapter the cannabis debate is analysed, but the wide implications of the questions which are being examined should be borne in mind. To begin with a brief account will be given of the law on cannabis, as it now stands, and some data provided on prevalence and patterns of cannabis use. An attempt will then be made to analyse dispassionately the arguments of the two opposing sides—the rhetoric of reform and its counter-rhetoric. The health implications will also be examined. Finally, a guess will be hazarded as to the future—cannabis a forgotten fashion or reefers sold by every tobacconist?

Cannabis—the law and how it now operates

The way the law stands on the statute books is easily determined by looking up the relevant sections of the Misuse of Drugs Act, 1971 (see p. 201). Cannabis is a Class B drug. Possession can carry up to a three-month sentence on Summary Conviction (before a Magistrates' Court), or five years on indictment before a Crown Court; there is also a parallel scale of fines. Growing cannabis places a person at risk of corresponding sentences of six months or 14 years, again according to the court involved, and "supply" or "possession with intent to supply" can exact precisely the same penalty levels (with or without a scale of fines).

How the law works in practice is a more difficult question to answer and is likely to vary in different parts of the country. In an urban area if a policeman finds a young person in possession of a few grammes of cannabis he may deal with the matter informally or offer a caution, and no official record will be made. In a country town possession of exactly the same quantity of the drug might lead to prosecution, a fine, and headlines in the local newspaper. Whether in the counties or the cities it is almost invariably true today that a first offence of possessing cannabis in a quantity likely to be interpreted as "personal use" will lead to a fine of £25–50, but not to a custodial sentence. Supplying the drug may put the offender at risk of imprisonment but it is only the bigger supplier who attracts condign punishment.

In brief, it is wrong to represent the law as it exists in practice as a savagely punitive system which will throw the first offender haplessly into gaol for personal use of the drug. However, it would be equally wrong to suggest that a stage has been reached where prison sentences have been abandoned for every type of cannabis offence. In fact between 1975 and 1985 custodial sentences for cannabis offences totalled 22,374.

Britain—extent of cannabis use

The precise level of cannabis use in this country is unknown. Illegal behaviour is, of course, always difficult to investigate and enumerate, and cannabis use is no exception. Even so, some data are available which give at least an indication of the extent of this drug's use, together with a description of those who use it.

For example, over sixteen surveys have investigated the extent of cannabis usage in the United Kingdom. Most of these studies have been confined to young people due to an assumption that these were by far the most likely users. In addition, most of these surveys have been restricted to a single or fairly narrow geographical locality and either to school pupils or to college and university students.

Four surveys of British secondary school pupils conducted between 1970 and 1980 showed that between 3% and 13% reported having ever used cannabis. A further nine surveys have examined the extent of cannabis use reported by samples of young people who were either college or university students or who were in their late teens and early twenties. These studies indicated that cannabis use was commonplace among such young people, with up to 34% of subjects having at least tried cannabis experimentally.

There is also information from two national sample surveys. In 1979 a poll showed that 12% of those interviewed (16% of men and 7% of women) had used cannabis. Cannabis use was reported by a higher proportion of people (14%) in the south of the UK than in the north (9%)*. Three years later, another survey was conducted of a sample of 1,326 young people aged 15–21. This showed that 17% of those interviewed (19% of those working and 10% of those in education) reported having smoked cannabis. Interestingly, a much higher level of use (27%) was reported by those who were unemployed. The young people who had used cannabis were asked from which source they obtained it. Altogether 71% reported getting the drug from "friends". Only 5% recalled obtaining cannabis from a "street seller"**.

*Fieldwork was conducted by MORI on behalf of NOW! amongst a representative quota sample. Interviews were conducted between 8th and 13th August, 1979.
**NOP interviewed this sample in 101 constituencies between 4th and 20th January, 1982. The sample was quota-controlled for age, sex and class. This survey was carried out for the *Daily Mail*.

Most but not all surveys have indicated that males are more likely than females to report having used cannabis. In addition, users came from all social and occupational backgrounds, political affiliations and income levels. Even so, there may be some truth in the popular belief that cannabis users are more likely than non-users to espouse "unconventional" political or religious beliefs and philosophical ideas, although the large majority of self-reported cannabis users are not remarkable in relation to their ideologies or their life-styles.

Besides these survey data one can get some indication of prevalence of cannabis use from official statistics on arrests for possession, supply or cultivation of cannabis, together with Customs and Excise data on seizures (Table 1). Such figures must of course be interpreted guardedly; only a small percentage of cannabis users are ever going to be arrested and only an uncertain proportion of cannabis itself will be seized. It is probably safer to regard these statistics as indicators of trend rather than prevalence, and even so it must be remembered that any change in police or customs activities may distort the picture. During the last decade or so police drug squads have been established throughout the United Kingdom.

Patterns of use

People who use cannabis are not to be seen in terms of a single identikit picture—they are not all hippies, all Rastafarians, or all young executives. Similarly, there is enormous variation in the actual patterns of use. All general population studies have shown that most of those who have used cannabis have done so only a few times and have then stopped.

A significant minority of cannabis users can however be identified as regular or frequent users. Different studies have applied varying definitions. Even so, several surveys have noted that a fifth or a quarter of those who have used cannabis have taken the drug regularly, i.e. weekly, or on many occasions. Such users are also particularly likely to be regular drinkers and tobacco smokers and to have used other illicit drugs. Indeed, polydrug use is fairly commonplace among regular cannabis users. It is necessary to stress, however, that not all heavy users of cannabis will be using other drugs.

Table 1: *Cannabis seizures and convictions 1975–1985*

	1975	1976	1977	1978	1979	1980	1981	1982	1983	1984	1985
Number of seizures*											
Cannabis (herbal)	3,835	3,912	3,238	3,986	5,664	8,830	8,500	8,775	8,929	9,730	10,388
Cannabis plants	436	628	872	820	1,324	2,351	1,787	1,708	1,296	1,806	1,594
Cannabis resin	4,969	6,108	8,080	8,247	8,826	6,964	8,911	10,670	13,976	13,978	14,991
Cannabis liquid	190	137	126	88	191	223	254	284	313	224	142
Persons convicted of or cautioned for cannabis offences	8,987	9,947	10,607	11,572	12,409	14,910	15,388	17,410	19,966	20,529	20,976

NOTE As the same seizure can involve more than one type of drug, rows cannot be added together.
(Source: Home Office 1986)

The following four case histories show the tremendous range of variations that exist among cannabis users. Each is a composite based upon several real individuals. None is presented as "typical".

Jean is a third-year dentistry student at a large university. She was introduced to cannabis smoking at a party in her home town shortly before going to university. Since then, she has smoked the drug once or twice a month, usually in the company of friends, but occasionally when alone. She is a moderate drinker and smokes twenty cigarettes each week. She has never used other illicit drugs.

Dennis is twenty and is unemployed. He last worked over a year ago as a labourer on a building site. He has applied for over sixty jobs since then, without success. He lives with his parents and an elder sister who is a typist. Dennis drinks and smokes as heavily as his restricted income allows. He associates mainly with a group of working class friends who are keen users of a wide range of illicit drugs. He has experimented with LSD, cocaine, barbiturates, diconal, heroin and amphetamines and has also sniffed glue and solvents. He smokes cannabis heavily and is frequently "stoned" or thoroughly intoxicated thereby. He had been admitted to hospital on six occasions following overdoses of alcohol combined with barbiturates or tranquillizers. He has received psychiatric treatment several times, both following these episodes and at other times for severe depression. Dennis is well-known to the police as a petty criminal and has convictions for theft, arson and for illegal possession of drugs.

Susan is fifteen and still attends secondary school. She has smoked cannabis several times while out with friends. These occasions were prompted by curiosity and she no longer uses the drug. This is mainly due to her aversion to smoking tobacco and her reluctance to forging links with hard drugs. She prefers drinking Martini, which she regards as more sophisticated and pleasant.

Brian is an artist who works with an advertising agency in London. Now forty, he has smoked cannabis since he was twenty-five. His use is mainly light, but it has been very heavy at times, especially when he feels depressed. On such occasions Brian smokes cannabis as an attempt at self-medication which he prefers to seeking tranquillizers from his family doctor. He concedes that such heavy use may not be a constructive response but maintains that it is a valuable form of release. He has used other illicit drugs, but not for ten years. His heavy drinking sometimes worries him.

Back to the debate

At the beginning of this chapter it was suggested that the reaction to the publication of the Wootton Report had to be understood in terms of the tendency for drug-related questions to bring out conflicting and basic attitudes and values, with the drug then cast as a moral symbol. The cannabis debate was seen as exemplifying the conflict between the libertarian and the authoritarian positions.

The fundamental positions of the two contenders might be described as follows. Libertarians, following the precepts of John Stuart Mill, contend that the State may only be justified in forcefully intervening to curb an individual's behaviour in order to prevent that person harming others. The contrary view is that private behaviour may, in effect, have a subversive impact upon society and, if regarded by the majority as immoral, may legitimately be subject to state control.

No doubt it is the dialectic of this debate that maintains the openness of our society, gives it its flexibility, and allows thinking to move forward. It would be inappropriate here to go much further into an analysis of these complex philosophical issues, but this is undoubtedly the context in which the debate on cannabis is embedded. It is apparent that the protagonists on either side of the cannabis controversy have over recent years argued their cases and bolstered their positions by some very selective borrowings from science. There are two opposing and very familiar sets of contention which have been put forward. An attempt will be made to summarise these contrasting positions as fairly as possible while at the same time insisting from the side-line that the rhetoric on either side requires scrutiny.

The rhetoric of reform

"Reform" has come to mean here the legalisation of cannabis — a nice trick of rhetoric in its own right. At least five commonly deployed lines of argument can be identified as constituting the current basis of the libertarian case. Each will be considered briefly in turn.

(1) The over-whelming consensus from international official enquiries is that moderate use of cannabis carries little if any health risk. Cannabis has been the subject of several weighty investigations and there can be no doubt that findings strongly support the position stated above. The first of these investigations was the Indian Hemp Drugs Commission which, after two years' inquiry and receiving the evidence of 800 witnesses, produced a report in 1894. It concluded that the widespread belief that cannabis use caused insanity was supported by extremely weak evidence while "moderate use" of this drug appeared to be harmless. A special committee appointed by the Mayor of New York reported in 1944 after six years deliberation. Their conclusions (usually referred to as the La Guardia Report) echoed those of the Indian Hemp Drugs Committee. They reported that marihuana causes neither true tolerance nor dependence and that even prolonged use could not be shown to be harmful. The Wootton Committee looked at its predecessors and in this regard repeated their findings:

> "Having reviewed all the material available to us we find ourselves in agreement with the conclusions reached by the Indian Hemp Drugs Commission appointed by the Government of India (1893–1894) and the New York Mayor's Committee on Marihuana (1944) that the long-term consumption of cannabis in moderate doses has no harmful effects."

In addition, many of the general conclusions of the Wootton Report and its two predecessors have since been echoed by a Report to the US President by the National Commission on Marihuana and Drug Abuse (the Shafer Report) and by the Interim Report of the Canadian Government Commission of Inquiry into the Non-Medical Use of Drugs (the Le Dain Report).

In summary, the contention that no-one has shown the moderate use of cannabis to be harmful is supported by a chorus of authority. But while accepting the validity of the conclusion in those terms, the medical critic will want to know what is meant by "moderate". He will also point out that the public health issue may hinge upon the likelihood that if an increasing number of people use cannabis "moderately" probably more people will use it "immoderately". This issue is discussed further below (p. 140).

(2) Why should cannabis not be legalised if alcohol and tobacco, which are far more harmful substances, are legally available? On any objective reckoning cannabis must at present get a cleaner bill of health than our legalised "recreational drugs". In terms of the libertarian argument to send a school teacher to prison for growing cannabis plants while allowing sports sponsorship by the tobacco industry is grotesque. However, the critic will argue that legalising cannabis would add to rather than diminish society's problems with alcohol and tobacco. The comparison is true in toxicological terms but, argues the critic, false in policy implications.

(3) The law is a worse evil than the drug. The argument which is advanced here is that stopping a young person on the street for a drug search is likely to alienate him from the police and lead to needless harassment, especially for members of ethnic minorities. Arrest and court processing is a costly business in terms of court time and it is a diversion of police efforts from more serious matters. Sending a cannabis user to prison is tangibly damaging and any conviction may carry secondary penalties such as employment difficulties or problems in getting travel visas. In sum, it is argued, the costs of criminalisation far exceed both in cash and human terms any demonstrable negative consequences of the use of the drug.

It is difficult to contest this position, but the critic will shift the debate by asking what the costs would be if legal controls were removed and cannabis use greatly escalated. And that leads directly to the next point in the libertarian argument.

(4) A limited decrease in sanctions directed at the user is unlikely to lead to any up-swing in prevalence or level of use. Here recent American experience is likely to be called in as evidence. Eleven American states have abolished sanctions on the possession of small amounts of cannabis since 1973. A recent review has concluded that this change has not led to alarming consequences; cannabis consumption appears unaffected or only very slightly affected, and most people believe that this lifting of sanctions has had little untoward result. In addition this so-called "decriminalisation" step has produced economic and administrative benefits for law enforcement agencies. These conclusions remain as yet tentative, but they might favour the libertarian case. Many systems of licensing or partial legal sanctions could be envisaged as alternatives to the present all-out repressive approach.

(5) So many people today in the UK use cannabis and public sentiment is so much in favour of this drug that the law is no longer workable. We have already reviewed the evidence on the prevalence of cannabis use and factually cannabis is a minority activity in every age group. As regards public sentiment, there are some interesting findings. Public opinion in Britain is over-whelmingly un-sympathetic to cannabis and to other illicit drugs. Opinion polls conducted between 1969 and 1975 have uniformly concluded that only a small minority, 8–12% of the general population, favour reducing cannabis-related penalties or legalising this drug. A survey of 15–24 year-old people carried out in 1979 concluded that, even among this age group, only 23% approved of legalising "soft drugs", while 71% disapproved. The same study also concluded that, consistent with patterns of cannabis use, males were more favourable than females in their attitudes to this issue. The most liberal views on the legalisation of "soft drugs" were evident among the unemployed, those with a grammar or independent school education, those with high incomes, those living in the South of Britain, those who described their life situations as "unhappy" and those who had passed 'A' levels or who had received a college or university education.

The argument that the law on cannabis no longer has any public support is therefore difficult to sustain. Of course the champion of the liberal cause could shift his argument and maintain that the true reformer should always be ahead of public opinion.

Counter-rhetoric—fighting the tide of permissiveness

In the preceding section the major elements in the "reform" platform have been outlined. The opposing case is put forward by those who contest cannabis reform because of a fundamental commitment to a belief that the State is properly the protector and arbiter of morality and social well being, with cannabis a threat to society's standards. Cannabis use is then evidence of feckless hedonism and moral decline. These views owe much to folklore about the excesses attributable to cannabis use. They also derive from a reality—the adoption of cannabis use by the young, radical and disaffected in Western countries during the 1960s and 1970s. The arguments on this side of the floor are generally less complex than those put forward by the reform lobby.

(1) Cannabis is all part-and-parcel of permissiveness, disaffection and the attack on established values. This was clearly the view of the spokesmen from both sides of parliament some of whose contributions to the debate on the Wootton Report were quoted at the beginning of this chapter. They are of course right insofar as cannabis has become a symbolic cause for exactly those movements in society which they decry and oppose. To an extent, the fighters against cannabis set up their own self-fulfilling prophecy. The ferocity of their attack on this drug amplifies the potency of cannabis as a symbol of opposition to the older generation and the establishment. It must also be noted that the argument is fundamentally mistaken if it assumes that all cannabis users are long-haired teenage revolutionaries. As already shown, this stereotyped view of the broad spectrum of cannabis users is contrary to the facts.

(2) Give an inch on cannabis and the wrong message on drugs in general will be put about. Here the fear is that if the public (and especially the young public) are led to believe that the government of the day is "going soft" on cannabis, encouragement will be given to every kind of more dangerous drug use. This position rests on the assumption that the country will be more naïve in its ability to discriminate between different drugs than may be true today.

(3) Cannabis use is likely to escalate to the use of heroin. One of the classic fears about cannabis is that its use may lead to more serious forms of drug use and to drug dependence. In fact, many of those who develop drug-related problems have previously used cannabis, along with alcohol and tobacco. It is clear that a person who uses cannabis is statistically more likely to try other illicit drugs than one who does not. Even so, the over-whelming majority of cannabis users do not use opiates or become dependent upon illicit drugs. Escalation or progression from cannabis to drug dependence is probably no greater than progression from moderate drinking to severe alcohol dependence. The risk is there but in the case of cannabis it has been greatly exaggerated.

(4) Cannabis has a wide variety of adverse social and medical effects—it causes violent crime, social incapacity, cancer, brain damage, foetal abnormality, sterility, promiscuity . . . and goodness knows what else. This statement as it stands unashamedly, and perhaps unfairly, caricatures the extreme position of those who see cannabis as a corrupting evil to be resisted at all costs—the moral crusaders who will exaggerate any shred of scientific evidence if they can twist it to suit their case. Such misuse of science to bolster fixed beliefs is, of course, anathema to the researchers who, guardedly and with endless provisos, report their tentative experimental results. As a corrective it is worth quoting the balanced and cautious conclusions of the 1982 report of the Advisory Council on the Misuse of Drugs on the "Effects of Cannabis use":

"1. There is insufficient evidence to enable us to reach incontestable conclusions as to the effects on the human body of the use of cannabis;

2. but that much of the research undertaken so far has failed to demonstrate positive and significant harmful effect in man attributable solely to cannabis;

3. nevertheless in a number of areas there is evidence to suggest that deleterious effects may result in certain circumstances;

4. there is a continuing need for further research, particularly of the epidemiological characteristics of cannabis use and on the effects of its long-term use by humans;

5. there is evidence to suggest that the therapeutic use of cannabis or of substances derived from it for the treatment of certain medical conditions may, after further research, prove to be beneficial''.

Selective quotation from the scientific literature on the toxicity of cannabis is no service to honest debate.

(5) An ultimate constraint is that Britain is signatory to the UN Single Convention and is thus bound by force of international agreement to outlaw cannabis. The first proposal to curb the availability of cannabis was advanced at the International Opium Conference held at The Hague during 1912. Twelve years later, the Second Opium Conference produced, in spite of British objections, the first international controls on cannabis. In 1961, Britain signed the international Single Convention. This treaty bound the 65 signatory nations to establishing a wide range of curbs on the availability of "addictive drugs". Cannabis was covered by this treaty even though the expert advisers to the Convention at the time had stated that cannabis was non-addictive. Whether the view formed by these advisers can still be regarded as correct in the light of later evidence is discussed later (p. 138). The Dangerous Drugs Act of 1965 implemented Britain's obligations under the Single Convention and included cannabis in its provisions.

It is true that Britain is at present bound by international treaty obligations. In fact, that treaty does enable signatories to opt out of its provisions unilaterally. This might be politically difficult, but is not unprecedented. Spain, for example, decriminalised cannabis in 1983. The symbolic commitment of Britain to international drug controls is important. Yet this need not be radically undermined by a change in the cannabis laws.

The health arguments

As stated at the beginning of this chapter, the facts which ought to form the basis of the cannabis debate all too easily become obscured by the sound and fury of the battle between those who make cannabis a symbol for two opposing factions which have little to do with the drug itself. To be squeezed by both sides of a hot and bitter contest is an unpleasant experience, and to have scientific data purloined as "evidence" to be used or misused by one or other contestant is saddening. This section of the chapter will attempt to spell out the factual basis and nature of a third and very different perspective, that of the individual's well-being and Public Health.

(1) **The decision as to whether cannabis should or should not be legalised is, at the end of the day, rightly and inevitably a value-laden social and political decision.** Scientists and medical practitioners can be called as expert witnesses but the primacy given to health considerations is determined by society, and society will get the health it deserves. "Health" can become as much a lobby as any other lobby but that in no way contradicts the argument that the scientific evidence on cannabis really does deserve calmer and less passionately clouded appraisal than has sometimes been the case. Health professionals themselves can all too easily go beyond their evidence.

(2) **The medical scientist does not think in terms of the absolute but rather the dose-related safety of a drug.** At present many self-designated "regular" users of cannabis in the UK are probably only using 5–10 mg or less of the active principle of the drug each day. In parts of the world where high-potency cannabis is readily available a daily intake of 100–200 mg is feasible. Current British and Western appraisal of the dangers

of cannabis may be based on a familiarity with it which would be parallel to a society's view of alcohol if only shandy were available.

The importance of considering dosage was aptly emphasised in a 1981 WHO report:

"Intermittent use of low-potency cannabis is not generally associated with obvious symptoms of toxicity. Daily or more frequent use, especially of the highly potent preparations, can produce a chronic intoxication which may take several weeks to clear after drug use is discontinued. The seeming inconsistency of this observation throughout the world may reflect differing exposures to THC (tetrahydrocannabinol) because of the large variation of potencies and smoking techniques, as well as different cultural preferences for the route of administration."

The first sentence of that paragraph is an accurate summary of the present state of knowledge. But one cannot just stop at that first sentence.

(3) Tolerance and dependence. It is useful to quote again directly from the 1981 WHO report as an authoritative summary of the present state of knowledge:

"Chronic administration of cannabis results in the development of tolerance to a wide variety of the acute drug effects in both humans and experimental animals. Though scientific opinion is more divided on the question of dependence on cannabis, there is now substantial evidence that at least mild degrees of dependence, both psychological and physical, can occur".

The clinical and Public Health significance of these findings is uncertain and it would be wrong to interpret this evidence as implying that cannabis is dangerously addictive. The scientist who is familiar with the history of early-warning signals on the dependence potential of different drugs (and the neglect of warnings) will however want to watch developments in this evidence very closely.

(4) There is persuasive evidence that at certain levels of exposure cannabis can be harmful to the individual. There can be no reasonable dispute that cannabis can cause acute mental impairment in terms either of intoxication or a transient but very bizarre and worrying psychological experience. The following paraphrase describes such events:

> "I don't know whether it was strong hash or I was just in a bad mood. But that time I smoked I got those paranoid feelings. You know, a lot of people get a bit paranoid when they smoke hash, specially at the beginning. But then I started to see everything going very small, sounds getting very loud, everything very threatening. Very frightening. But it only lasted a couple of hours or so and my mates sort of said 'don't worry', calmed me down".

Such transient perceptual distortion, anxiety, and mild paranoid reaction seem indeed to be regarded by cannabis users as none too remarkable. Although adverse consequences are unlikely to arise from this kind of brief disturbance what is more significant is the now persuasive evidence that cannabis can in some circumstances give rise to an exaggeration of this type of disturbance which may be manifest as a spectrum of intensity and duration with, at times, very unpleasant symptoms lasting for a day or more. Indeed, the picture in many ways can resemble an LSD "bad trip". There is also the possibility of a further parallel to the LSD experience in that "flashbacks" from an adverse cannabis experience can occur over a period of weeks or months. The potential hazard to the developing minds of young people cannot in this context be ignored. Thus at present it is the evidence of the adverse psychiatric consequences of this drug that is more conclusive than any proof of physical harm, while data which show that intoxication with cannabis can seriously impair a person's control of a motor vehicle must also be taken into the reckoning.

(5) Cannabis is a drug with a number of features which in terms of general pharmacological principles invite reasonable caution. Pharmacologists, when confronted with a new drug, will often try to place it in its "family" and thus to an extent predict its behaviour in terms of family resemblances. A new opiate will, give or take a little, often behave rather like other opiates. Cannabis has general depressant properties (see p. 20) and one would therefore expect that in equivalent doses it would have some of the intoxicating and incapacitating effects of say alcohol, and perhaps also the same kind of dependence potential. It also has a family resemblance to the LSD-type of hallucinogenic drugs. This combination of features should by itself be seen as reason for caution but in addition there is evidence that THC (the active principle) or its break-down products can remain in the body tissues for many weeks and perhaps lead to cumulative effects. To the pharmacologist the drug's profile is not reassuring.

(6) The lesson of history is that the dangers of a drug are far more often under-estimated than over-estimated. Today it is realised that tobacco smoking causes about 100,000 deaths each year in the UK, but the fact that tobacco is dangerous has only been established over the last 30 years. Heroin was introduced as a non-addictive substitute for morphine. History is littered with such instances of neglect, denial and late discovery. With that perspective in mind the public health specialist is going to be extremely wary of encouraging the wider use of a drug such as cannabis which in his judgement is already known to have some worrying characteristics.

(7) Public Health has to think in terms not only of the individual but also the population at risk. The medical doctor must be concerned for the individual health of every single person in the community, but the Public Health tradition also emphasises the enormous importance of thinking about health at the aggregate or population level. Within this framework the question is not just whether cannabis in certain doses can adversely affect the individual, but also that of ensuing implications for the health of the *population*. What methods of control will therefore lead to fewer people using a potentially harmful drug and to fewer people using it at the higher dose levels? Here thinking is likely to be influenced by research on alcohol and associated problems, which suggests that the best way to decrease the prevalence of excessive use is to limit the general level of use. Keeping down the level of cannabis use by our present control strategies may be the best available Public Health strategy despite its social costs.

The future for the cannabis debate—and for cannabis

There is a genuine division of opinion on whether or not certain types of behaviour warrant State intervention and whether such behaviour should be permitted to continue, albeit in private. If cannabis is approached from the libertarian angle, it should clearly be legalised and the costs of current punitive controls to the individual and society removed. The libertarian position does not require cannabis to be risk-free for this decision to be taken, and the integrity of the position is only weakened if its proponents wrongly dismiss the evidence for potential dangers.

As for those who want to fight cannabis because of their innate commitment to resisting threats to old established values, their views deserve respect but the argument of this chapter is that in tilting at cannabis they may be setting their lances at an inappropriate target.

Making a symbol or a counter-symbol of this drug is dangerous in the actual encouragement it will give to its use and in the further symbolisation of cannabis as a fountain-head of liberty. That is how the debate can be summarised at present. Respect must be given to the right of others to hold to their values but it is also fair to ask that in doing so they should cease mis-representing the health evidence in either direction.

Health is only one of several issues at stake and the health perspective does conflict with libertarianism. It is for society to make the decisions as to what ranking it gives to illness and health as opposed to other costs and benefits. But a dispassionate evaluation of what is known and not known at present about cannabis within the health perspective does not recommend its wider use.

It is difficult to foretell the future so far as society's relationship with any particular drug is concerned. Perhaps cannabis will fade away as a forgotten fashion or its popularity come and go like the skateboard craze. Perhaps people will wake up one morning to find that cannabis has been taken over by the tobacco manufacturers and the Government is subsidising its cultivation. On the evidence reviewed in this chapter and because of health considerations and the overwhelming public antipathy towards either partial or complete legislation, it is not likely that a radical change in the law will be politically acceptable in the foreseeable future.

Chapter 13
Solvents

"Glue sniffing" first became headline news in the UK in the mid-1970s. As had so often happened previously with drugs misuse this country was once more in a way catching up with the USA, where there has been concern over this issue since the 1960s. Now the problem is one of international dimension and there have, for example, been major outbreaks of a similar kind in such different parts of the world as Scandinavia, Mexico and Japan.

"Glue sniffing" is not in fact a particularly apt term, given that it is the organic solvent rather than the glue itself which is the sought-after drug, and given also that the usual mode of intake is more likely to be inhalation than sniffing. For these reasons this chapter will use the term "solvent misuse" instead of "glue sniffing" as the preferred designation. Some experts use the phrase "volatile substance misuse", which is scientifically correct but perhaps too cumbersome for ordinary purposes.

At times in the last few years in Britain solvent misuse has been a cause of acute public and political anxiety. A parliamentary speech recorded by Hansard in May 1984 is quoted as an instance of an extreme expression of alarm:

"Individual cases have been reported to me of people being left with no minds as a result of solvent abuse. They emerge from prison, for example, having committed offences while under the influence of the vapour which they have inhaled. They are wholly unimproved on leaving because their minds have been extinguished by the abuse of solvents. It is extremely serious".

Such a view of the dangers of solvent misuse has been amplified in many lurid newspaper headlines which give the impression that this habit has become a national plague which is corrupting every school playground, with no child too young to fall victim.

It is easy to react against the absurdity of this alarmism. What *is* an "extinguished" mind? Are there not some more common and less drug-related reasons for people coming out of prison "unimproved"?

It might well be felt that playing on public anxieties as reflected in that Hansard report constitutes disservice to the community. But over-reaction to that type of distortion should not lead to the opposite extreme with a dismissive response. It is legitimate for a community to be worried by the new and unknown, and the local newspaper which carries the story of a teenage "glue sniffer" being found dead with a plastic bag over his head is reporting a personal and family tragedy which is of understandable concern to that neighbourhood. It is not the reporting of the facts which is wrong but the frequent lurid exaggeration which is built up around such tragedies.

In this chapter an attempt will be made to describe briefly this phenomenon and its dangers. What is challenging and difficult here is that the "drug" is not a foreign product foisted upon the country by drug smugglers, nor even a medical substance, but the stuff of ordinary everyday household materials. There is no easy police or customs barrier against model aeroplane cement. Society is dealing in this instance with the mundane, unromantic, low-prestige "kid's" end of the drug problem spectrum, but it is one which somehow strikes directly under our guard.

What substances and how are they taken?

The chemicals with which this chapter is concerned have in common the fact that they are hydrocarbon compounds which are commercially useful because of their solvent properties and hence for instance their use as a carrier solution for glue. They also share the property of being "volatile" which means that they readily give off a vapour or evaporate. Although these solvents have certain similar essential properties they represent a diverse range of chemicals which are to be found in such products as glues and adhesives, hydrocarbon fuels, paint strippers and nail varnish removers. It is of course the vapours from these solvents which are actually misused. A rather different but related class of substances acting as aerosol propellants has also been misused.

Solvents are taken by inhalation and one highly dangerous practice has been to pour solvent into a plastic bag which is then placed over or around the head, a technique which carries the danger of death by suffocation. Although other methods of administration are probably well known to young people who are exposed to misuse, there is little merit in further publicising them here.

Who is at risk?

The majority of solvent misusers are teenagers, although some 10 year olds may be drawn into the habit, and occasionally people are found still inhaling solvents in their twenties. The problem most typically affects the school-age population aged between 12 and 16. Solvent taking, like so many other forms of deviant or rule-breaking behaviour, is more often a group than a solitary activity, and more frequently involves boys than girls.

Many different patterns of misuse exist. Solvents may be the only substance being misused, or there may be heavy drinking or experimentation with a variety of illicit drugs going on at the same time. A young person may "glue sniff" on only one or two experimental occasions or become more regularly involved in this habit over a few months or years. Some adolescents may inhale solvents only once or twice a week or perhaps less often, while others may do so with much greater frequency. After a few years the majority of solvent misusers will abandon the practice and look upon it as juvenile and unprestigious, and will then probably steer clear of any move towards further or more serious drug involvement. However, a minority will not be so fortunate.

Solvent misuse appears to be more common in urban than in rural areas. Although experimental use may occur haphazardly, chronic, intense, and more dangerous patterns of use are particularly likely to occur among adolescents who are vulnerable to a cluster of problems, such as those who come from disadvantaged families, where, for example, a parent is drinking excessively, or where there has been a breakdown in the marriage.

How many cases?

The difficulties inherent in the "how many" question become very evident in this sector of the drug problem. How many *what*? What is "a case"? The figures can be made to reach frightening totals if one counts everyone who has ever sniffed a solvent experimentally, even just once or twice. No doubt the juvenile delinquency statistics could be made to appear at least equally alarming by counting as a delinquent any adolescent who has ever cheeked a policeman. A false impression of the solvent misuse problem is created by totting-up young urban experimenters who in the course of fairly normal adolescent development are rashly but transiently breaking many of society's rules and occasionally using solvents in that context. What is said here must not of course be misinterpreted as viewing the problem lightly; any solvent misuse, even on one occasion, can carry serious dangers.

A more important question relates to an estimate of the proportion of adolescents who are engaged in persistent solvent misuse. An honest answer to that question would probably go something like this:

"I don't know—it must depend on the city, the borough, the school, the street. 'Average' figures don't have much meaning. I would guess that in some urban areas, in some schools or on some housing estates, 10–20% or more of adolescents may have experimented with solvents but far fewer—at worst perhaps 1 or 2%—will have been seriously and dangerously involved. But I am projecting from very inadequate data".

At present, epidemiological surveys cannot give more definitive information than is carried in such a guarded statement. That a small percentage of young people in some localities is seriously involved in a potentially damaging habit is of course sufficient reason for concern.

To over-interpret those data as in the following further extract from Hansard is however not too helpful:

"Some researchers into the numbers who so abuse solvents have produced estimates that show as many as 10 per cent of the population in any one school may be abusers. That does not apply to all schools but perhaps it applies to the average school".

Against this statement should be noted that the "ever used" figure for "glues" obtained in a National Opinion Poll of 1,326 young people aged 15–21 from 101 constituencies in Britain in 1982 was given as 2.8%. There is the possibility of misuse of statistics as well as of drugs, and perhaps the solvent story brings this particular difficulty into unusually sharp focus.

The wanted effects

As mentioned in Chapter 2, solvents may have both depressant and hallucinogenic effects. It is both these types of experience which can make solvent misuse attractive to the adolescent user. The intoxicant properties of these substances provide a quick means of reaching a mental state which in many ways is equivalent to that produced by alcohol. The fact that inhalation is a technique for getting a drug rapidly to the brain means that the solvent taker will go from sobriety to intoxication within a few minutes and far more speedily than is possible by drinking alcohol on an empty stomach. This abrupt form of intoxication gives the solvent experience a special psychological attraction.

The hallucinogenic effects are usually mild and may include subtle distortions in the form and intensity of what is being experienced. The room may, for instance, go out of perspective, light may be altered in quality, sounds become louder, an imaginary voice may be heard. These happenings can however merge imperceptibly with the more bizarre and frightening consequences described under the "Bad Consequences" heading below.

The intoxication produced by one acute experience of solvent inhalation may last about 45–60 minutes. The user may then feel sleepy or "a bit hung over". He or she may stop at this point or repeat the process. The sophisticated user may attempt to maintain a state of mild intoxication over some hours, measuring intake against the mental state.

This discussion so far has dealt with the desired *pharmacological* impact of solvents on the brain. These direct drug effects are certainly important to an understanding of why young people "sniff glue". But as with so many other drugs it is also necessary to realise that the lure lies in more than the chemistry alone. Solvents are attractive because their use is a group activity and provide thrills in a landscape where more legitimate excitement may be hard to find. Risk-taking has its own attractions, as has breaking the grown-up rules and provoking the anxiety and perplexity of worried adults. Solvents are also attractive to some isolated youngsters who may use them as a form of escapism.

Bad consequences

Most transient misuse of solvents is likely to cause no damage at all and this statement is necessary to place anxieties in proper perspective. This point must however be properly balanced with the warning mentioned before that any such use of solvents carries some degree of risk and even some possibility of serious disaster.

The Russian roulette quality of the problem makes solvent misuse worrying. It is because so many in that little circle of adolescent users get away with their experimentation and come to regard "glue" as an ordinary plaything that the reaction is likely to be one of particular horror when to everyone's surprise fun turns into tragedy and someone is suddenly killed.

Deaths which result from solvent misuse can happen for different reasons. Occasionally death can occur without warning as a result of sudden heart disorder. The young person who has been inhaling with a plastic bag may fall unconscious and suffocate with the plastic bag over his head, or he may die from inhaled vomit. Many of the risks from inhalant intoxication are similar to the hazards of simple drunkenness. Instances have also been reported where under the influence of solvents, someone has become acutely disturbed and suffered the sort of fatal event, for example the jump from a window, which can occur with LSD and similar drugs, although, as with the latter drug it is necessary to guard against exaggerated horror stories. Solvent misuse may sometimes be scapegoated for a tragedy which had some quite other cause. It is however possible that any form of continuous drug-induced intoxication in a young person can result in a morbid disturbance of mood and personality, and this has to be understood as the special danger of the impact of drugs on the young mind.

It is not just the random and occasional risk of acute intoxication which causes anxiety. There is also concern about the nature and extent of possible damage to various tissues of the body which may result from solvent misuse. Some of the more toxic organic solvents (benzene or carbon tetrachloride, for instance) are capable of causing serious harm to the body over long periods of exposure. They can damage the liver, kidneys, heart muscle, bone marrow and nerves supplying the limbs. Poisoning by these substances can indeed cause toxic death. However, a question mark still hangs over the issue of whether exposure to solvents in the course of intermittent adolescent sniffing and inhalation is likely to result in such gross physical damage. In particular, attention has been focused on possible damage to the brain. The evidence on this point is inconclusive.

Turning from the physical to the psychiatric dangers, the immediate drug effect sometimes goes beyond the wanted experience of pleasurable intoxication to something approaching the LSD "bad trip" or a short-term delirious state, which in rare circumstances can give rise to behaviour that is a danger to the individual or to others. It has also been stated that exposure to solvents can result in transient depression, or in a more prolonged emotional disturbance.

Lastly, under the "Bad Consequences" heading, it is necessary to examine the possible social or lifestyle consequences of solvent misuse. As has already been mentioned, adolescents who have been involved in experimentation with solvents are likely to move out of that phase after a few years, find their first job, and put petty deviance behind them; that is the natural history of most adolescent acting-out. For a small minority the experience with solvents may provide a gateway to continuing deviance and alienation, and an introduction to a sub-culture which itself poses a threat to ordinary social development and integration. It is among this minority that more dangerous and persistent patterns of drug use (including heavy drinking) may emerge.

Dependence

A young person who is heavily involved in solvent misuse and whose friends are also engaged in this activity may find it very difficult to break from the habit. Solvent misuse only very rarely gives rise to significant dependence in the formal sense in which that term is being used in this book (Chapter 4). Solvents thus illustrate the possibility of a drug giving rise to misuse without usually inducing dependence.

How to respond?

The furtive use of solvents by a group of adolescents on a piece of waste land or on the stairway to a block of flats is not something which can be eradicated by the heavy artillery of drug laws and enforcement.

"Control of supply", for instance, cannot possibly be considered in terms of banning a host of ordinary household products or in seeking to control these substances under the Misuse of Drugs Act. It is not an offence to misuse inhalants or to be in possession of any of these substances with the intention to misuse, but recent legislation (The Intoxicating Substances (Supply) Act of 1985) has usefully strengthened control over sales. It is now an offence for anyone to supply a substance to a person aged under 18:

> "if he knows or has reasonable cause to believe that the substance is, or its fumes are, likely to be inhaled by the person under the age of eighteen for the purpose of causing intoxication".

Successful prosecutions have been brought under this Act and conviction can lead to a fine or a prison sentence of up to 6 months.

Modelling glue will inevitably go on being sold in the toy shops but shopkeepers can be expected to exercise due care. Responsibility must lie with the good sense and alertness of the individual manager and shop assistant, and useful guidelines have been prepared and distributed to advise shopkeepers and their staff on how to meet their responsibilities. Dangerous products should not, for example, be displayed where they can fall easy prey to shop-lifting.

Suggestions have been made that the problem might also be ameliorated by "product reformulation", by industry finding less dangerous solvents or aerosol propellants. This is desirable wherever practically possible but there are limits to feasibility. It is technically rather difficult to find chemical additives which can be put into products so as to make them generally acceptable but aversive or unattractive to the potential misuser.

A great deal of responsibility for treatment and prevention lies with the integrated efforts of a wide network of general agencies at local level—the social services, schools, voluntary agencies, GPs and others. The ability of parents to deal with these problems at home needs to be strengthened and supported. A family in which a boy or a girl is suddenly discovered to be misusing solvents may be in need of counselling so as to respond appropriately to what at first appears to be a frightening crisis or a family disgrace. To refer young solvent misusers to the police is inappropriate and indeed unethical, but if the police are involved they can steer the youngster informally toward help. Help for the young solvent misuser must always treat that youngster as a person in distress and take note of the context of his or her life, including the total environment of family, housing, schooling, work, leisure and friendship. Solvent misuse again underlines the fact that "treatment" of a drug problem is never a matter of a master-stroke focusing just on a drug or on a "problem" taken out of context. Both preventing solvent misuse and helping the misuser must rely essentially on multiple, simple and undramatic community-based responses rather than on any grand or too forceful strategy.

Chapter 14
Psychotropic drugs

The word "psychotropic", in its literal meaning of affecting or influencing the mind, encompasses all the drugs discussed in this book. However, in this chapter the term is being used in a much more restricted way to indicate those manufactured drugs that are prescribed by doctors for the treatment of mental symptoms. Thus it includes *hypnotics*, for the treatment of insomnia, *minor tranquillizers*, used for treating anxiety and *stimulants*, sometimes used as appetite suppressants. Specifically excluded from this heading are the major tranquillizers (phenothiazines and butyrophenones) which are used in the treatment of psychotic illnesses and seldom misused. Antidepressants are sometimes included among the psychotropics but they have only very low misuse potential and will not be considered here. Amphetamines have been accorded a chapter to themselves (Chapter 10).

Why should these medically prescribed substances — the stuff of the bathroom cupboard — be included in a report which is dealing with the problems and pains which society is encountering with illicit drugs? A critic might argue that we are blurring the proper boundaries of concern, and that it is a slur upon the good names of useful medicines to bracket them with black-market heroin.

It is exactly this question of boundaries on which this chapter will focus. Are psychotropics within the territory of "drug problems"? In examining national prescription trends for psychotropic drugs the data conclusively show the extraordinary penetration which these drugs have made into our society. It is therefore important to examine the possible effects of psychotropics on people in daily life, and to consider problems related to overdose and self-poisoning as well as recent evidence on the dependence potential of the benzodiazepines. On this basis the question of whether psychotropics are part and parcel of "the drug problem" will be considered and some conclusions drawn.

Prescription trends

The increasing consumption of psychotropic drugs, described by one authority as the "march of the psychotropic juggernaut", is reflected in the number of prescriptions for these drugs. The figures for 1975 in the United Kingdom provide a good starting point for discussion. In that year such prescriptions reached their peak. There were 47½ million prescriptions for psychotropic drugs (including barbiturates) dispensed at retail pharmacists in England and Wales. These figures represented an 8% increase over the 1970 levels (although during the same period there was a 15% increase in the prescription of non-psychotropics too, so the juggernaut does not only carry psychotropics), and the increase for psychotropics was in fact lower than in the previous five years when it was at 19%.

A more detailed analysis reveals that of the 47½ million prescriptions, 43% were for tranquillizers, 35% for hypnotics, 17% were for antidepressants and 5% for stimulants and appetite suppressants. Although there had been a marked reduction in the prescribing of barbiturates due to an increased awareness by the medical profession of their dangers, this was compensated for by an increase in the number of prescriptions for the newer and safer tranquillizers, the benzodiazepines.

If the figures are then traced forward from that peak year the DHSS statistics on the number of prescriptions for antidepressants, benzodiazepines and barbiturates show that from 1975 to 1979, the annual figure was steady at about 43 million with the continuing fall in barbiturate prescriptions still being compensated for by increased benzodiazepine prescriptions. Since 1979, however, there seems to have been a reduction. The benzodiazepines, originally welcomed in the 1960s because they were "non-barbiturate", are now at the root of current concern about psychotropic drugs. In 1985 a total of 25 million National Health Service prescriptions were issued for this class of drug. In less than 15 years diazepam (Valium), the best known of the benzodiazepines, became the largest selling drug in the world. In 1986 the benzodiazepines were put within the controls of the Misuse of Drugs Act (Schedule IV).

Such is the frequency of prescription of tranquillizers that it is estimated that 5% of men and 12% of women in the UK consume these drugs on a daily basis for one month or more during the course of the year. Greater use of tranquillizers by women and their frequent dependence on this class of drugs is well documented and has been interpreted as an undesirable side-effect of the status of women within society as a whole.

Of course anxiety about psychotropic drugs is not limited to the UK and they are increasingly being used in other industrialised countries and in the developing world. While not wishing to deny the people of developing countries the advantages of modern drugs, there is concern among international organisations that the Third World should not import all the problems experienced in the West with the widespread use of these substances. The diversion of scant medical resources away from preventive medicine and other areas of high priority and the damage to community systems for coping with distress may be too high a price to pay for importing psychotropic drugs.

Effects of psychotropics on daily life

What effect are these pills likely to have on the user? Leaving aside for the moment questions of overdose or dependence it is important first to note the effects of minor tranquillizers and sleeping pills on ordinary everyday functioning.

The most obvious adverse effects of these drugs include drowsiness, confusion and a general slowing-up of activity. These side-effects are familiar to those who take the drugs and who may complain of feeling "muzzy", particularly during the first few days of medication. Later on, if they continue taking drugs, these sedative side-effects may become less troublesome and patients may not realise that their ability to perform daily tasks is still compromised. This can have serious consequences if the individual concerned is driving a car or is in charge of machinery where quick reactions and decisions are essential. After an hypnotic (i.e. sleeping) dose of benzodiazepine the night before, a hangover effect disrupts early morning performance. Impairment of performance after benzodiazepines appears to be related to the age of the patient and to the dose consumed.

Despite much expressed concern there is comparatively little reliable information available about the contribution, if any, of psychotropic drugs to road traffic accidents. No doubt such accidents have multiple causes and it may be difficult to apportion the contribution made by any one factor. For instance, the underlying condition that led to the prescription of a psychotropic drug may itself cause poor driving. The statistics about the association of these drugs with road traffic accidents cannot be regarded as wholly reliable but available data for sedatives and hypnotics suggest that their use in therapeutic doses may double the risk.

The question has also been raised as to whether benzodiazepines can cause "disinhibition" which may then result in anti-social behaviour uncharacteristic of the individual. The defence lawyer may see this as a possible line of argument when a woman, with an otherwise unblemished record, is charged with shop-lifting and it is revealed that she had recently started to take diazepam (Valium) on her doctor's prescription. Even more than with traffic accidents it is difficult to make confident statements about the possible role of a drug in such a complex event which is the end result of many different circumstances and influences.

Before leaving the effect of psychotropic drugs on daily life, it must be emphasised that the adverse effects on performance and arousal may be compounded if other drugs (including alcohol) are taken simultaneously.

Psychotropics and overdose

Against the background of wide availability that the prescription rates indicate, the health problems associated with the misuse of psychotropics have become apparent. Undoubtedly the most important adverse consequence in terms of sheer numbers must be drug overdose. The frequency of these events is such that the margin of safety between the therapeutic dose of the drug and the dose required for serious overdose or death is at times a pharmaceutical feature with commercial significance.

The problem of drug overdose has been described as an epidemic. In a month long study carried out in London in 1975 when all drug-related problems attending the Accident and Emergency Departments were monitored, 1,641 cases of drug overdoses were recorded. Obviously there were other cases that never came to hospitals. Minor tranquillizers were the drugs most frequently involved (27% of cases), followed closely by barbiturates

(22%). Studies in other countries have had similar results. The Drug Abuse Warning Network (DAWN) that monitors drug problems all over the USA, reported that nearly one-quarter of all "drug mentions" in the survey were related to benzodiazepines. Although benzodiazepine overdose is rarely life-threatening the effects are potentiated and may be fatal if they are taken, as they often are, together with depressant drugs such as alcohol.

A drug overdose may be taken either accidentally in the course of dependence and in the search for heightened effect, or deliberately in a suicidal gesture or attempt, the so-called para-suicide. Undoubtedly psychotropics are the drugs used most frequently for para-suicide, and it has even been suggested that the mounting frequency of para-suicide can be attributed to the increasing quantity of prescriptions for psychotropic drugs.

The drugs used in para-suicide do reflect prescribing trends and the reduction in the proportional use of barbiturates for para-suicide is mostly due to the increasing use of benzodiazepines and similar drugs. Given the far higher safety margin of benzodiazepines in comparison with barbiturates this must be good news. But although the margin of safety between the therapeutic dose and the dose required for serious overdose or death is considerable for benzodiazepines, it is much narrower for other sedatives and hypnotics, and when taken in overdose, the latter cause profound sedation and depression of respiration.

Barbiturates

In any discussion of the misuse of psychotropics the barbiturate class of drugs deserves special mention. The barbiturates were introduced into medical practice in 1903. It appears likely that one of the reasons for the medical profession and the public rather easily surrendering the wide use of opium as a sedative and hypnotic was the arrival of the barbiturates as drugs which in many ways provided a substitute. Such preparations as Luminal (phenobarbitone), Nembutal (pentobarbitone), Seconal (secobarbitone), Amytal (amobarbitone) and Tuinal (a combination of secobarbitone and amobarbitone) became household words. Over 2,500 different barbiturates were synthesised. A patient going into hospital for whatever reason would automatically be written-up for a range of barbiturate sleeping tablets. Over the years prescriptions and repeat prescriptions for barbiturates were written by the incalculable millions until in the 1960s benzodiazepines began to be substituted for barbiturates, even as decades earlier barbiturates and bromides had taken the place of laudanum and other opium preparations. There were several reasons for the tide turning against the popularity of the barbiturates. Overdose and para-suicide were reaching worrying levels and it was evident that barbiturates were particularly dangerous because of the relatively narrow margins between a therapeutic dose, a "suicidal gesture" and a fatal outcome.

Evidence also began to accumulate that barbiturates had a high dependence potential and that withdrawal could cause epileptic fits or a clinical picture resembling delirium tremens. The most damaging blow to the reputation of these drugs came perhaps in the 1970s when barbiturates began to make a major appearance as "street" drugs. The young injecting poly-drug users discovered that it was possible to grind up barbiturate tablets and prepare a solution for injection. The hazards inherent in such a procedure were appalling but the use of barbiturates in this manner spread rapidly. The grossly drug-intoxicated and disinhibited intravenous barbiturate user became a familiar and disruptive figure in the hospital Accident and Emergency departments.

The arrival of this very serious variety of epidemic barbiturate misuse forced an awareness of the need for stricter control on prescribing. Most of the barbiturates which were circulating on the black-market originated from lax medical prescribing or pharmacy thefts. A campaign was organised in the mid-1970s to persuade doctors to cut down voluntarily on their deployment of barbiturates and in 1985 these substances were put within the controls of the Misuse of Drugs Act.

Barbiturates still have a currency on the black-market and still make some contribution to deaths by overdose. The extent of their use and misuse has today enormously declined, but it would be incautious to assume that barbiturates could never make a comeback. What has happened with the barbiturates vividly illustrates the possibility of ebb and flow in drug problems and the dynamic nature of the drug ecology. Within the larger theme of the present chapter the barbiturates demonstrate that the licit and illicit use of a drug must often be seen as matters of interlocking concern, and much the same can be said about the amphetamines.

Psychotropics and the risk of dependence

Apart from the amphetamines (Chapter 10) and barbiturates, consideration must also be given to non-barbiturate sedatives such as methaqualone, meprobamate, glutethimide and chlormethiazole and the benzodiazepines. As so often happens in the history of addictive drugs, the story is one of initial claims for safety being confounded by later experience. All the non-barbiturate sedatives have a more or less serious potential for dependence, and clinicians have learnt to handle them warily.

Realisation that benzodiazepines also carry serious risks of dependence dawned more slowly. To begin with most reports of dependence were of individual cases, and the patient's underlying propensity for drug misuse was blamed rather than the inherent properties of the drug itself. However, as psychotropic drugs have been prescribed more widely their dependence-producing liability has become more apparent and has increasingly become the subject of scientific enquiry.

It has been argued in defence of the benzodiazepines that only a small fraction of the total number of patients who are prescribed them will run into problems with dependence. A "small" fraction might look worrying in terms of the count of patients even if this argument were accepted, given the extent of benzodiazepine prescribing. But how small is a "small" fraction? While the answer to this question is not known the research evidence which is accumulating is far from reassuring. Perhaps 15% of long-term benzodiazepine users are going to experience withdrawal symptoms when they try to stop. The ancillary question of how long is "long-term" then arises, and research suggests that a four to six week exposure to benzodiazepines can put a patient at risk of dependence. What is also worrying is the evidence that withdrawal symptoms can occur after therapeutic or "normal dose" exposure to benzodiazepines. It is not necessary to build up tolerance or to exceed the prescribed dose to encounter this trouble.

One reason for the delay in recognising that benzodiazepines can give rise to a withdrawal syndrome in dependent subjects was that the anxiety and psychological distress resulting from withdrawal were wrongly interpreted as a resurgence of the psychological symptoms for which the patient was originally prescribed the drug. In fact the cluster of symptoms that make up the withdrawal state often goes beyond anything which could be confused with a return of the psychological complaints which originally led to prescribing the drug. These withdrawal symptoms may include an exaggerated and unpleasant response to ordinary sensory stimulation (to light, sound or touch), tingling sensations, giddiness, muscle spasms, headaches, sleep disturbance and more rarely hallucinatory experiences. Such a bizarre and multiple set of complaints may all too easily be dismissed by a doctor, unfamiliar with the benzodiazepine withdrawal state, as "neurotic" or "just putting it on".

The duration of these symptoms is variable but they are capable of persisting for longer than more familiar drug withdrawal states. Benzodiazepine withdrawal symptoms usually start a few days after the drug has been stopped and may continue with unpleasant intensity for four to six weeks. Recent reports suggest that a degree of withdrawal distress may persist for as long as one year in some cases.

Are psychotropics part and parcel of "the drug problem"?

Amid all the concern about psychotropic drugs, and the catalogue of problems consequent upon their use, it should not be forgotten that it has been members of this broad group of drugs that have revolutionised psychiatric care since 1950. To suggest that some of these drugs should be considered an integral part of "the drug problem" is not to underestimate the enormous value of many of them when properly prescribed. Starting with the introduction of chlorpromazine (a phenothiazine) and continuing with more recent anti-psychotic drugs, the number of mental hospital in-patients has fallen markedly, although this is balanced by increased admission rates, shorter repeated lengths of stay and greater emphasis on community care. The immense value of anti-depressants in the treatment of severe depressive illness is also well documented. These advances in psychiatric treatment should not be perceived only in terms of the number of in-patients and the economic benefits of out-patient care, although such factors may well be important at times of scarce resources. The real advance lies in the reduction of human suffering, both of patients and their families.

A nihilistic and across-the-board denunciation of drugs in the treatment of psychiatric patients would therefore be absurd and inappropriate. With that point established the question of "boundaries" raised at the beginning of this chapter deserves serious debate. If widely prescribed drugs like the benzodiazepines (and the barbiturates before them) not uncommonly give rise to unpleasant and serious dependence problems it is hard to dismiss out-of-hand the argument that this type of psychotropic drug is indeed part of "the drug problem". That some psychotropics are of great benefit when correctly used has to be readily conceded, but *some* psychotropics does not mean *all* psychotropics, and the boundaries between proper medical prescribing and the "drugging of society" are sometimes blurred.

It might help to summarise the arguments which can be marshalled to support the case for placing some psychotropic drugs within the boundaries of "the drug problem":

(1) People who by any reckoning have "a drug problem" and who are, for instance, heavily involved in the misuse of cocaine or heroin, are likely these days to be mixing a number of psychotropics with these illicit substances. They do so "to get a better buzz", to dampen the excessive excitement induced by cocaine or to counteract the sedation produced by an opiate. They do so because these diverted medicines are easily available and because someone offered this "handful of pills". Psychotropics are therefore part of the poly-drug scene. As mentioned earlier, psychotropics are also part of the self-poisoning scene. Non-barbiturate sedatives and benzo-diazepines are also increasingly misused by patients with drinking problems, sometimes with disastrous consequences.

(2) Many people are taking benzodiazepines and similar drugs not for relief from any circumscribed or definable medical condition but for the malaise and anomie that comes from an unsatisfactory social situation or unresolved personal problems. Close analysis of a spectrum of individual cases suggests that it is not stretching the boundaries of "the drug problem" too greatly to propose that there are all too many instances where "the pills the doctor gave me" are astonishingly similar in meaning and function to "the pills I got at the disco". There is increasing realisation that the medical treatment of social ills is a step with grave implications. At worst it could be the first step towards producing a "drugged" society too tranquillized to react to social wrongs.

(3) In Chapter 7 evidence was discussed suggesting that the greater the national per capita consumption of alcohol the higher will be the rate of alcohol problems. "Normal drinking" is the base of the pyramid, and the bigger and broader that base the greater the tip of problems. In Public Health terms there cannot be more drinking without having more drinking problems. Some research has now examined the possibility that the true drug pyramid is not just an illicit drug pyramid or a psychotropic pyramid or an alcohol pyramid, but a construction which is built out of all these chemicals put together. More psychotropics at the base may imply a bigger tip of illicit drug use. If it is accepted that adults may think it entirely proper to reach into the medicine cupboard at the slightest tinge of psychological distress, it is also likely that such an attitude will generalise and provide exactly the background to encourage the strained, bored or frustrated adolescent to reach for illicit drugs.

So much for some of the arguments which bear on the boundary debate. Having examined the evidence and the arguments, what conclusions can be drawn? The extreme position that "medicines" have nothing to do with the "drug problem" must be untenable. Equally, the view that psychotropic substances are an unmitigated evil should be dismissed as a dangerous exaggeration. The truth is to be found in the middle ground, and there the boundary is an uncertain and shifting line which needs constant surveillance.

Part III
Responding to drug problems

Chapter 15
Prevention

Facile optimism, facile pessimism

Drug misuse is rather like sin. Most people who regard themselves as upright citizens will be against it, without having considered in any detail what *it* is. In a similar way, many people will be in favour of virtue in the guise of prevention, without having considered what exactly is to be prevented or how prevention is to be achieved. Pressure is thus generated which can lead to well-intentioned but hopelessly inappropriate drug prevention campaigns. Such campaigns are nearly always targeted on school-children and are based on the simple-minded belief that if children are told that drugs are dangerous they will not take them.

The disappointed reaction to failure following such unduly optimistic approaches is often inappropriate pessimism. Failed campaigns and over-ambitious expectations give prevention a bad name and the temptation is to retreat to the gloomy view that nothing can be done.

The position taken in this chapter is guardedly positive. If multiple, sustained and rational strategies are employed headway can be made, and prevention is in the truest sense better than cure. Nevertheless substance misuse is unlikely to be totally eradicated. Although prevention can achieve positive benefits, it must be admitted at the same time that it is a difficult business. Seemingly commonsense strategies may not always succeed and can have unexpected and untoward effects. An examination of these difficulties is therefore made as an important preliminary to any new look at this subject and this will be followed by proposals for a set of ground rules for effective prevention strategies. Finally, examples will be given of elements which can contribute to a total prevention strategy under the headings of "supply" and "demand" reduction, and what is meant by these terms will become clear.

165

Prevention—traps and barriers

Uncertainty as to the target problem

Drinking problems provide an illustration. In the past many campaigns have focused on the prevention of alcoholism with the target narrowly conceived as distinct from the whole range of alcohol-related problems. As a result, efforts have only been directed at a very small sector of the total burden of pain and damage inflicted on society by the excessive use of alcohol, and the greater part of the spectrum of undramatic but pervasive ways in which this drinking affects mental health and social adjustment is excluded.

The same questions about goals have to be asked in relation to psychotropics, smoking, or illicit drugs. Is the goal to be prohibition or amelioration? Is it substance use itself which is the target, or the adverse consequences of use? Is the strategy to focus on early experimentation or more established patterns of use? Different goals may require different methods for their realisation.

Uncertainty as to the target audience

This heading is closely related to the issue of goal definition but here the concern is not with the type of problem but with the type of drug-misusing population to be targeted. A prevention strategy suitable for adolescents may need to be different from one directed at adults. Women and men may require different approaches. Prevention strategies go wrong when it is assumed that the target group should be restricted to one sector of the population, such as young people, while ignoring the drinking and drug taking of older people, or alternatively when it is assumed that the target group is of homogenous class and ethnic background.

The lure of master-strokes

It is all too easy when faced with complex social problems like those of drug misuse to retreat to a simple solution in terms of a personally favoured master-stroke. Some would advocate a major emphasis on class-room education and teaching children to say "no". Others would argue that the class-room approach is unproductive, and that the answer lies with stricter police enforcement. Still others would insist that an improved urban environment is the only legitimate remedy. Simple and reductive answers of this or any other kind will not solve complex problems.

Targeting on one substance, forgetting the others
It has been repeatedly stated in this book that drug problems must
be seen as embracing not only illicit drugs but also cigarette
smoking, the misuse of alcohol and the excessive use of
psychotropics. It generally makes sense to tackle problems in
proportion to their severity unless there are good reasons for doing
otherwise; yet in relation to health issues more prominence is
frequently given to problems of lesser significance, because of their
notoriety and the glamour attached to combatting them, than to
those which are less spectacular but more pervasive. Carrying out
heart-transplants is a more attractive proposition in all respects
than maintaining the sewers, but the health implications of the
latter vastly outweigh those of the former. In the area of addiction
it is perhaps more glamorous to crusade against heroin, but far
more people die as a result of drinking and smoking. The mood
of the time supports the message that "Drugs Kill", whereas
cigarette packets still carry only a coy message on health, and
alcohol carries no message at all.

Any truly effective prevention policy must correct these
imbalances. It is important that many more people realise and
accept that alcohol-induced symptoms like hangovers and "the
shakes" are mainstream drug-related phenomena which they
experience in common with so called "junkies", that lawful and
unlawful drug use are not totally separate realms of experience,
and that falling over and being sick because one has had too much
to drink is in no way a superior form of behaviour to a similar
state of intoxication achieved through some other substance. It
is instructive to ponder the reasons which make it seem all right
to say "don't worry about him, he's just drunk", and not all right
to say "don't worry about him, he's just taken heroin".

Lack of commitment
Prevention is only likely to succeed when there is a high level of
national conscience and community commitment to sustain the
necessary action. Without such commitment there will only be
token gestures or opportunistic political posturing, and the
considerable forces which are arrayed against prevention are then
all too likely to win the day.

Tobacco provides a telling example of the difficulty in
generating a true national commitment to prevention. Cigarette
advertising continues at an intensive level, and sports sponsorship

more than defeats the effects of the ban on direct television advertisements. Every poster which proclaims the gentle charm or the manly image of cigarettes makes nonsense of any idea that society is truly committed to action on smoking. The official stance is shown up as being one of timidity and duplicity. In the same way the commitment to action on alcohol problems is quite unconvincing; and it would still be unsafe to assume that most Western countries have yet made the necessary degree of commitment to preventive action on illicit drugs. Commitment has to be argued, demanded, generated and sustained if prevention is to be more than a token of political expediency.

Commonsense which is not necessarily sensible
At the beginning of this chapter reference was made to the misplaced faith in a type of common-sense education campaign based on the premise that if children are told that drugs are dangerous they will observe the warning. Sadly the research evidence is otherwise, and at least among part of the adolescent population scare-mongering in the name of education appears to be counter-productive and may encourage the misuse of drugs. Propaganda or crude efforts at persuasion must not be confused with education in its truest sense. A strong warning must be issued against exaggerated tactics such as telling schoolchildren that drug taking leads to inevitable doom and exposing them to pictures of emaciated, over-dosed or dead heroin users. This caricature is not too remote from some schoolroom practice.

It is necessary to bear in mind that much human behaviour is supported by social associations and symbolic meanings, while other activities are relatively free of these influences. In the former the behaviour in question will be more resistant to change, since it is embedded in a reinforcing set of factors. Activities like drinking, smoking and taking illicit drugs have enormous symbolic value as already discussed in Chapter 5. For example, drinking among teenage youth is partly motivated by the belief that drinkers are more sociable, sexually attractive and mature than youth who do not drink. For teenagers at least these motivations are probably as important as the effects of alcohol itself. By contrast, brushing or not brushing one's teeth carries less symbolic meaning, and no-one seriously tries to demonstrate his maturity, manliness or toughness by letting his teeth decay. In consequence information on tooth brushing can profitably be confined to facts and problems surrounding the teeth, brushes and toothpaste, whereas education about alcohol has to tackle widely different issues on a number of fronts, including toughness, maturity, sexual attraction and so on.

If the message concentrates on negative aspects or consequences which are unrelated to sources of motivation, it will miss the mark. For example, if a youngster drinks to appear mature an appropriate counter message might point out that alcohol does not make that adolescent mature, and that in addition it is not a worthwhile goal to strive for maturity in that way. An inappropriate message might say that drinking too much makes a person ill—a message which does not impinge on the reasons for drinking. Someone "addicted" to mountaineering will not be dissuaded by the information that it is dangerous and that people can get killed. He knows that already and it is not because he is unaware of the possible consequences that he is climbing rocks.

Prevention can have back-lash
Education campaigns illustrate one type of conflict which can sometimes occur between "common sense" and more careful reasoning. Conflicts can also be identified in other areas of prevention and whatever the particular arena, clumsy and poorly thought out intervention can all too easily lead to a back-lash or unwanted side-effects.

For instance, availability of drugs is clearly an important factor in drug use, and one could reasonably expect fewer users in a situation where a particular substance is made difficult to obtain. However, this approach is not without its problems and these are of the type associated with any prohibitionist policy. When supplies of a drug are curtailed the first result is a price increase because of scarcity and greater demands on the remaining sources of supply. The addict may compensate for this market shift by committing more acquisitive crime. Secondly, there is an increase in the "cutting" that takes place; the drug concerned tends to be mixed with other possibly dangerous and impure substances, with increased health risks. Thirdly, drug users will turn to substitutes, as when heroin addicts have switched to the very dangerous use of intravenous barbiturates when heroin has been in short supply.

In a word, the drug-culture becomes more extreme, and although there may be fewer drug users those who are using are likely to be heavy users experiencing mounting problems. They will need to find ways around the increased price and scarcity of the substance, and a bigger gulf is created between society generally and the drug culture with all that this entails. Thus any rigorous interdiction of supply involves costs as well as benefits.

It is also worth examining the possible double-edged effect of increased police powers and larger penalties for possession and dealing in drugs. To provide police with substantially increased powers of search and arrest on the basis of possible preventive efficacy may go beyond the normal concept of what is just and fair in our society. If it is argued that by "making an example" of some people others are deterred, it has to be clear that what is taking place is scape-goating. In the process young people would increasingly end up in gaol with all the alienation and waste of human potential that this entails.

Messages need credible messengers

The significance and quality of the messenger must be considered in relation to any type of drug education. Experts such as doctors and police may sometimes prove to be less effective than the schoolchildren's own teacher. This is especially likely if those outsiders cannot communicate at the appropriate age level, if they confuse or daunt the children by their presence, if they over-stimulate them by their stories and pictures, or if they exaggerate the facts and so lose credibility.

Employing ex-addicts as spearheads for prevention campaigns, in the belief that their evidence is especially real, is often misconceived. The enticing and implicit message, "I've been there, man, so I know" is alluring, containing as it does the hidden conceit that the only way you ever really "know" is to "go there". Admittedly, people who have "been there" are likely to have a personal view which is perhaps more detailed and richer than that of other people, but it is less, not more, objective. The central involvement of ex-addicts in educational campaigns may give a subtle kudos and credence to the very activity it is wished to discourage.

Different audiences may be more or less responsive to different messengers and the essential lesson is again the need for diverse approaches to diverse target groups. Most fundamentally there is an issue here which leads back to the question of whether Society itself is a credible messenger. Is it not pharisaic when Society warns young people about the dangers of illicit drugs while at the same time it displays such a half-hearted response to the damage done by alcohol and tobacco or the misuse of sedatives and tranquillizers?

Prevention—learning from experience

The reason for having catalogued the difficulties which frustrate the purpose of prevention is not to lend support to pessimism. It is to learn from experience and so gain a view of the prerequisites of a successful prevention policy. In the past there has been a marked tendency in this field to recycle ineffective or mischievous approaches.

Learning from experience must be a constant and continuing process. Different drugs are going to require different approaches in different circumstances. Within this perspective it is useful to review the main strategies which should find a place in an overall prevention policy (a total list of everything that has been done in the name of prevention would be amazing and exhausting). These can usefully be placed under three broad headings namely, those which aim at controlling the *supply* side; those which aim at reducing the *demand* for drugs; and those which aim at *risk reduction*. These three major themes will be discussed in the ensuing sections of this chapter.

Prevention—controlling the supply side

Under this heading can be placed every type of action which aims to prohibit, curtail or control the individual's or the population's access to the dangerous substances concerned.

Curtailing cultivation

Heroin, cocaine, alcohol and tobacco are among the leading substances misused on a world-wide scale and it is interesting that they have in common a botanical derivation. Although today there is a range of entirely synthetic substances which also contribute to the drug problem, it is remarkable that despite all the advances in pharmacology and technology these plant substances remain at the centre of the international drug stage.

In considering prevention strategies it is therefore necessary to examine a range of difficult issues affecting the economic development of poor countries, the widespread activities of multi-national business corporations and even EEC agricultural policies. For example, efforts have been made in Thailand to introduce crop substitution programmes which aim to persuade peasant farmers in the northern hill territories to grow peppers and other lawful crops instead of the opium poppy. The gains have only been limited. There are vast remote areas of the world in which it is all too easy to slash or burn a patch of jungle or hillside for cultivation, plant an illicit crop and reap quick and certain profits.

It is unlikely that, in the long term, problems of opium cultivation in Eastern countries or of cocaine in Central or South America can be met by taking drug cultivation out of the context of the much wider issue of socio-economic development. Equally difficult questions arise when an African country which stands greatly in need of a cash crop is encouraged to invest in tobacco production. European agricultural policies that bear on the wine markets are dictated by economic rather than health interests. Whatever the difficulties, there can be no doubt that, in the future, authorities seeking to intensify prevention will be forced to give increasing attention to these difficult and politically charged issues; and international co-operation will have to be strengthened. It is insufficient to conceive of an interdiction of heroin, cocaine or cannabis, only in terms of the very last links in the long chain that leads to the drug's presence on the streets of our own cities.

Customs and police action

The operational costs, the ingenuity of the smuggler, the length of the coastline, the freedom and complexity of traffic all mean that only 10% to 30% of illicitly imported drugs are likely to be seized by Customs in the UK. This is not an argument for abandoning Customs efforts, and the situation would be much worse if vigilance was lowered.

Much the same can be said about police interdiction of supply once a drug has crossed the borders. Even the most massive deployment of police resources and diversion of manpower from other important police work would not eliminate drug misuse. The big dealers are cautious and have accurately calculated that the chances of arrest are not great, while the small-scale dealers at the street and housing-estate level are so many and their activities so diffuse that they often defy effective action. As with Customs, it must be appreciated that continuing police action aimed at curtailment of supply is vital but nevertheless limited.

Locking up the pharmacy
This is an example of the type of small and undramatic measure which is unlikely to catch the headlines but which can contribute to the success of preventive endeavours. It is useful at this point to introduce this example to underline the fact that prevention is about small remedies as well as grand strategies. A few years ago pharmacy break-ins in Britain were serving to swell the flow of drugs available to the black-market. The Home Office successfully met this problem by making detailed recommendations as to how pharmacy security could be improved.

Control of prescribing
Today the system whereby certain drugs can only be obtained on medical prescription is accepted without question, but this is a very different state of affairs from that of the last century. One by one dangerous psycho-active drugs have been brought under varying degrees of control, and there are highly formal national regulations and international agreements designed to prevent drugs with serious dependence potential from being available over the counter or carelessly introduced to medical practice. Such regulations are reviewed from time to time.

Liquor licensing
The system of liquor licensing has grown up piece-meal and it is tempting to see it as an historical relic aimed only at frustrating the Britisher and his visitors who want to drink at a time of day (or night) of their own rather than Lloyd George's choosing. The urgings of tourist and trade interests for reform or relaxation of liquor licensing are well organised and a partial liberalisation has already taken place in Scotland. The pressure from the temperance organisations and other campaigners is just as strong for the preservation of the *status quo*. The actual efficacy of any of these licensing measures is difficult to determine and does not easily lend itself to experiment. Total prohibition is clearly counterproductive, but controls may have a symbolic as well as a more direct impact and serve to support the message that alcohol does indeed have potential danger and ranks differently from a cup of tea. The extent of adolescent drinking and the ease with

which young people can obtain alcohol must be viewed with concern.

Taxation
Taxation constitutes a yet further method for controlling consumption of lawful substances, and the important potential of price regulation in relation to alcohol and smoking is discussed elsewhere in this book.

A variety of approaches to prevention which bear on supply have been identified, but many other variations of this type of intervention could be listed. Taking cigarettes out of hospital shops, adding unpleasant-tasting contaminants to surgical spirits or outbidding the black-market by buying up and burning the opium crop in Thailand are but a few.

Prevention—attempts to reduce demand

Although measures to control supplies are necessary to a total prevention strategy there is a bluntness about these attempts to alter human behaviour which before long reveals its limitations and incompleteness. If policies are merely repressive and do not address themselves to the demand for drugs no amount of pushing down on the problem will prevent those who "need" drugs from obtaining them. A brief respite will be followed by a further epidemic outbreak; or the misuse of one class of chemical substance will be substituted by another. Some of these difficulties have already been noted. Supply strategies must therefore go hand-in-hand with demand policies. Reducing a population's demand for drugs is no easy business but there are encouraging examples.

Sustained and multiple efforts at education
Over recent years adult cigarette smoking in the UK has changed from being a majority to a minority behaviour. In 1972, 52% of British males and 41% of females aged over 18 were smokers. Ten years later these figures had fallen respectively to 38% and 33%. The historical background to this decline in smoking was discussed in Chapter 8. Relevant factors included the first scientific demonstrations of the harmfulness of smoking dating from 1950, the impact of a series of highly influential reports by the Royal College of Physicians, the formation of Action on Smoking and

Health as a campaigning organisation, the work of the Scottish Health Education Group and the Health Education Council, the ban on direct television advertising of cigarettes and the restrictions on smoking in public places. The conclusion must be that if education is truly to change social awareness, attitude, and behaviour, the commitment has to be found for a very full, varied and sustained effort. Prevention through education does not win its victories in a day. Such a perspective is different from the "miracles" expected from an occasional classroom lecture. It has to take into account the whole social context which shapes and forms relevant attitudes and responses.

Linking drug prevention programmes to other social movements

Many developing countries are now taking the threat posed by excessive drinking seriously, and campaigns against drunkenness can be effectively linked to wider issues of national development. Such processes mirror the links between the public health movement and the religious (moral) revivalism which occurred in the last century in Europe and the USA supporting anti-opium and temperance campaigns. Today's alliance of public health may be with the growing popular concern for individual fitness and sport as demonstrated by "health maintenance", jogging, concern over diet and so on. Reducing the demand for drugs, alcohol, tobacco and needless medication may increasingly find its links with these strands of health consciousness. Some American anti-smoking campaigns, for instance, have been placed deliberately within the broader positive health context.

Community development and finding positive alternatives to drug use

The complex relationship between social deprivation and misuse of drugs and alcohol has been discussed in an earlier chapter (p. 49). In Western society today drug and alcohol misuse occur among the privileged as well as the poor but there is suggestive evidence that there can in some circumstances be a relationship between urban deprivation and such manifestations as glue sniffing, heroin use, and certain patterns of drinking. Attempts have been made in other countries to tackle drug misuse through strategies of "community development". The underlying premise is that if people living in a community can themselves be engaged in renovation or development of their area, and if youth activities can be supported and leisure facilities built, then the factors which invite drug misuse are likely to be undercut. This has been described as an "upstream" approach to demand prevention. The attack is not directly on drugs, but on the housing, education, employment, leisure and living conditions; in fact, the quality of life itself.

The parents' movement
This has become a major grass-roots manifestation over the last few years in the USA. Such a development relates in part to the issues of community development which have just been discussed, but parents' organisations are becoming active in anti-drug campaigning in many different sectors of American society, not just the less privileged areas, and are now a force with political influence. However, their view of the problem is sometimes anything but balanced.

Treatment as prevention
Treatment and prevention cannot be sharply separated. The individual who is successfully treated is a one-person example of demand reduction, while treating a community's heroin addiction reduces the mass of those engaged in using and dealing in drugs. There have been examples of intensive community treatment campaigns curtailing a local heroin epidemic. The fact that there are several recovered alcoholics who do not drink at a party makes abstinence more socially acceptable.

Advertising
There is evidence from Norway that a total ban on cigarette advertising may constitute an important health measure. The debate continues about the efficacy of curtailing alcohol advertising and whether the benefits would justify further interference.

The media
Concern has been expressed that the many images of addiction which appear on the television screen, together with the plethora of sensational newspaper headlines dealing with the latest society or pop-music drug scandal may actually stimulate the appetite for drugs. At times this slavering interest in "The drug menace" has

gone far beyond anything which could be described as balanced reporting and could better be described as fairly cynical commercialism. There is also worry about the subtle conditioning influence of the television play in which the hero is forever romantically lighting cigarettes for his girl, and about the soap-opera in which heavy drinking is portrayed as part of the good life. The argument put up for the defence of the former is that the media have a responsibility to report social problems and it is unfair to blame the messenger who brings the bad news. As for smoking and drinking the point will be made that there must be artistic licence to portray life as it is actually lived rather than as a sanitized health educator's version of reality. It will be argued that health concerns cannot be allowed to impose a new type of censorship.

At times those professionals whose primary commitment is to health have tended to show little understanding of those in the media whose primary responsibility is to report or entertain. There is a need to bridge this gap and in reality there is much potential common ground. Part of the overall prevention strategy on the demand side must involve a better dialogue between the two professional sides in which both explore together how the health interest of society can be strengthened rather than undermined in this important context, with discussion of how to provide the media with necessary technical advice and information.

Prevention—attempts to reduce the risk

The thinking behind this third approach is that if drug use itself cannot always be prevented a secondary aim can be to diminish the risks which result from its use.

Cigarette smoking provides an example. While many millions of people continue to smoke despite major efforts of health education campaigns and warnings, lives may be saved by persuading addicts to smoke less dangerous cigarettes. This may be done by switching to low tar or filtered cigarettes or by other changes in the manufacturing process which reduce the toxic qualities. Cigarette smokers may also be persuaded to change to less risky types of tobacco use such as pipe or cigar smoking. Some years ago an unsuccessful attempt was made to market an entirely synthetic smoking material (New Smoking Material), allegedly very low in cancer potential.

The experience of these various attempts to make cigarette smoking safer points to the positive and negative consequences which are likely to be associated with risk-reduction strategies. On the positive side it seems probable that many lives have been saved by cigarette smokers changing to less dangerous modes of taking nicotine. It makes good sense to acknowledge that not all these dependent individuals are going to abandon their habit or do so quickly.

The negative aspects also deserve attention. Smokers who go over to filtered cigarettes may negate any health advantage by smoking more of each cigarette. Cigarette smokers who are inhalers may turn to inhaling cigars with no consequent decrease in the health threat. The most fundamental objection to the message that it is possible to go on smoking but smoke more safely comes from those lobbyists and educators who see such a statement as detracting from the true health message — stop smoking. The idea that it is possible to smoke safely is seen by them as dangerously undermining the broad and fundamental health campaign, and as a defensive ploy on the part of the manufacturers.

With variations, much the same debate has more recently focused on certain types of drug prevention strategy. There have been sharp arguments as to whether it is proper to distribute educational material giving instructions on how to inhale solvents in ways that avoid the current highly dangerous techniques. Is such an initiative truly health education or is it providing dangerous covert encouragement to glue sniffing?

The same arguments arise as to whether sterile disposable needles and syringes should be given to heroin addicts in an attempt to prevent person-to-person transmission of the HIV virus causing AIDS. This issue is also considered in Chapter 16 (p. 193) but it is raised here to highlight the important question, whether risk-reducing messages may sometimes in the long run do more harm than good by giving reassurance to those who are engaging in intrinsically dangerous behaviour, or by recruiting others to such behaviour.

It would be unwise to adopt an inflexible attitude on the very difficult matters raised in this debate. Each problem needs to be approached separately on its merits and carefully studied, with data gathered to determine outcome. The dangers of introducing risk-reduction strategies without great caution and measured observation should be borne in mind, but it would be unwise on doctrinaire grounds to rule out such approaches in all circumstances. There is danger in making the best the enemy of the good.

Prevention—everyone's or no-one's business

The prevention of substance misuse ought to be everyone's business. First and most importantly, the avoidance of chemical misuse must be seen as essential to every individual's personal responsibility for maintaining his or her good health. Encouraging a concern for health in the child and adolescent is a fundamental duty of each parent and the transmission of healthy attitudes toward drugs, alcohol, and tobacco stands in the whole context of home, school, college, industry and society at large.

Prevention of drug and alcohol misuse and the elimination of cigarette smoking is a task for every community and for very many sectors within a community. These problems should be the active concern of School and College authorities, Youth Clubs, Sports Clubs, Women's Groups, Residents' Associations, Church Groups and of all the many other formal and informal groups that make up the mosaic which is the local community. Prevention cannot be left just to central and Government action.

To insist on the necessity for individual and community commitment is not to ignore the simultaneous and equally vital need for central and national contribution. No amount of effort to deal with a heroin outbreak in one particular borough is itself going to succeed without the background of adequate and sustained national effort. Exactly the same can be said about joint local and national action in relation to alcohol misuse, cigarette smoking and the misuse of prescribed drugs. Action at one level is only likely to succeed if it is in alliance with action at every other level.

The sad truth of the matter at the present time is that such a view of prevention of drug and substance misuse reads like empty and pious exhortation. Prevention is more often neglected at every level and despite all the fine talk remains nobody's business at all. It is a responsibility always left to someone else. The community will leave it to the Government, while the Government suddenly discovers an enormous faith in the virtue of each person's captaincy of his own soul. Government will preach the individual's responsibility for "sensible drinking" while it allows the price of alcohol to slide downwards and all the national indicators of excessive drinking to move upwards. Government spending on television advertising against heroin cannot be pleaded as a redeeming example of commitment. Such a campaign makes a big splash and can be portrayed as evidence that "something is being done". An anti-drugs campaign is therefore politically attractive, if in reality ineffective, while banning sports sponsorship by tobacco firms is unattractive in the same political terms. So far as prevention is concerned the game is largely one of passing the buck, and little is achieved.

It has been argued throughout this chapter that prevention in this field is difficult but feasible. There is much experience from which to learn and some of this has been described. There are opportunities at every level. The final point, however, must be strongly stated. There can be no real prospect of successful prevention until the talk of "everyone's business" becomes more than a platitude.

Chapter 16
Treatment

There is no single group in society which is the only one involved in drug misuse. It follows that treatment must be sufficiently flexible and sensitive to match the needs of an astonishingly mixed collection of people in trouble. Here are just a few examples:

Miss A. Aged 19, living in Glasgow, unemployed and with no prospect of a job. She has been smoking heroin for three years and more recently has occasionally been injecting the drug. She was pushed toward help after her parents discovered a syringe.

Mr B. A building foreman aged 55, who has suffered his second coronary thrombosis. He smokes 40 cigarettes per day.

Doctor C. A medical practitioner aged 47, has just been convicted of drunk driving which brought to light a serious drinking problem of 10 year's standing. He has also been prescribing for himself large quantities of minor tranquillizers and sleeping pills.

Ms D. Aged 22, working in Manchester in the music business, smokes cannabis heavily, has developed "these weird feelings that keep coming and going, like things round me aren't real".

Mr E. Aged 29, lives in a squat in London. He presents to a Casualty Department after what might be an accidental overdose or might alternatively constitute a suicide attempt. "You name it, I've used it. Everything". His life revolves around "getting the next fix".

Those five cases are drawn at random from the vast array of people who are in trouble with one or another drug and who are in need of help. Five brief case profiles can only touch on the true and total picture of need but they serve to demonstrate the absurdity of any approach to treatment which is conceived in terms of a single formula. Treatment services must adapt to the changing characteristics of the population which they seek to serve. Today's policies may be outmoded tomorrow.

It is not possible to make any final judgement about the value claimed for one treatment method against all others. Different people will require different types of help. This recognition is vital and a range of services must develop side-by-side, each working with the other. There is a need to tailor the choice of treatment to individual requirements. This is similar to the work of a real tailor; the cloth must be of good quality but it is also important to ensure that the size and the style meet the requirements of the client. It is not that one size or style is universally correct and others are wrong. Perhaps in practice different basic types of treatment can be seen as different ready-made suits, so that initially a reasonably good "style and fit" may be found, following which adjustments can be made to make treatment yet more appropriate.

There is a steadily increasing recognition of the importance of a wider definition of treatment and rehabilitation so that interventions do not just concern themselves with getting a person off drugs but also with helping that person to make the necessary changes so that he or she is more likely to remain off drugs. It is important to understand that treatment and rehabilitation are different threads in the same seamless garment.

This chapter will deal particularly with the treatment approach to problems associated with opiate misuse. This focus is justified by the needs of this group and the important issues which must be examined in relation to the rapid expansion of relevant treatment services. Among the questions which have to be considered is the fundamental one of whether treatment is in any way worthwhile. Is recovery from addiction possible? With that question answered, the chapter will move on to a brief review of the historical background to current treatment developments — the "how did we get here" question. This will be followed by consideration of a number of different elements within the total array of treatment and rehabilitation approaches.

Before going into these matters of detail two general points must be made. The first is that although the focus of the chapter is largely on what might be termed the "heavy end" of the drug spectrum, it would be wrong to equate this simply with heroin. The drugs which have required a rapid development in treatment and rehabilitation services and which have been tackled by Drug Dependence Units certainly include heroin, but the young patient who newly arrives on the doorstep of such a centre may also be drinking to excess, or involved on a fortuitous basis with the misuse of a number of different illicit drugs. Opiates are only part of the "heavy end".

The second point, which is already evident from those five brief introductory case histories, is that although the "heavy end" justifies a special focus, drug problems and the needs of treatment cover a much wider spectrum. An adequate response to the problems of substance misuse must imply that help is available not only for the person who is injecting heroin but also for someone who wants to stop smoking, for the adolescent who is inhaling a solvent, for the middle-aged patient who is "finding it difficult to stop those tablets", for the individual who is worried about drinking and for a host of other drug patterns besides. With the space available the main focus of discussion has to be limited to specific areas of current concern, but the wider context of treatment needs must not be forgotten, and reference will be made at various points to alcohol, tobacco and other drugs.

Addicts are not untreatable

A popular misconception is that addicts are incurable, that once "hooked" there is no way out. In fact the truth is different.

One important study reported on the long-term outcome for heroin addicts who had enrolled at London drug clinics in the late 1960s. This research found that over a ten year period there was a steady trickle of people coming off and staying off drugs, and usually making a good adjustment to a drug-free lifestyle. At the end of that time 42% were drug-free, 33% were still using drugs and 15% had died (the remainder were of uncertain status). These figures show both the appalling seriousness of this condition and the significant possibility of recovery among a group of heroin addicts who have no special advantage. Very similar results have been found in follow-up studies of patients with drinking problems. Both younger and older people who have given up cigarette smoking are no longer a rarity and are to be found at every party.

Treatment in historical perspective

The historical context within which current treatment approaches for opiate misuse were slowly to evolve were outlined in Chapter 6, and in particular the landmarks of the Rolleston Committee was noted. That Committee recommended in 1926 that opiate addicts should be viewed as suffering from a disease characterised by a desire to continue taking the drug. It was appropriate therefore for such people to be treated as patients rather than punished as criminals. They should receive their drug on prescription in order to help them to withdraw, or alternatively they should receive on-going supplies of such drugs if withdrawal seemed impossible or contra-indicated. The Rolleston report shaped the treatment of drug addiction in Britain for the next 40 years.

In 1965, when overtly hedonistic drug-use by adolescents was increasingly observed, the second Brain Committee made specific recommendations which led to the development of the Drug Treatment Clinics. The first specialised National Health Service Drug Dependence Units (DDUs) in the United Kingdom were opened in 1968. The focus was very much on heroin.

The manner in which DDUs operate has been subject to considerable evolution over the last 15 years. Most recently the emphasis has been on increasing community involvement, with the clinics acting only as one part of the network in which the medical practitioner and other primary health care workers have come to play an important role. There has also been a marked shift from the original long-term prescribing of "maintenance" opiates to more active policies. The contribution made by non-statutory agencies has become a vital part of the total response. An important up-dating of views on the direction in which treatment services should be moving was given in the Advisory Council on the Misuse of Drugs 1982 report on *Treatment and Rehabilitation*. This underlined that concern must now be with the provision of a diversity of resources to help a wide range of "problem drug takers" rather than focusing exclusively on the person who has developed severe dependence. The task is to organise an accessible and flexible treatment system that can respond to each individual's personal needs. These needs may include the treatment of dependence but are also likely to include that of social or psychological difficulties and health problems. The emphasis is broadened from dependence as the central treatment target to the totality of drug-related problems.

A somewhat similar history could be charted in the treatment of excessive drinking in the context of prevailing medical and moral views. Since the 1950s the NHS has made a purposive and expanded contribution to the treatment of drinking problems and over recent years the move has also been towards a re-definition of the role of specialised agencies and an emphasis on local practitioner and community care. Alcoholics Anonymous has not only made an important direct contribution but has also provided an example of what can be achieved by a self-help organisation. Treatment of cigarette smoking has a very recent history but here a behaviour which was previously considered a mild indulgence or a bad habit now invites enrolment at an anti-smoking clinic. Self-help groups are beginning to develop for people who have become dependent on minor tranquillizers.

Coming off drugs—the immediate treatment of withdrawal

It has already been stressed that treatment of dependence involves more than withdrawal from the drug. Nevertheless, withdrawal is the gateway to what will follow if the individual is to be helped to discover a life without drugs. It is therefore important that there should be quick and competent professional help within the total provision of treatment services for the person who wants to take this step.

Withdrawal from opiates is often handled by a brief in-patient admission of perhaps two to four weeks, but with adequate support it may also be managed on a hospital out-patient or day-care basis or by a general practitioner. The choice should depend on the patient and his circumstances. The characteristics, the speed of onset and the duration and severity of the withdrawal syndrome vary according to which pharmacological group of drugs is being considered. Thus, a classical opiate withdrawal syndrome is recognised which applies to all opiate drugs, but the timing of the syndrome will vary according to the specific opiate being taken.

Physical dependence and the resulting withdrawal syndromes are not solely a feature of illicit opiate drug-use. They can also occur with sleeping tablets and minor tranquillizers, such as the barbiturates and benzodiazepines, and with alcohol. Special help may be needed with each of these different groups.

Two basic approaches are available for the treatment of a drug withdrawal syndrome. The specific drug of dependence or a drug from the same pharmacological group can be prescribed, so as to restore, on a temporary basis, the drug-influenced *status quo*, following which small stepwise reductions in the daily intake can be made. The alternative approach is to avoid prescribing the drug of dependence or any similar drug altogether, choosing instead to provide purely symptomatic relief of the withdrawal illness. When such active treatment is properly implemented, it is surprising how comfortably an addict can come off opiates, or an alcoholic off alcohol.

Staying off drugs—
treatment of the dependence itself

Dependence is a phenomenon that goes beyond the mere biological adaptation that has taken place in the body following the constant presence of the drug. Giving up a drug habit involves more than giving up the drugs; it involves giving up a habit, and habits die hard. "Junk is not a kick—it is a way of life"—these words were written by William Burroughs in his autobiographical book "Junkie" published in America in 1953. Part of the problem of giving up any habit is the desperate feeling of emptiness that results, and this fundamental issue must be tackled in treating dependence. If not, the lack of both other interests and strong motivations will leave the ex-addict all too vulnerable to the lure back to the comforting drug. It is necessary to examine the role filled by drug-use, and to look at other ways in which the addict's needs might be met. This applies whatever the drug.

Many opiate users are reassured to discover that supervised withdrawal is not as frightening as they imagined. However, they often give insufficient attention to the difficulties involved in staying off drugs and find themselves ill-equipped to deal with the various situations which put them at risk. Exactly the same can be said in relation to other drug or alcohol problems. These risk-situations may be associated with mood changes (such as anxiety or depression) or with protracted minor withdrawal symptoms (such as continued sleep disturbance), or when environmental stimuli create a nagging urge to repeat what was previously familiar behaviour. These environmental cues may include particular people, places, the paraphernalia of drug-use itself, or for the cigarette smoker the familiar cup of coffee, a piece of work successfully accomplished, or sitting back after a good meal. The alcoholic may relapse when he is anxious or angry, when he is elated or when the perfect summer day seems to invite a glass of beer.

It is a common experience for drug-addicts who have managed to come off drugs to feel comfortable while cocooned in a protected environment such as a hospital ward or rehabilitation centre. However, when they return to their everyday unprotected life, with its trials and tribulations, they find that all kinds of events serve to prompt a further episode of drug-use. For many people, this lapse is not a deliberate decision to return to drug use but has close similarities to the ex-cigarette smoker who decides to have "just one cigarette" to enhance an enjoyable social situation or to cope with some crisis. This single episode of drug use may then precipitate a catastrophic relapse. Treatment must therefore include both a study of those stimuli which trigger off the relapse and embrace a shared examination of ways in which to handle and curtail a brief lapse before it escalates into something worse.

A wide range of both individual and group psychotherapies are employed by different agencies in treating these issues. Such psychotherapeutic techniques are valuable tools for dealing with personal and relationship difficulties which lead to drug or alcohol use, as well as those which develop later but perpetuate the dependence. Nevertheless, it is important that in their enthusiasm the helpers themselves do not fall into the trap of believing that a single approach will be universally appropriate. What is required is a range of social and psychological strategies so that a package can be constructed which is both relevant and effective for a particular person. The work of the therapist must be to nudge that individual along the most natural and possible pathways of recovery. These basic principles of therapy are widely applicable whatever chemical substance is involved.

Drugs in the treatment of opiate dependence

Methadone maintenance evolved as a treatment approach for heroin dependence in America in the 1960s, and since then it has been applied in many other countries. It has had both its detractors and its ardent supporters. The basis of this approach is that it may be better to prescribe medically for the addict a small once-daily dose by mouth of this relatively long-acting synthetic drug rather than leave him "running on the street", repeatedly injecting his veins with black-market heroin with all the attendant risks of infection or overdose, and paying for his habit by a life of acquisitive crime. Methadone gives a mild plateau drug effect and little subjective intoxication when prescribed in a low maintenance dosage. The patient is spared the peaks and troughs of intermittent drug intoxication which results when shorter acting heroin has to be injected several times each day. Some of those who favour this method compare it with the treatment of diabetes, seeing dependence as a "metabolic disorder" which will respond to appropriate drug treatment. They would advocate that if necessary the addict should be encouraged to continue with methadone over a period of many years until he is ready to give up his addiction. By 1980, 37,000 addicts were receiving this treatment in New York alone. It is important to understand that it is the use of methadone as a maintenance drug and not its use in short-term detoxification which is being discussed under the present heading. The primary purpose of maintenance treatment is to stabilise the addict in society.

The critics of drug maintenance, although conceding that oral methadone is clinically preferable to the risks of injecting heroin, contend that in the long term the substitution of one drug for another is no answer to drug dependence. The individual is still tied to a drug habit and still has drug taking as a shadow over his life. He has not finally broken free. There is also a fear that the argument that methadone maintenance reduces crime is moving the medical profession out of treatment and into social control.

There can be no final and overall assessment of the efficacy of methadone maintenance because results will depend on the social and cultural setting in which this treatment is applied. The important questions are empirical and not doctrinal. It is not a question of whether methadone maintenance is in some intrinsic sense "good" or "bad" but whether it is likely to be the best option for a particular patient in particular circumstances. In Britain today long-term maintenance of this type is not greatly favoured but it is possible that worry about AIDS may lead to wider use of long-term methadone if it is shown that such an approach is effective in keeping patients away from injected drugs. There is at present no research to bear on this question and it would certainly be wrong to take AIDS as an excuse for promiscuous prescribing.

Some drugs have the power to reverse the effect of opiates. These drugs are called *opiate antagonists* (p. 55). An important application of their use is in the emergency treatment of opiate overdose. An injection of naloxone can be life-saving and a patient will dramatically recover from coma within a minute or two of such treatment. In recent years in the United States there has been research into an oral version of a similar antagonist drug called naltrexone, and it is possible that this product may be of value to patients who have become drug-free but feel that without it they would have difficulty in controlling the occasional impulsive wish to use opiates.

Minor tranquillizer and sleeping tablets such as the benzo-diazepines may help with associated anxiety or sleep disturbance, but do not have a substantial part to play in the treatment of dependence and there is always the risk of substituting a new form of addiction.

General practitioners and the primary level of care

The immediate withdrawal phase and the subsequent treatment and rehabilitation of a patient should all be pictured as one continuing process. Rehabilitation is that part of the helping process concerned with the individual finding his way towards a chemical-free and stable life-style. In the UK treatment is mainly provided by the National Health Service on an out-patient, day-patient, and in-patient basis, both for drug and alcohol problems. The choice between these options will be determined by the availability of local services, by characteristics of the presenting patient and by the preference of both the patient and the treatment centre itself. Some agencies will deal with illicit drugs, alcohol or tranquillizers in the same setting while others specialise in a selected part of the chemical spectrum. In the London area, a network of specialist Drug Dependence Units exists which deal with large numbers of drug-takers on an out-patient basis. There are also a few specialist in-patient DDUs, although the availability of beds is limited.

For those living outside London, the NHS service for drug-takers is usually part of the overall service provided by local general psychiatric resources and is not a specialist commitment. There are about thirty specialised NHS Alcoholism Treatment Units in the UK. But whether drugs or alcohol constitute the problem, a major part of the responsibility for work with these patients is being undertaken today by general practitioners, by other members of the primary health care team (social workers and community nurses) and by voluntary agencies.

Reference has already been made in this chapter to the importance of a community and primary health care approach in the treatment of drug and alcohol problems, and it is important to clarify what is meant by this approach. The phrase "community care" can sometimes become a slogan but in this particular area of work the need to develop a treatment system with a firm community perspective cannot be doubted. During any one year, for example, most patients with alcohol problems are likely to be in contact with their general practitioner, complaining of symptoms such as stomach upsets or bad nerves or asking for sickness certificates. It is the practitioner who is the primary contact and who needs to be equipped with the competence to raise the possibility of a drinking problem with the patient, to talk matters through, and to give immediate advice and counselling.

Until recently, to have suggested a similar approach with heroin addicts would have appeared to many professionals as dangerously wrong-headed. It was the received wisdom that drug addiction was the province of Drug Dependence Units and general practitioners were strongly advised to leave these patients to the hospital services and not to meddle. Over the last few years it has become apparent not only that Drug Dependence Units have insufficient resources to deal with the surge in numbers of heroin users but also that the primary health team is very much the appropriate front-line for early detection and response. General practitioners, community psychiatric nurses and social workers can in this way make a highly important contribution without taking the drug user out of the community. A recent report has suggested that family doctors in England and Wales overall are seeing about 40,000 heroin users over a 12-month period. Community Drug Teams have been set up in some parts of Britain with specialised staff acting in support of the primary health care system.

Voluntary organisations

The NHS's contribution today to the total treatment and rehabilitation effort is increasingly made in partnership with the voluntary or non-statutory sector. Voluntary work in relation to drinking problems dates back to the last century when the Salvation Army and other church organisations played a leading role in responding to slum drinking and to many other problems of the expanding industrial cities. If voluntary action on drug addiction has only arrived on the scene comparatively recently it has done much to make up for the lost time. There has been a burgeoning of day centres, hostels, therapeutic communities and telephone hot-lines, all stemming from voluntary initiatives.

There is the true voluntary sector in which self-help or local support groups are established to help drug-takers or their families. Such groups are usually run by others who have been, or still are, in a similar situation and can provide invaluable support. They can also act as pressure groups which identify deficiencies in the services and bring pressure to bear to improve the quality of local care.

The other part of this network is more accurately described as the non-statutory sector and depends on full-time paid employees with considerable skills and experience, some of whom may be ex-addicts. Within this non-statutory sector the largest contribution is the provision of long-term rehabilitation houses. Here residents are expected to remain for a period of about 12–18 months, during which time they become involved in the life and work of the therapeutic community and may begin training or re-training for work outside.

There are different types of rehabilitation house. "Concept" houses provide a clear hierarchical structure and a demanding and confrontational programme through which the residents must progress. Privileges and responsibilities increase as the resident works his way through the programme. There is likely to be a strong work ethos and considerable involvement in group therapy and Encounter sessions.

A number of houses have recently been set up in Britain which are based on an American approach called the Minnesota Model, placing emphasis on the disease model of addiction and stressing the importance of the individual's affiliation to Narcotics Anonymous or Alcoholics Anonymous. People usually live in these houses for two to three months. General houses also exist in which there is less emphasis on hierarchical structures and the intention is to provide a supportive environment with individual and group counselling. Some rehabilitation houses stress the importance of religion to the recovery process.

The majority of these rehabilitation houses are registered charities and much of their cost is met by national supplementary benefit. However, additional funds are usually required to make up the balance for a resident to enter such a house. Although the Social Services Department of some Local Authorities may provide top-up funding, there can be great difficulty in obtaining this in other areas. Many of the voluntary drug projects in England and Wales are linked to the Standing Conference on Drug Abuse (SCODA) which acts as their national co-ordinating organisation.

In recent years there has been a considerable growth in Britain of the Narcotics Anonymous movement, especially in the London area. This self-help organisation is similar to the longer-established Alcoholics Anonymous and it constitutes a valuable resource. Both organisations provide a caring support structure and are run by ex-users for ex-users, carefully preserving the anonymity of the individual. Belief in the principles of Narcotics Anonymous is often held with great conviction.

Narcotics Anonymous view drug addiction as a life-long disease and consequently see ex-drug-users as people who still suffer from the disease but who have managed to keep it in check for the time being. Consequently, they adopt an approach similar to Alcoholics Anonymous where total abstinence from all drugs at all times is seen as fundamental to the survival of both the individual and the group. They also provide a structured action programme involving the "twelve steps" through which members work while striving towards recovery, and this is accompanied by close support and a system of personal contact with each member. Associated organisations called Alanon and Families Anonymous exist to provide special support to spouses and relatives of those with alcohol or drug problems.

Treatment and prevention of physical complications

Some physical complications of drug misuse can be a direct result of the substance itself, such as liver damage associated with heavy drinking and chronic constipation resulting from opiates. Other complications stem from the way in which a drug is used. If, for instance, a drug-taker injects drugs without ensuring that the needle and syringe are sterilised there is a risk that a local infection will occur at the site of the injection. Local inflammation may progress and lead to an abscess. If the body is unable to deal with this local infection (even with the help of prescribed antibiotics) the infection will spread via the blood stream to other parts of the body and septicaemia will develop.

Other hazards of intravenous drug-use are associated with the sharing of needles and syringes between drug-takers (see p. 23). A particularly virulent form of liver infection, known as Hepatitis B, is caused by a virus which is mainly transmitted from one person to another in minute quantities of blood, although it can also be transmitted more rarely by other body fluids.

In the United States and in some European countries, a similar picture is developing with the transmission of the HIV virus. A proportion of those who are infected with this virus will go on to develop the Acquired Immune Deficiency Syndrome (AIDS). Over 50% of tested injecting drug users in Edinburgh are HIV positive; although to date that city is an exception so far as Britain is concerned, the risk of this virus spreading is likely to become an increasingly important issue. This is not only because of the direct danger to the drug-using population but also because addicts may spread the infection by sexual contact to partners who are not drug-users. There is in addition the danger of transmission from an infected mother to her unborn child.

Prevention measures must become an important part of the health response to both Hepatitis B virus and HIV virus infections. Stopping drug-taking is obviously the best way of avoiding these risks, but while drug-taking continues there are practical measures which should be taken to reduce the likelihood of Hepatitis B and AIDS by avoiding the sharing of needles and syringes.

A common risk with injected opiates is accidental overdose and the same danger arises when a drug-taker injects ground-up barbiturate (sleeping) tablets intravenously. Hospital casualty departments have immediate responsibility for dealing with such accidents and with other physical and psychiatric complications of drug misuse.

The medical complications of excessive drinking are legion and as a consequence many patients with drinking problems are admitted to general hospitals. If the staff concerned are alert and recognise that drinking is involved the hospital admission may provide the opportunity for treatment of the alcohol dependence itself and prove a turning point in the patient's life. A cigarette smoker who presents with a cough and breathlessness should be treated for cigarette addiction and not simply for the chest condition.

Treatment of psychiatric complications

Some drugs can cause serious but usually transient psychiatric complications and these have been noted in the chapters dealing with specific substances. With a drug-taker who has become distressed or potentially suicidal, or where unpleasant symptoms are continuing or recurring after a few hours, medical help will be needed. LSD and cannabis can be responsible for unpleasant psychiatric reactions lasting a day or two, and stimulants such as amphetamines and cocaine can induce a short-term psychosis. Emergency medical and psychiatric help may be needed for any of these reactions. It should not be forgotten that excessive drinking can also give rise to a variety of psychiatric complications including acute and chronic depression, suicide attempts, violence and the acute psychosis of delirium tremens.

Children of drug users or excessive drinkers

Abrupt withdrawal from drugs during pregnancy may precipitate abortion or premature labour. The pregnant addict should therefore be advised against stopping her drug abruptly and instead the reduction should be gradual. Some experts recommend maintaining the mother-to-be on her drugs until after the birth of the baby. Infants born to opiate addicts are often of low birth weight, although this is less likely with mothers who have maintained a stable drug regime and taken care of their general physical health. Retardation of foetal growth has also been linked to the use of alcohol, barbiturates, amphetamines and nicotine.

Opiates, like other psycho-active drugs, pass through the placenta into the foetus. The baby is then at risk itself of becoming physically dependent and in this case the birth will be followed by an acute withdrawal syndrome. Although such a state of affairs attracts anxiety and perhaps censure from both hospital staff and general public it is important to appreciate that the infant's withdrawal syndrome can be managed effectively by prescribing a scaled-down reduction regime over a period of a few weeks, following which there is no need for the baby to receive any more drugs. It would generally seem preferable for pregnant opiate addicts to be off their drugs by the time of the birth, but it is important to remember that an unsympathetic professional response will only serve to deter the pregnant drug addict from seeking help. Services adopting a user-friendly approach in their management of the pregnant drug addict will be more likely to ensure early presentation and regular attendance. The same issues arise in relation to women who drink heavily, and the significance of the foetal alcohol syndrome is discussed in an earlier chapter. The pregnant mother who is a smoker also needs professional help while the mother who continues to smoke after the birth of the baby will put her young child at added risk of chest infections.

Questions arise as to the competence of a mother who continues to use drugs or who is dependent on alcohol to look after a baby or young children. Situations can occur where both parents are drug addicts or heavy drinkers. The dilemma which faces the social worker who is asked to assess such a family is that although parental addiction does not necessarily imply that such parents are unfit to look after their children, the potential danger to a child cannot be overlooked. In general the decision is best made by reference to overall aspects of the mother's or father's parental competence, responsibility, attitudes toward and involvement with the child, rather than by focusing exclusively on the drug or the drinking.

Alternative treatments

Acupuncture has been proposed as an effective treatment for a wide range of withdrawal syndromes and as a technique for dealing with craving. Theoretically such an approach is attractive as there is evidence that acupuncture can stimulate production of endorphins, which are the brain's own opiate like substances, the production of which may have been suppressed by taking drugs.

The most popular form of acupuncture in the treatment of drug dependence is electro-acupuncture (also called neuroelectric-therapy) and there are a number of reports by the proponents of this approach which describe impressive success rates. Regrettably these good results do not usually seem to be repeated when the technique is applied by independent observers. For example, a study at the Maudsley Hospital in London found that drug addicts who were treated with neuroelectric-therapy often reported the experience as similar to unmodified abrupt withdrawal of drugs (cold turkey). The conclusion must be that this approach does not warrant claims of a break-through in the treatment of drug addiction.

Recent developments

The larger population now involved in drug use and the less deviant nature of some of this population make it appropriate to consider more normal options of response. When drug takers were clearly different from the rest of society and acted as an outgroup it was appropriate for the treatment and rehabilitation services themselves to be highly specialised and separate. However, when drug-takers present as unremarkable casualties closely identified with the ordinary community, it is reasonable to develop services as part of the local provision of general health and social care. A number of local projects are now being established in Britain which attempt to integrate people who have recently come off drugs with ordinary training and re-employment programmes.

An important area of clinical investigation involves the detailed assessment of the nature of different and especially risky situations to which the addict may be exposed and for which specific psychological behavioural treatments may be designed. Work on "relapse prevention" is beginning to attract attention, especially in relation to drinking problems.

Some interesting work has been done on techniques of "motivational interviewing" as, for example, when the drug-taker or heavy drinker is encouraged to draw up a personal inventory of problems associated with the abuse. This quickly clarifies important issues for both the patient and the therapist and leads to more productive work and planning.

Treatment of cigarette dependence over the last 10–20 years has attracted a wide variety of psychological therapeutic techniques. Today there is a special focus on two possible lines of advance. First, the fact that smoking is essentially an addiction to nicotine has led to attempts to wean patients off cigarettes by substituting nicotine impregnated chewing-gum. The results appear promising. Nicotine itself is relatively harmless compared with the dangerous chemicals which a cigarette delivers to the lungs. A second approach comes from the demonstration that simple advice to stop smoking given by a patient's family doctor is indeed often effective. There is perhaps an important general message here that more significance should be attached to what people can say to each other under certain conditions and in special circumstances, and that this can sometimes be more effective than complex and expensive techniques.

Private practice

Private medical practitioners have a legitimate role to play in the treatment of patients with drug problems. Difficulties may arise if private doctors prescribe opiates beyond the requirements of short-term medication for the treatment of withdrawal, or if they are lured into incautious prescribing of other substitute psycho-active drugs.

Such untoward happenings sometimes give private practice in this field a bad name which is unfair to the majority of private doctors who work to the same high standards as anyone else. It cannot however be denied that problems potentially exist when fees are charged for medically prescribed opiates. Private practitioners may also be handicapped by not having the social work or community nursing support available in the NHS.

Not giving up trying

At different stages in the course of their drug taking and drinking, patients will be responsive to different types of intervention or sometimes responsive to none. At an early stage a prevention approach might be appropriate while at a later stage it may be the law that has to intervene; but it is always to be hoped and expected that at some point a patient will listen to advice and accept the need for treatment and rehabilitation.

As emphasised earlier the possibilities for recovery from even the severest type of addiction do exist even if there are risks and difficulties. The message to the individual trapped in substance misuse should definitely be "Do not give up trying". The same message is equally important to the medical profession and to society at large. Drug users and excessive drinkers are not hopeless and deserve the same quality of compassion and help as anyone else in need.

At the same time cigarette smokers must be warned that they are exposed to a dangerous addiction and society as a whole must be helped to overcome this terrible habit. This applies equally to the massive use of tranquillizers which can insidiously dominate peoples' lives.

The endeavour of all concerned must be to reduce the numbers of those involved in the destructive use of drugs, alcohol and tobacco, and to help patients to escape from these tyrannies by offering effective and appropriate avenues of recovery.

Chapter 17
Drugs and the law

Legal responses are an inevitable part of the complex and interlocking totality of any country's attempts to prevent and deal with the misuse of drugs. Different aspects of the legal dimension have already been discussed at many points in this book. The law enters the arena in relation to such diverse issues as the control of public house licensing hours, regulations which supposedly prevent the sale of cigarettes to children, the prohibition of cannabis cultivation, drunk driving legislation, and of course the extensive provisions of the Misuse of Drugs Act.

Why and how did the law come to be involved in the business of drug control? Does it achieve its stated or implicit purposes or is the legal presence in this field too pervasive? Certain aspects of these large and difficult questions have been debated in earlier chapters and particularly in relation to cannabis (Chapter 12) and to general issues of prevention (Chapter 15). The present chapter will concentrate on legislation dealing with illicit drugs rather than the law as relating to psychotropics, alcohol or tobacco. It will start with a note on the development of drug legislation in this country—the "how it got there" question. The provisions of the Misuse of Drugs Act will be summarised.

Attention will then turn from an examination of the way the law is written to its consequences in actual practice. Compulsory treatment and treatment within the penal system, the criminality of addicts and the number of drugs users in prison will also be considered. However, details of police practice, court processes and the customs operation are outside the scope of this book. The final section returns to a general appraisal of the role of law and law enforcement in aid of the public health.

The development of drug legislation in the United Kingdom

Legislation to control the non-medical use of drugs through the criminal law can be a response to various social anxieties and influences. A change in the age pattern, with increased drug use by young people, is a situation which is likely to lead to a call for strengthening legal prohibitions. Any perceived link between drug misuse and crime also tends to give rise to new legislation and harsher penalties.

In charting the development of drug legislation in Britain it is first necessary to recall some of the crucial legislative events which were identified in Chapter 6, in relation to the opiates. Until the mid-nineteenth century there were no legislative controls on drug misuse in the United Kingdom. The first drugs legislation was the Arsenic Act of 1851. The Pharmacy Act of 1868 restricted the sale of morphine and opium to pharmacists and by the 1890s some opium-containing patent medicines were also brought under the Act. Until the beginning of the First World War it was possible to purchase drugs such as heroin and cocaine from pharmacists; the only restriction was that the purchaser had to be known to the pharmacist and had to sign the Poisons Register.

The United Kingdom participated (at times unwillingly) in a series of international conferences concerned with the suppression of the opium trade in the Far East, culminating in the Hague Convention of 1912 which resolved that opium, morphine and cocaine should be confined to medical use. The signatories agreed to adopt a system of controls on these drugs.

During the First World War there was concern in Britain about the allegedly widespread use of cocaine by soldiers on leave, and the effect that this might have on the efficiency of the armed forces. As a result Regulation 40B was introduced in 1916 under the Defence of the Realm Act, making it an offence to possess cocaine and opium.

After the War the Versailles Peace Treaty required signatories to implement controls on narcotic drugs in accordance with the Hague Convention, and Regulation 40B was replaced by the first permanent legislation, the Dangerous Drugs Act of 1920. Opiate drugs and cocaine thus became available only on medical prescription. The Act introduced controls over the importation, manufacture and sale of these drugs with inspection of records together with fines and imprisonment as penalties. The 1920 Act became the basis of subsequent drugs legislation in the United Kingdom and its essential features are still in force. A succession of Dangerous Drugs Acts revised and extended the controls and penalties, and cannabis was first included in a Dangerous Drugs Act in 1925. The 1926 report of the Rolleston Committee (p. 61) made medical prescribing to addicts legitimate.

The 1960s saw the breakdown of an equilibrium which had lasted for many years, and a rapid change in the patterns of non-medical drug use. The government responded with a succession of further legislative measures. The first of these was concerned with amphetamines and was a response to widespread amphetamine abuse by young people (see Chapter 10). The Drugs (Prevention of Misuse) Act 1964 made unauthorised possession of amphetamines an offence. In 1966 LSD and later methaqualone also became controlled under this Act. Parallel with the concern about amphetamines it became clear that there had been a disturbing increase in the abuse of heroin and cocaine.

The recommendations of the second Brain Committee (see p. 63) were implemented by the Dangerous Drugs Act of 1967 and by regulations issued under the previous Dangerous Drugs Act of 1965. Thus legislative controls had grown up piecemeal, in response to a series of crisis situations, first with amphetamines and then with heroin and cocaine. The Misuse of Drugs Act 1971 replaced the Drugs (Prevention of Misuse) Act 1964 as well as the Dangerous Drugs Act of 1965 and 1967, and so rationalised legislation by bringing the various drugs of abuse under the control of a single Act. This rather dry chronicling of legal provisions is necessary to an understanding of how the law on drug misuse in the UK reached its present form.

The Misuse of Drugs Act 1971

This Act and the regulations made under it are the main current legislation concerned with the prevention of drug misuse in the United Kingdom. It is a comprehensive law dealing with a variety of subjects and such is its importance that it is useful to give a brief summary of its main provisions.

Section 1 provides for the establishment of an Advisory Council on the Misuse of Drugs, whose purpose is to "advise Ministers" on a range of matters relating to drugs covered by the Act, and to whom Ministers may refer relevant issues.

Section 2 deals with controlled drugs and their classification. In a schedule to this section the drugs controlled under the Act are specified. The drugs are divided into 3 classes. Class A includes the natural and most synthetic opiates, cocaine, LSD, injectable amphetamines and cannabinol (the active ingredient of cannabis). Class B includes the oral amphetamines, phenmetrazine, cannabis and cannabis resin, codeine and dihydrocodeine. Certain barbiturate drugs have also been included. Class C includes methaqualone and certain amphetamine-like drugs.

Section 2 also provides for the addition or removal of any drug from the Schedule or for a drug to be transferred from one class to another, by an Order in Council. The aim here is to achieve a flexibility of approach by modifying the controls over particular drugs without the need for new legislation. A recent example is the inclusion of certain barbiturates in Schedule 2 as Class B drugs.

Section 4 makes it an offence to produce, supply or offer to supply a controlled drug, and *Section 5* makes it an offence to possess or attempt to possess a controlled drug or to possess a controlled drug with intent to supply it to another. These provisions are aimed at creating a distinction between unlawful possession of drugs and trafficking in drugs.

Section 23 confers powers of search on the police (if a constable has reasonable grounds to suspect that any person is in possession of a controlled drug).

Section 25 deals with penalties, and under Schedule 4 of this section maximum penalties are laid down for offences under the Act. A summary of the penalties is shown in Table 2. It will be seen that there is a difference between penalties for simple possession and those for trafficking offences, and the penalties vary also with the class of drug involved. Class A attracts the most severe penalties.

Sections 12–17 are concerned with offences by doctors and pharmacists, and the prevention of irresponsible prescribing.

Table 2: *Misuse of Drugs Act 1971. Maximum penalties for certain offences*

Class of drug	Supply		Possession with intent to supply		Possession	
	Magistrates Court*	Crown Court	Magistrates Court*	Crown Court	Magistrates Court*	Crown Court
A	6 months or £1000 fine, or both	Life imprisonment or unlimited fine, or both	6 months or £1000 fine, or both	Life imprisonment or unlimited fine, or both	6 months or £1000 fine, or both	7 years or unlimited fine, or both
B	6 months or £1000 fine, or both	14 years or unlimited fine, or both	6 months or £1000 fine, or both	14 years or unlimited fine, or both	3 months or £500 fine, or both	5 years or unlimited fine, or both
C	3 months or £500 fine, or both	5 years or unlimited fine, or both	3 months or £500 fine, or both	5 years or unlimited fine, or both	3 months or £200 fine, or both	2 years or unlimited fine, or both

*Sheriff's Courts in Scotland.

Section 10 confers powers on the Home Secretary to make various regulations for preventing the misuse of controlled drugs. The most important of these regulations is the Misuse of Drugs (Notification of and Supply to Addicts) Regulations of 1973. These require doctors to notify details to the Chief Medical Officer at the Home Office of any patients whom they consider to be addicted to certain controlled drugs. The drugs concerned are cocaine, opium and the major opium derivatives and synthetic opiates. The Regulations also prohibit doctors from prescribing heroin or cocaine to addicts except when licensed by the Home Secretary. Because of the increase in the misuse of dipipanone (Diconal) in recent years, this drug was added to the list on 1 April 1984. The regulations, however, do not prohibit doctors from prescribing any of these drugs for the treatment of organic disorders or injury.

The formal framework for legislative control of drugs in this country is now both comprehensive and complex. Matters have come a long way since 1851 and the Arsenic Act.

The law in practice

How does this apparatus operate in practice? This chapter cannot examine that question in detail from the lawyer's point of view. The discussion which follows focuses on the overlap between drug problems and criminal behaviour, and on the relevance of the law to treatment provisions and prevention strategies.

Drugs and crime

Why is it that so many drug misusers and addicts commit crimes, and what sort of crimes do they commit? It is generally agreed that no drug has inevitable and inherent criminogenic properties. Whether or not drug misuse leads to crime depends more on the personality of the user and on the socio-cultural context of drug use than on the pharmacological actions of the drug itself. Lawrence Kolb in 1925 noted in picturesque and hyperbolic language that chronic narcotic intoxication has the effect of turning "drunken, fighting psychopaths into sober, cowardly, non-aggressive idlers".

Nevertheless there is a frequent association between certain types of drug abuse and crime. Most studies have been concerned with the relationship between criminality and opiate dependence. In the United Kingdom several studies of addicts notified to the Home Office and of addicts attending drug dependence clinics have shown that between one-quarter and one-third of male addicts are convicted of an offence prior to any admitted drug use, significantly more than would be expected for the general population of comparable age. About two thirds are convicted before notification to the Home Office, and over 90% of males attending London drug dependence clinics have a history of convictions. For females, one study found that 12% had a conviction prior to any drug use and 76% eventually acquired a conviction. Over 70% of all convictions are for non-drug offences and of those the majority are offences against property (mostly theft and burglary). Offences of violence are not common.

When comparison is made with the United States it is a striking feature of the British scene that on the whole addicts here are not involved in serious crimes in order to support their drug habit. There may be several reasons for this relatively benign situation. Drugs on the UK black-market are relatively cheap. The welfare system also contributes to the possibility of supporting a drug habit without resort to serious crime. Perhaps an important factor is that there has been no evidence so far in the United Kingdom that people who become involved in drug use come from a grossly deprived urban environment with a sub-culture of violence, or from alienated racial minorities.

It is also a striking observation that treatment at a drug dependence clinic and the prescription of opiates does not lead to any reduction in the overall crime rate, although there is a change in the pattern of offences so that paradoxically there is a significant increase in the proportion of drug offences as opposed to non-drug offences. In consequence the criminal history of opiate users becomes progressively more limited to drug offences.

Although it may be true that the prescribing policies of the clinics are conservative, this in itself cannot account for the continued involvement of clinic attenders in criminal activity, and there is no evidence that liberal prescribing of opiates leads to a reduction in the misuse of other drugs, such as barbiturates. The expectation that a free supply of drugs from licit sources would minimise illicit drug-related crime has proved incorrect.

The number of addicts in prison

There is evidence that over 50% of notified male addicts receive a prison sentence at some stage in the course of their addiction, although the actual number of addicts or serious drugs abusers in prison is difficult to determine. Criminal statistics (in figures rounded to the nearest 100) show that the number of cautions and convictions for drug offences increased from 11,800 in 1975 to 26,600 in 1985. The proportion of drug offenders given a custodial sentence has remained steady at 16% of the total during the last 5 years and stood at 5,776 in 1985.

About 80–90% of drug offences are for simple possession, and over the past decade in nearly 90% of these offences the drug involved was cannabis. For simple possession of cannabis the proportion of offenders given an immediate custodial sentence is about 5%. Nevertheless, in over two-thirds of all drug offenders who receive a custodial sentence the drug involved is cannabis.

Drug offenders formed 6% of the total male and 16% of the total female prison population serving a sentence on 30 June 1985. The proportion of drug offenders in prison who are seriously dependent on drugs is not known. It is unlikely that many of the large number of cannabis-related offenders come into this category. The relatively high proportion of drug offenders in the female prison population is probably due to the fact that women are often used by drug smugglers as couriers. Recent surveys of a female remand prison that drug offenders formed an average of 22% of the prison's population, ranking second only to theft offenders. Over 70% were charged with illegal importation of drugs (in most cases cannabis). The majority of those sentenced were serving long sentences of more than 18 months. Over 70% were foreign born, nearly half of them coming from African countries.

Perhaps the best estimate that can be made of the number of addicts coming into contact with the penal system are the figures published in the annual reports on inmates of the Prison Department, who are notified by prison medical officers as "showing some degree of dependence on drugs". The Prison Department has developed its own notification system which, unlike the Home Office Index, deals with all types of drug abuse. The number of these notifications remained fairly stable between 1,000 and 1,200 annually during the years 1974–1979. There has been a rapid increase in the 1980s with 1,827 notifications in 1983.

In summary, the evidence available on the number of people with drug problems in prison is patchy. The number of drug offenders imprisoned gives no indication of the number of prisoners who have a serious drug problem since the majority of these are charged with non-drug offences. The situation is complicated by the fact that many people with drug problems may be remanded in custody for lengthy periods but do not in the end receive a prison sentence.

The law and treatment

Compulsory treatment
Compulsory treatment for drug dependence under the civil law has not been regarded as justifiable in this country. Within the British framework of treatment facilities, the idea of compulsion has been increasingly rejected. Limited, short-term compulsory powers to detain patients undergoing withdrawal at treatment centres was advocated by the second Brain committee but was the only recommendation of the Committee which was not implemented.

Compulsory admission under the Mental Health Act of 1959 was very rarely used for the treatment of addicts. The new Mental Health Act of 1983 has now explicitly excluded dependence on drugs and alcohol as a reason for compulsory detention when there is no other evidence of mental disorder. The experience of other countries also suggest that there is no evidence that compulsory treatment can be justified on the grounds of its effectiveness.

These liberal principles — the affirmation of the medical model of response to addiction and the rejection of compulsory treatment — are the declared intentions of UK policy. However, there is evidence that, to an extent, the reality has turned out differently. Parallel with the medical response to drug problems there has also developed a very different response of which the public is relatively unaware. In fact, a large number of people with serious problems of drug misuse or dependence are "treated" within the penal system. In addition, the Probation Service also deals with a substantial number of addicts.

In 1983, 12% of *new* notifications came from Prison Medical Officers. Less than 5% of opiate addicts notified from prisons in 1983 were being treated with prescribed drugs at treatment centres or by their general practitioners prior to their admission to prison. These figures suggest that there are a large number of illicit drug users who at the time of their arrest were not in contact with a treatment agency. A study of the outcome of treatment at two London drug dependence clinics found that a quarter of the patients who left the clinics did so because of imprisonment, a slightly higher proportion than those who left as a result of successful withdrawal from drugs during the course of their clinic treatment.

There is therefore reason to believe that the relative rarity of compulsory hospital treatment for addicts is in a sense counter-balanced by the fact that many addicts are compulsorily resident in prison. If unintentional, it is nevertheless a matter of fact that the penal services play a substantial role in the way in which this country deals with its drug problem. Exactly the same conclusions must be drawn in relation to alcohol except that here the numbers involved are much greater. Drink-related crime probably makes the single largest contribution to the prison population. The fact that the majority of people found drunk on the streets will be "detoxified" in a police cell rather than given more appropriate help is sad and absurd.

Treatment in the penal system

On admission to prison, physically dependent addicts are with-drawn from drugs usually under medical supervision in a prison hospital setting. In response to the rising number of addicts in prison during the 1970s, some penal establishments set up new treatment facilities for convicted addicts, or they included addicts in their existing psychiatric treatment pro-grammes. Among the many difficulties experienced by these units have been their relative isolation from contact with the drug dependence clinics and voluntary agencies and their difficulty in providing aftercare. These special units require a large investment in terms of trained staff, and the prison system itself is already seriously over-burdened with many other problems. The response to these pressures has been an increasing trend towards a philosophy of secure containment rather than therapeutic endeavour and experiment. The difficulty in helping the addict in prison is but one facet of the wider problem presented by the treatment of mentally abnormal offenders within the penal system.

The law and prevention of drug misuse

There are many aspects of the law's functioning in this context which few people would wish to question. It would, for instance, be difficult to give serious support to a case for dismantling legal controls over the prescribing of potentially dangerous or addictive drugs. Most people would be happy to accept that heroin should not be made available for over-the-counter sale in unrestricted nineteenth-century fashion. It is taken for granted that such controls are useful measures in the prevention of drug misuse.

It also seems likely that most commentators today would not argue against the necessity for continued customs and police action aimed against importers and large scale traffickers as part of a needed overall prevention strategy. But what should be the limits of society's expectations in regard to prevention, in terms of increasing costs of enforcement and escalating penalties? One response to the growth in drug trafficking over recent years has certainly been an increase in penalties. The number of drug traffickers sentenced to more than five years imprisonment nearly doubled in one year, from 123 in 1982 to 238 in 1983. Recent legislation has increased the penalties for trafficking in Class A drugs to life imprisonment, and measures have been introduced to deprive drug traffickers of the proceeds of their activities by confiscating their assets. Prevention measures and policing have also been strengthened by increasing the number of customs officers to deter drug smuggling, by the stationing of investigators abroad, and by strengthening drug squads.

Conclusive evidence on the effectiveness of measures aimed at the importer or the major dealer is by its nature difficult or perhaps impossible to obtain. There is no possibility of a controlled experiment. In these circumstances it is likely that society will very reasonably continue to invest money and effort in such directions. What must be cautioned against is an exaggerated belief in the efficacy of ever more draconian sentences. The need to strike a balance between "supply" and "demand" strategies has been discussed at greater length in Chapter 15.

Where there is room for debate and for further analysis of policy options is in regard to the preventive value of punishment directed at the user himself or at the user who is also a small-scale supplier. Different arguments may be relevant to drugs which carry greater or less health risks. The idea that the law can operate as a "general deterrent" in relation to a heroin addict's attempt to acquire and possess heroin for his own use, within exactly the same deterrent model as is valid in relation to parking offences or evasion of TV licences, is not very convincing. It is perhaps here that the most worrying uncertainties lie over "law as prevention". The scanty research evidence that is available does not support the view that punishment is likely to deter the drug user from further drug involvement.

Over recent years both in the United Kingdom and elsewhere there has been a tentative search for alternatives and a move to relax the rigidity of legal controls. At a practical level rigid enforcement of the law has become extremely expensive. As a result there has been a significant increase in the use of cautioning for unlawful possession of cannabis—from an average of 250 cases per annum in 1978–1979 to 500 in 1982 and nearly 1,200 in 1983. The Customs and Excise have experimented with the imposition of "on the spot" fines for illicit importation of small amounts of cannabis instead of taking the matter to court.

The law in perspective

The conclusion to be drawn from a brief review of some of the diverse ways in which legal provisions bear on the treatment and prevention of drug use might well be that the operation of the law in this particular field has the same potential and limitation as observed in other areas. Very similar issues could be debated in relation to the law and road safety, the law as an instrument to regulate industrial relations, the law and juvenile delinquency, or even the Official Secrets Act. Whatever the area of its necessary operation the law can always be described as an ass or a blunt instrument.

Inevitably the law makes its entry into the drug problem area as it will in many other contexts where behaviour is thought to be against the public interest. Even a brief review of how the law works in practice must suggest that the meeting-points between drugs and the law require vigilance. Hard laws easily escalate to harder ones, and at times of social anxiety the pressures and rhetoric will all too easily encourage such escalation.

Chapter 18
Finding a way forward

What is the likely future for drug problems? How far can any country hope to influence the course of events or must it be a matter of drifting on the tide? One way of approaching these questions can be found in examining two vividly contrasting and hypothetical situations.

Take first the view of the future which assumes that by the year 2000 (or thereabouts) everyone will have happily come to terms with the fact that they are going to live in a drug-soused world. All the defences will have crumbled and current objections to such drugs as heroin, LSD or cocaine will be viewed in retrospect as having been quaintly symbolic of the cautious resistance to the inevitable tide of progress like the man who walked in front of the early motor car with a red warning flag. Not only will there no longer be any warning flags, but the drugs of today compared with the designer drugs of the future will appear as antique as the earliest horseless carriage compared with the sixteen valve turbo-charged sports car.

Come the new drugged dawn (say the prophets of this first scenario) and every citizen, young or old, will colour his or her moods and perceptions with a multi-hued chemical paintbox. They will buy their drugs at the corner shop (just like opium in the old days) and the home laboratory will be as ordinary as the home computer; the host and hostess being appreciated as much for their sophistication as chemists as for their skill in cuisine. Gone will be the bad old days when the human experience of psychological growth was a matter of learning to deal with reality. Instead maturity will be defined by the capacity to manipulate and enjoy an ever-expanding range of chemically-induced experiences, thrills and unrealities. It will be as easy to turn on the channels of the mind as to flick over the channels on the television set. The occasional individual or epidemic disaster will be accepted as the price paid for getting rid of the warning flag and the repressive and costly apparatus of control.

For a moment let us leave that picture of a drugged future without comment and move on directly to the extreme alternative. The contrary scenario for the year 2000 assumes that the war against drugs will have been conclusively and gloriously won. Peasants in Thailand will be growing red peppers on every hillside rather than white poppies, while the Bolivians will have turned from cocaine to the production of coffee. Adolescents will have been averted from all use of drugs by horrifying video-portrayals of addiction and by severe legal sanctions. The trade in drugs will have been stamped out by bringing in the Armed Forces in support of Customs and Excise and by swingeing sentences directed at every detected dealer (and all dealers will have been detected). Drugs will have gone the way of bubonic plague—a slightly horrifying memory of less morally hygienic days. Where alcohol, tobacco and medicines are to stand in this projection is unclear.

Before immediately dismissing either of these two sketches of the future as caricatures unworthy of serious consideration it must be realised that there are already some protagonists today who would want to see the world's relationship with drugs move in one or other of these directions. Those who would actually champion either of these positions as a realistic basis for policy—the goal at which to aim—are perhaps relatively few in number. The importance of these two images lies not in the numerical count of their public advocates but in the power which such visions can exert as latent images influencing the thinking of many more people than would wish to be identified with these extremes. Such simplistic assumptions easily influence important aspects of decision-making.

What will be argued in this chapter is that future policies on drugs should studiously avoid the lure of extreme solutions and instead stand firmly on the middle ground. Extremist solutions for drug problems cannot work and would do much damage. Realistic policies can only be based on an acceptance that the world and this country will have to co-exist with drugs and meet the challenge of determining how best to handle the problem and adjust to it in rapidly changing circumstances.

It is within this context that the following recommendations are offered as a basis for further debate. The intention will be to identify the broader issues which need to be examined when setting a course for the future rather than taking these recommendations to the level of fine-grained detail. There have been a number of recent authoritative publications which have also made recommendations which this book strongly supports. These include the Prevention and the Treatment and Rehabilitation reports of the Advisory Council on Misuse of Drugs, the Royal College of Psychiatrist's publication on alcohol called *Alcohol: Our Favourite Drug*, and the Royal College of Physicians' report on *Health or Smoking*.

The way in which drug issues are defined and debated determines the aptness of the way individuals and communities react to drug problems and to national policies. Careful attention should therefore be given to strategies which can ensure that the quality of the debate on drugs is enhanced and better informed.

In certain countries, and at certain times, the quality of the debate has become so distorted and remote from the realities that it has led to dangerous misjudgements. The American response which led to Prohibition, for instance, can be seen as a telling example of how a fantastic misreading of the realities could lead to extravagant and inappropriate government action. There are many similar examples in the field of drug misuse.

There is a need for constant watchfulness to ensure the good sense of the debate and to guard effectively against the dangers of polarisation. The following proposals might contribute some practical remedies.

(a) *In the political arena the possibility should be considered of multi-party political agreement on basic elements in a non-partisan national drug policy*. There is a danger that the political appeal in slogans of "getting tough on drugs" will lead to an ever-increasing escalation in legal stringencies and a heavy investment in other high-profile and competitive but ineffective strategies. The problem of drug misuse must not become a political football.

(b) *Co-operation should be sought with the media in designing a system which can make authoritative information on drugs and drug problems readily accessible, in providing continuing seminars for useful exchange of ideas between media experts, scientists and health experts and in initiating agreed methods for long-term monitoring of media trends.* The media's role in shaping public debate on drugs is of such crucial importance that the direction of that debate cannot be left with safety to considerations dictated by circulation wars and viewers' ratings.

(c) *Any school-based programme of education on drugs should cover the nature and significance of the debate.* Drug education is still essentially at an experimental stage of development. Young people should not be given one-sided didactic information but be helped to develop an awareness of the arguments which are likely to be deployed in this arena as offering examples of the way in which discussion on personal and social problems can be debated and understood.

If the debate is to be rational there must be a sustained flow of reliable information to determine the nature and extent of drug problems, the causes of these problems, the characteristics of the people affected, and the best possible methods of prevention and treatment. Attention must also be directed at the nature of the policy-making process itself.
It is a convention in official reports to recommend "more research". What is intended here is more than a routine and meaningless bow in the research direction. The intention is to give a strong priority to a recommendation for the establishment of an adequate research base in this field.

Research in this context is not a luxury. The understanding derived from research provides the essential under-pinning for a wide range of necessary practical actions. Research costs money, but actions which are uninformed by research (treatment of uncertain efficacy, prevention measures which in fact may actually encourage drug use) waste money and resources on a large scale.

The contribution which the research councils (MRC and ESRC) and government departments have made to research funding in this area should be acknowledged but it is insufficient. The essential requirement is a sustained injection of new research money. Of course it is the word "money" which is likely to cause alarm in official circles. The reality must not, however, be fudged. Research in this country on drug misuse has been grossly underfunded up to the present time and the matter will only be corrected by greater and more appropriate spending.

The manner in which the USA has dealt with research funding for alcohol and drug problems may provide useful lessons. It became clear some years ago in America that if bids for alcohol and drug research were left to take their chance in a general budget allocation for health research, they were often squeezed out to the margins by the big battalions of more established research interests. Ear-marked budgets were therefore created and handled in each instance by government agencies with specialised responsibilities.

The case should be explored for setting up a similar mechanism of research funding in the UK jointly to support alcohol and tobacco research together with work on the misuse of illicit and prescribed drugs. It is reasonable to suggest that the total budget should be built up over a few years to a level of about £3–5 million annually. At present most young research workers entering this field do so on the basis of very insecure funding and an absence of career structure. Not surprisingly they tend before long to move off to other areas.

Misuse of both illicit drugs and licit mind-acting substances raise many similar or inter-connecting questions. It should be fully acknowledged that "the drug problem" involves this very broad spectrum of chemicals. Policies in relation to illicit drugs, alcohol and tobacco, as well as sedatives and minor tranquillizers should be more closely integrated.

This heading bears in part on matters of public attitude, and further underlines the importance attached to the quality of public debate. Media treatment of these issues should, for instance, avoid the error of presenting "the drug problem" as essentially the heroin epidemic, while leaving the misuse of alcohol with only an occasional mention.

The basic and common questions relate to society's use and misuse of every and any chemical which can alter perception and feeling, whether that substance is prescribed by the doctor, bought on the black-market, or purchased at the off-licence and corner tobacconist.

As well as its bearing on the background debate, this recommendation must suggest a range of practical strategies. Educational material aimed at prevention should not disconnect drug, alcohol and tobacco misuse. There is little justification for a Community Council which deals only with drug problems while remaining aloof from drinking problems. An alcohol problems clinic which is only interested in alcohol and offers no help to its patients who are smoking 40 cigarettes a day is not practising good medicine. A community nurse who helps the medical practitioner with drug problems but whose terms of reference do not include pills which doctors prescribe is conniving in a false definition of "the drug problem". Relevant professional education should be based on a broad spectrum.

This recommendation is not to be interpreted as a doctrinaire proposal that each policy initiative, treatment service or prevention campaign has always to deal with every single chemical substance at one and the same moment. In practical and everyday terms the suggestion is that in every relevant new or on-going project the question should be asked whether the existing pattern of only concentrating on one or two substances is helpful or harmful, and policies adjusted accordingly.

International collaboration must be strengthened.
Major responsibility for dealing with substance problems must lie at both national and international levels. Opium led the way in forcing awareness that drug problems have an international dimension and require international co-operation in their resolution. The export of opium from British India to China in the 19th century caused intense reformist alarm. The Single Convention of 1961 now sets out a framework for control of opiates, cocaine and cannabis, and the International Narcotics Control Board and UN Commission on Narcotic Drugs provide the necessary organisational support. Interpol provides a basis for international co-operation on police action directed against drug trafficking. The 1971 Convention on Psychotropic Substances extends international controls to a range of substances beyond those covered by the 1961 convention.

The direction taken with formal agreements on international co-operation in this field have thus clearly centred on drugs other than alcohol or tobacco, and on control and enforcement rather than collaboration in relation to health issues. International co-operation on health matters in general and on anything to do with alcohol and tobacco is left to ad-hoc initiatives by the World Health Organization. Alcohol and tobacco are no concern of the formal UN control apparatus.

Few people would suggest that the UN drug control apparatus should be asked just to extend its remit to cover alcohol and tobacco. However, exploration of the possibility of initiating international co-operation to offer some control over the production and marketing of these "recreational" substances does require attention. It seems extraordinary that world trade in these substances should be left entirely to the play of market forces while there is an international system of accounting for poppy straw.

In the long term there must be a place for establishing some international control on the alcohol and tobacco trade. What is urgent and more immediately feasible is a strengthening of international collaboration on health issues (as opposed to control) relating to drugs, alcohol and tobacco. There is a need for improvement in the flow of international information on health matters. At present there is no mechanism for a continuous exchange of updated information on treatment and prevention and on wider policy experiences among people working on drug problems in the countries of the EEC, let alone between Europe and other continents. A valuable start has been made on co-ordination at the official and governmental level by such organisations as the Pompidou Group but it is in relation to international contact at the ordinary working level that the present system is weak. Most treatment personnel in Britain have only the sketchiest ideas of the developments in German or Italian handling of drug problems, or of Scandinavian attempts to deal with cigarette smoking, or of what the Dutch are doing about drugs or alcohol.

As regards other possible ideas for international health collaboration there is pressure from Third World countries for practical assistance in the development of treatment and prevention work. There is a call for assistance in training and education of health professionals. There is also an international dimension to research which requires further attention. Individual governments tend to fund research projects which are only national in scope while no one contributes the money for work on vital matters which literally cross national boundaries. Examples of these are the economic structure of the international trade in alcohol and tobacco, the relationship and the flow of Western-manufactured tranquillizers and sedatives to developing countries, and the political and economic issues in which cocaine and opium production are embedded.

**Professional training should be
strengthened across a broad range of disciplines.**
A doctor who qualified even ten years ago will probably have received little teaching on these issues and may never have seen a patient with opiate dependence during his clinical training nor even heard an informed discussion on inhalant misuse. In many medical schools teaching on how to recognise and deal with a drinking problem remains inadequate. Yet general practitioners are encouraged by government policy to take a major frontline responsibility in dealing with drug misuse and alcohol problems. The same dilemma confronts doctors in other branches of the broader medical field as well as clinical psychologists, nurses and social workers; and the enormous training needs in the voluntary sector are not being met.

Over the last few years proposals affecting treatment and treatment delivery systems have moved ahead of the means for strengthening the training base. Each profession involved in these matters would do well to carry out its own review of basic and post-qualification training so as to ensure that new professional responsibilities are matched by new training programmes.

Legal controls are an essential part of society's defences against drug problems and to recommend their dismantling would be absurd. However, there are limits to what laws can achieve and there are social costs as well as social benefits to legal enforcement. The function of the penal response to drug misuse should therefore be kept under review. Any slide toward greater criminalisation and harsher penalties imposed only for wishful and symbolic reasons should be resisted.
This recommendation is intended as a cautionary note. The tendency in some countries has been for the emergence of a progressively more extensive legal apparatus in response to drug misuse together with an ever increasing set of penalties until even life imprisonment or the death penalty become mandatory. We should be forewarned in Britain of the futility of believing that such draconian measures can ever succeed in beating the drug

problem out of our society and we should learn from the negative experiences of other countries in this context. However this is not to be interpreted as recommending a soft response towards the criminal purveyors of drugs.

It would be absurd to believe in what was once a British myth and to imagine that this country operates only in terms of a beneficent medical response to drug problems in contrast to the punitive systems which characterise certain other countries. This country, in fact, operates with a mixed penal and health response with some luck and arbitrariness effecting the path along which individuals will travel. The way that this system actually operates needs to be better understood and an effort made to ensure that it does not too often result in inappropriate routeing. More adequate treatment should be provided within the penal system for those drug users (and drinkers) who still go to prison and clinical research and evaluation should be encouraged.

Three recommendations are suggested in relation to treatment. (a) Greater attention needs to be given to determining the efficacy of treatment methods provided for drug problems. This recommendation echoes what has previously been said about the general importance of research. It must be acknowledged that evaluating the efficacy of treatment in this field is a difficult business and what works for one person may not be helpful for someone else. There is logic therefore in providing a choice in available facilities. Indeed, over recent years both compassion and political imperative have encouraged an expansion in treatment services, but these have sometimes moved ahead of proven evidence on efficacy.

In the long run no-one's interests are well served by spending the available but inevitably limited funds on treatment facilities in an unquestioning manner. The recommendation that there should be concern with value for money should not be misread as unsympathetic. Compassion is not well served by investing in a treatment approach which may in reality offer no sustained improvement or which may even result in harm. That these difficult points have not been pressed harder in the past may be forgivable in the context of urgent pressure for action. However, optimistic perseverence with unproved remedies must not be the formula for the future.

(b) Where, as a result of careful professional assessment of British or international experience, there is reason to believe that a given approach is likely to offer substantial benefit, the availability of that treatment should be expanded and marketed. The identification of any treatment methods which might meet such criteria should be the subject of very detailed review. It is impossible within the confines of this book to engage in such appraisals, and it would therefore be premature and wrong to comment on claims to success. However, to take a particular aspect of treatment briefly as an example may be useful. There is some evidence to suggest that in-patient detoxification may give significantly better results than detoxification attempted on an out-patient basis; if this is substantiated it would be desirable to expand in-patient facilities to meet any current needs. What is implied by the idea of "marketing" in these terms is that in-patient detoxification for opiate users should then be put positively on offer and appropriate patients should be strongly encouraged to come forward. Such an active attempt to recruit patients into early treatment is a very different policy from that of just reacting to urgent problems; and of course tolerating long waiting lists and passively declaring "our beds are full" is quite unacceptable.

Turning from this particular example to the general principle, it is this entrepreneurial zeal which should be encouraged in strengthening the treatment response to many types of drug problem. However, such policies must be based on convincing evidence that the approach which is being marketed is indeed effective.

(c) A continued place exists for doctors working privately in the treatment of drug misuse. There is, however, a danger of some private practitioners lacking adequate professional and peer group support and so failing to observe the good practice necessary to the treatment of drug dependence. The same difficulty may also at times affect the isolated practitioner within the NHS. Where private fees are involved undue pressure may be put on a doctor and overprescribing may result. The medical profession must be seen to keep its own house in order and constant care must be taken to avoid abuse.

Methods of prevention directed at drug problems should be sustained, multi-faceted, and usually a matter of small focused remedies rather than grand strategies. In general, mass media campaigns cannot be recommended. Sensitive measures which attempt to reduce demand for any type of substance will be overwhelmed if the supply of that substance is allowed to get out of hand.

It is worthwhile taking aeroplane glue off open shelves where any adolescent shoplifter can easily slip a packet into his or her pocket, and it is important to remind shopkeepers of their responsibility in this context from year to year. It is sensible to teach doctors to prescribe minor tranquillizers only with great caution and to maintain their professional education.

The recommendation made here is that many seemingly small preventive measures are in sum what an effective and integrated preventive policy is all about, and the emphasis must be on the need to sustain the pressure of continuous preventive action rather than engage in one-off efforts which are soon forgotten. Echoing what was said in the chapter on Prevention, the plea must again be made for extreme caution in relation to media campaigns which although politically attractive may otherwise be useless or even harmful. Finally, a concern for research evidence is as important in relation to prevention as it is for treatment. Drug education campaigns, whether conducted through the media or in schools or some other setting, should be regarded as experimental and very carefully evaluated.

This recommendation also ties up with an earlier theme on the importance attached to the interplay between demand-side and supply-side strategies. The present book is written primarily within a health and social perspective, but in terms of a total strategy on drugs it is necessary to provide adequate support for enforcement and customs agencies. If the streets are awash with heroin no amount of education aimed at modifying attitudes and values is going to have much impact. Exactly the same argument applies to alcohol and tobacco but here it is price and taxation rather than police and customs which operate significantly.

Lastly under this heading the implication should be noted that what happens to a country's drug problems cannot realistically be separated from what happens to the social fabric of that country in the course of many years. The conclusion which policy makers should be invited to draw is that they should be actively thinking about drug issues and the context in which people may or may not misuse drugs when they are planning for many other matters affecting the quality of life and its opportunities.

The threat posed by the relationship between AIDS and injecting drug misuse demands an urgent, vigorous and sustained programme of action, aimed at the AIDS/addiction link.

AIDS and HIV infection constitute an appalling health threat. To react dismissively because the number of people so far infected is not yet at a disastrous level would be culpable. What is needed is action *now*, while there is still an opportunity to get ahead of events and stop an explosive spread.

Much has already been done both as regards the wider AIDS problem and in terms of the relationship between drugs and AIDS. The DHSS has given commendable leadership. Action on drug misuse must constitute a vitally important component in an overall national policy on AIDS. The recommendations which are made below are linked to what has already been said about the need to provide adequate support for prevention and treatment of drug problems, but within the context of concern over AIDS these pleas gain added cogency:

(a) Prevention and treatment of drug misuse must be accorded greater priority not just because drug problems are important, painful and costly in their own right, but also because such investment can vitally contribute to reducing the transmission of HIV infection.

(b) When drug misuse has already occurred, individual counselling and health education should concentrate on discouraging progression of injecting misuse.

(c) When injecting drug misusers cannot be persuaded to give up this route of use, efforts must be made to dissuade them from continued sharing of needles and syringes, and they must be counselled on how to clean their apparatus. Needle exchange schemes, recently introduced, need to be monitored but may have national application.

(d) The intravenous drug user who has become infected with the HIV virus requires compassionate individual help, but must at all costs be dissuaded from further needle sharing or other risky behaviours.

To sustain an adequate action programme combining the elements listed above will, of course, require extra funding for service provision and for the counsellors and educators who will be needed. In plain terms every drug addict who is today persuaded to relinquish the needle habit represents a very significant gain for public health. Money spent at this juncture on curtailing the AIDS/addiction link will save ten times the resources which will otherwise have to be spent on treating the load of terminally ill cases in a few years' time.

The case for reasonable optimism

This chapter has identified a set of recommendations for debate. The basic message is that there are tangible possibilities for thinking things through more productively than in the past, with a real chance of finding new and better ways of handling drug problems, and with hope for more effective preventive strategies and a better way ahead. There must be a greater emphasis on determining what really works rather than persevering with old treatment or prevention strategies that do not work.

This is essentially an optimistic message. If these issues can be dealt with in terms of informed and unpolarised debate so that gaps in evidence and clashes of value are openly admitted, then there is every possibility of amelioration in this difficult and worrying field.

On the other hand, if the quality of the debate is allowed to degenerate, facile and polarised solutions will be offered on the basis of a prejudiced analysis. In those circumstances not only will drug problems become worse but society will inflict on itself a second-order of damage by blunt and inappropriate remedies. The result will either be excessive punishments, burgeoning criminalisation and a contaminating rhetoric leading to a dangerous misunderstanding of human behaviour, or alternatively a misreading of libertarian principles leading to the cruel abnegation of responsibility.

As has been stated many times in this book the way in which drugs are debated will have important practical consequences. Judgement as to whether the future can be seen optimistically or pessimistically must be coloured by the evolving evidence as to whether or not in difficult circumstances the quality of this essential debate can be enhanced. This is everyone's business.

Further reading

The selected references which are given below will provide further information on many of the key issues discussed in this book. Although items have been arranged in accord with the main heading of the text, some of the more general references will, of course, have a bearing on several sections.

Background to understanding

ADLER, P. (1985) *Wheeling and Dealing: An Ethnography of an Upper-Level Drug Dealing and Smuggling Community*. New York: Columbia University Press.

BRITISH JOURNAL OF ADDICTION (1987) Special Issue: Psychology and Addiction. *British Journal of Addiction*, **82**, 329–449.

BRITISH NATIONAL FORMULARY (1987) *Controlled Drugs and Drug Dependence*, pp. 30–32. London: British Medical Association and the Pharmaceutical Society of Great Britain.

JACOBS, M. R. and FEHR, K. O'B. (1987) *Drugs and Drug Abuse: a Reference Text*. 2nd ed. Toronto: Addiction Research Foundation.

GALIZIO, M. and MAISTO, S. A. (1985) *Determinants of Substance Abuse: Biological, Psychological and Environmental Factors*. New York: Plenum.

HOME OFFICE (1987) Statistics on the Misuse of Drugs in the United Kingdom. London: Home Office.

JAFFE, J. H. (1985) Drug Addiction and Drug Abuse. Chapter 23, pp. 532–581. In: Goodman, H. G., Goodman, L. S., Rall, T. W. *et al* (eds.) *Goodman and Gilman's The Pharmacological Basis of Therapeutics*. New York: MacMillan.

KANDEL, D. B. (ed.) (1978) *Longitudinal Research on Drug Use*. New York: Halstead.

KENDELL, R. E. (1984) The beneficial consequences of the United Kingdom's declining per capita consumption of alcohol in 1979–1982. *Alcohol and Alcoholism*, **19**, 271–276.

MADDEN, J. S. (1984) *A Guide to Alcohol and Drug Dependence*, 2nd ed. Bristol: Wright.

ORFORD, J. (1985) *Excessive Appetites: A Psychological View of Addiction*. Chichester, Wiley.

PLANT, M. A., PECK, D. F. and SAMUEL E. (1985) *Alcohol, Drugs and School-Leavers*. London: Tavistock.

WORLD HEALTH ORGANIZATION (1981) Nomenclature and Classification of Drug- and Alcohol-Related Problems: A WHO Memorandum. *Bulletin of the World Health Organization*, **59**, 225–242.

Drugs and society

ADVISORY COMMITTEE ON DRUG DEPENDENCE (1968) *Cannabis*: London: H.M.S.O. [The Wootton Report].

ADVISORY COUNCIL ON THE MISUSE OF DRUGS (1982) *Report of the Expert Group on the Effects of Cannabis Use*. London: Home Office.

BERRIDGE, V. and EDWARDS, G. (1987) *Opium and the People: Opiate Use in Nineteenth-Century England*. New Haven: Yale University Press.

CONNELL, P. H. (1958) *Amphetamine Psychosis*. Maudsley Monograph Number 5. London: Oxford University Press.

GABE, J. and WILLIAMS, P. (eds.) (1986) *Tranquillisers: Social, Psychological and Cultural Perspectives*. London: Tavistock.

GHODSE, A. H. (1986) Cannabis psychosis. *British Journal of Addiction*, **81**, 473–478.

IVES, R. (ed.) (1986) *Solvent Misuse in Context*. London: National Children's Bureau.

KAPLAN, J. (1983) *The Hardest Drug: Heroin and Public Policy*. Chicago: University of Chicago Press.

PACINI, D. and FRANQUEMONT, C. (eds.) (1986) *Coca and Cocaine: Effects on People and Policy in Latin America*. Cambridge, Mass.: Cultural Survival Inc.

PARKER, H., NEWCOMBE, R. and BAKX, K. (1987) The new heroin users: Prevalence and characteristics in Wirral, Merseyside. *British Journal of Addiction*, **82**, 147–157.

PETURSSON, H. and LADER, M. (1984) *Dependence on Tranquillizers*. Maudsley Monograph 28. Oxford: Oxford University Press.

PLATT, J. J. (1986) *Heroin Addiction: Theory, Research and Treatment*, 2nd ed. Malabar: Robert E. Krieger.

ROYAL COLLEGE OF PHYSICIANS (1983) *Health or Smoking*? London: Pitman.

ROYAL COLLEGE OF PSYCHIATRISTS (1986) *Alcohol: Our Favourite Drug*. London: Tavistock.

SCHULTES, R. E. and HOFFMAN, A. (1980) *Plants of the Gods*, London: Hutchinson.

SPITZ, H. I. and ROSECAN, J. S. (1987) *Cocaine Abuse: New Directions in Treatment and Research*. New York: Brunner/Mazel.

STIMSON, G. V. and OPPENHEIMER, E. (1982) *Heroin Addiction*. London: Tavistock.

TAYLOR, P. (1984) *Smoke Ring: The Policies of Tobacco*. London: Bodley Head.

TIMS, F. M. and LEUKEFELD, C. G. (eds.) (1986) *Relapse and Recovery in Drug Abuse.* NIDA Research Monograph 72. Rockville: Department of Health and Human Services.

VAILLANT, G. E. (1983) *The Natural History of Alcoholism.* Cambridge, Mass.: Harvard University Press.

Responding to drug problems

ADVISORY COUNCIL ON THE MISUSE OF DRUGS (1982) *Treatment and Rehabilitation.* London: Department of Health and Social Security.

ADVISORY COUNCIL ON THE MISUSE OF DRUGS (1984) *Prevention.* London: Home Office.

ASHERY, R. S. (ed.) (1985) *Progress in the Development of Cost-Effective Treatment for Drug Abusers.* NIDA Research Monograph 58. Rockville: Department of Health and Human Services.

BAKALAR, J. B. and GRINSPOON, L. (1984) *Drug Control in a Free Society.* Cambridge: Cambridge University Press.

BELL, C. S. and BATTJES, R. (eds.) (1985) *Prevention Research: Deterring Drug Abuse among Children and Adolescents.* NIDA Research Monograph 63. Rockville: Department of Health and Human Services.

BRUUN, K., PAN, L. and REXED, I. (1975) *The Gentlemen's Club: International Control of Drugs and Alcohol.* Chicago: University of Chicago Press.

BUCKNELL, P. and GHODSE, H. (1986) *Misuse of Drugs: Criminal Law Library No. 2.* London: Waterlow.

COURTWRIGHT, D. T. (1982) *Dark Paradise.* Cambridge, Mass.: Harvard University Press.

EDMONDSON, K. (1987) Government drug agencies and control of drug misuse. *British Journal of Addiction,* **82,** 139–146.

HOME OFFICE (1986) *Tackling Drug Misuse: A Summary of the Government's Strategy.* London: Home Office.

MUSTO, D. (1973) *The American Disease: Origins of Narcotic Control.* New Haven: Yale University Press.

NURCO, D. N. (1987) Drug addiction and crime: a complicated issue. *British Journal of Addiction,* **82,** 7–9.

PORTER, L., ARIF, A. E. and CURRAN, W. J. (1986) *The Law and the Treatment of Drugs-and Alcohol-Dependent Persons.* Geneva: WHO.

WOODY, G. E. and O'BRIEN, C. P. (1986) Update on Methadone Maintenance, Chapter 8, pp. 261–278. In: Cappell, H. D., Glaser, F. B., Israel, Y. *et al* (eds.) *Research Advances in Alcohol and Drug Problems Vol. 9.* New York: Plenum.

WORLD HEALTH ORGANIZATION (1986) *Drug Dependence and Alcohol-Related Problems: A Manual for Community Health Workers with Guidelines for Trainers.* Geneva: WHO.

Index